"Even Lincoln would have been impressed!"

—Steve Forbes, President and CEO, Forbes Inc.

"Present Your Way to the Top is full of practical insights that will help anyone deliver presentations that connect with audiences. This is not a book of abstract theories. David Dempsey gives us guidelines that have been tested and proven. Pick it up. It's a great investment."

—United States Senator Bob Dole

"If you know your next public speech will be drop-dead wonderful, this may not be the book for you. But should you belong to the remaining 95 percent of the world, David Dempsey's *Present Your Way to the Top* is full of easy to absorb, readily read ideas that will stay with you. Guaranteed applause at the end of your next talk."

—Gerald Grinstein, CEO, Delta Air Lines, Inc.

"With my busy schedule, I appreciate that David Dempsey has organized this book into quick, easy-to-read tactics for improving public speaking. I have found many informative and entertaining suggestions in *Present Your Way to the Top.*"

—James C. Kennedy, Chairman and CEO,
Cox Enterprises, Inc.

"From cover to cover, *Present Your Way to the Top* delivers on its promise to make anyone a more powerful and persuasive presenter. David Dempsey's real-world experiences and proven tips show you exactly how to get the bottom-line results you want from a business presentation. In my opinion, he is *the* Public Speaking Expert for no-nonsense executives."

—Peter Schwarzenbauer, President and CEO,
Porsche Cars North America, Inc.

"David Dempsey's book, *Present Your Way to the Top*, written with wonderful humor, takes you on a journey of building a dynamic presentation. It is packed with invaluable lessons for all speakers and shouldn't be missed."

—Dr. Ken Blanchard, coauthor of *The One Minute Manager* and *The Secret*

"*Present Your Way to the Top* is a superb tool for any executive who wants to influence, persuade, and inspire every audience! It provides a precise blueprint for crafting and delivering an outstanding speech that will have your audience members sitting on the edge of their seats. The writing is engaging, the information is insightful, and the organization is excellent. The resources and Web sites listed are a great bonus. Any speaker would benefit enormously from reading and applying the advice in this book. It is an essential book for every leader."

—Jack Guynn, President and CEO,
Federal Reserve Bank of Atlanta

"*Present Your Way to the Top* is a great resource! This excellent book shows you how to speak in a way that will cause audience members to sit up and listen. It demonstrates how to have a meaningful, heartfelt conversation that connects with your audience, how to stand out in today's cluttered, speaker-filled world. Every speaker would benefit tremendously from reading this book and applying its principles."

—John R. Alm, CEO, Coca-Cola Enterprises, Inc.

"Many people do not understand the importance of communicating clearly. David Dempsey's book, *Present Your Way to the Top*, is packed with numerous personal tales from the trenches and great ideas that he has learned through his lifelong experience in the speaking arena."

—Garry Betty, President and CEO, EarthLink, Inc.

"Clear, honest, precise, and consistent communication is the ultimate tool for effective leaders and is essential in captivating presentations. *Present Your Way to the Top* is a virtual toolbox of useful suggestions and guideposts to help you become the best, most effective communicator possible."

—John Schuerholz, President and General Manager,
Atlanta Braves

"*Present Your Way to the Top* shows you how to prepare and deliver better talks and presentations than you ever imagined. When you follow its advice, you will look and sound like a star."

—Brian Tracy, author of *Maximum Achievement* and
The Psychology of Selling

"The last 30 years, I have spent my life giving speeches before a wide variety of audiences. I am constantly on the lookout for books and articles that can help me give an extraordinary message each time I speak. There is no better resource than David Dempsey's *Present Your Way to the Top* when it comes to helping you experience extraordinary results when you stand to give your speech. I can honestly say that David is one of the best speakers in America today, and it's always wonderful to learn the secrets of the best!"

—Dr. Dwight "Ike" Reighard, Executive Vice President
and Chief People Officer, HomeBanc

"I am always looking for books that will help me be a better communicator. I really liked *Present Your Way to the Top*. David is proving himself tops in the field of speech making, and you need to read it!"

—Bobby Bowden, Head Football Coach,
Florida State University

"*Present Your Way to the Top* inspires me! It teaches every speaker how to craft and deliver a passionate message."

—Marc Hebert, Chief Marketing Officer,
Virtusa Corporation

"When Dempsey was a young trial lawyer, his knees once wobbled so violently during his summation to a jury that he overheard them dub him "Jell-O Boy." In *Present Your Way to the Top*, he describes the presentation wisdom he has learned since then that has helped him to become a professional communication skills trainer and coach. By detailing the minutiae involved in great presentations, including essential tips for conquering question-and-answer sessions, his professional advice can take the anxiety and uncertainty out of any presentation."

—Soundview Executive Book Summaries

"There's a reason most people are afraid of public speaking: They're bad at it. Really bad. They're either paint-drying dull or, worse, embarrassing. And many of those who are comfortable with public speaking are nowhere near as good at it as they think. (Yes, we're talking about you.) Since we're not likely to convince everyone to sit down and shut up, the next best thing would be to get them to read *Present Your Way to the Top*. Author David Dempsey, who learned public speaking as a trial lawyer and university professor, offers step-by-step advice to help you stop boring us to tears."

—*Accounting Today*

"The communication ideas and insights in *Present Your Way to the Top* are exceptional. My executive team and I speak around the world to a variety of audiences (customers, prospects, employees) and in a variety of venues (Town Hall meetings, investor calls, large user conferences, sales meetings). We have worked with David for several years in his dual role as a speechwriter and presentation skills coach. He utilizes all the battle-tested principles discussed in this book to help us craft and deliver dynamic messages—presentations that truly make us stand out. These techniques and his approach have produced excellent results for Infor."

—Jim Schaper, Chairman and CEO, Infor

"With *Present Your Way to the Top*, Dempsey gave me an actionable road map to rapidly transform my own presenting style . . . as well as my clients'. This is not a book about theory: you'll see a profound and positive impact the very next time you speak in public."

—Claudia Patton, President, Southeast Region, Edelman

"For several years, David and his team have coached and trained many senior executives of Siemens, including me, so I have a unique perspective. I know from first-hand experience that his recommendations for creating and delivering exceptional presentations outlined in *Present Your Way to the Top* work and, most importantly, produce results. They will help any executive deliver more engaging, persuasive presentations. What really distinguishes his approach is that the advice he offers has been tested and proven in the most important arena of all: the real world. This is a treasure trove of great ideas."

—Scott Macdonald, Vice President, Siemens Industry, Inc.

PRESENT
YOUR WAY
to the
TOP

DAVID J. DEMPSEY, JD

New York   Chicago   San Francisco   Lisbon   London   Madrid   Mexico City
Milan   New Delhi   San Juan   Seoul   Singapore   Sydney   Toronto

Copyright © 2010 by David J. Dempsey, JD. All rights reserved. Printed in the United States of America. Except as permitted under the United States Copyright Act of 1976, no part of this publication may be reproduced or distributed in any form or by any means, or stored in a data base or retrieval system, without the prior written permission of the publisher.

1 2 3 4 5 6 7 8 9 0   DOC/DOC   1 5 4 3 2 1 0

ISBN   978-0-07-173994-8
MHID   0-07-173994-7

McGraw-Hill books are available at special quantity discounts to use as premiums and sales promotions, or for use in corporate training programs. To contact a representative, please e-mail us at bulksales@mcgraw-hill.com.

This book is printed on acid-free paper.

Library of Congress Cataloging-in-Publication Data

Dempsey, David J., 1954-
    Present your way to the top
/ David J. Dempsey.
          p.   cm.
    Includes bibliographical references and index.
    ISBN-13:   (invalid) 978-0-07-173994-9
    ISBN-10:   0-07-173994-7
    1. Business presentations.   2. Public speaking.   I. Title.
HF5718.22.D46   2010
658.4'52—dc22   2009052622

This book is dedicated to Kathy, my best friend and the love of my life, and to Dee, a true inspiration and the family pillar of strength.

Contents

Acknowledgments

Where to begin? Many people contributed enormously to this book. Their insights and suggestions greatly enhanced the final product, and I am forever indebted to them for their contributions. Several deserve special recognition.

Michelle Weaver, the executive vice president of Neon Zebra, LLC, patiently and painstakingly critiqued, revised, and polished the manuscript; honed the language; and unquestionably made it a much better book as a result. She has an amazing eye for details. She is a consummate professional who left an indelible imprint on the book. Her contributions were invaluable.

As the book evolved, Kathy Rose, senior vice president of Neon Zebra, LLC, constantly added an objective perspective that was necessary when we were so deeply entrenched in the details that we lost sight of the big picture. She reviewed dozens of iterations of this book and was a perfect voice of reason when reason was called for.

John Aherne, senior editor, McGraw-Hill Professional, and Janice Race, senior editing supervisor, McGraw-Hill Professional, added valuable and insightful perspectives at every stage of the production process. They carefully considered all of the critical decisions, patiently responded to my incessant edits and my many undoubtedly inane questions, and guided me through the entire book production process with pleasant, patient, and reassuring manners. They are creative, energetic, and most important, utterly professional.

Rita Rosenkranz of Rita Rosenkranz Literary Agency, New York, is a rich treasure trove of knowledge for any author. She is an expert at representing authors and protecting their interests. She anticipated, raised, and resolved critical issues that frankly would have whizzed right by me without her wisdom and experience. I cannot imagine having made the journey from my nascent idea for a book to my first book signing without her steady hand guiding me all the way. I recommend her without reservation.

Finally, to the many business leaders across the country—far too many to list—whom I have had the honor of coaching and training over my 25-year journey as a communications consultant: You display enormous courage every time you step into the speaking arena searching for the best way to connect and stand out when you speak. You inspire and reassure me constantly that the principles in this book work. You have allowed me to experiment and refine these ideas and theories in the most important laboratory of all—the real world.

I sincerely thank each of you.

Introduction

According to most studies, people's number-one fear is public speaking.
Number two is death. Death is number two. Does that seem right?
This means to the average person, if you have to go to a funeral,
you're better off in the casket than doing the eulogy.

—Jerry Seinfeld

The beginning of my legal career was not merely inauspicious—it was disastrous. Ever since I was a small child, I had dreamed of becoming a courtroom wizard, mesmerizing the jury with my eloquence and goring hostile witnesses with insightful questions. I was always the victor, never the vanquished. I would not simply be *a* trial attorney; I would be *the* trial attorney. Visions of grandeur played in my head. Alas, reality diverged so dramatically from those visions!

My first jury trial is indelibly seared in my memory. To this day, more than 29 years later, I can describe the sights, the sounds, and the layout of that courtroom in minute detail. I can picture the faces of the jurors and recall the name of the judge.

I remember being supremely confident before the trial—and why not? My argument was brilliant, and my logic unassailable. When the judge instructed me to begin my opening statement, I slowly and dramatically swaggered toward the jury.

For the first five minutes of my opening statement, I waxed poetic about the enormous injustice that had befallen my client. I described his grievous injuries and exhorted the jury to do its grave and solemn duty and right this wrong with a whopping award of damages. Just as I had envisioned, the jurors were nodding in agreement. They were putty in my hands, and my chest swelled with pride.

Then, I misspoke twice. I was attempting to say the word *statistically*. On my first stab, I said, "Surrealistically." Several jurors snickered. In a futile attempt to correct myself, I blurted, "Sadistically." All the jurors burst into laughter. I became hopelessly tongue-tied, and almost instantly I began to unravel. My right knee began to twitch, gently at first, and then more violently. Within seconds the left knee joined in, bobbing in time with my right. As I struggled to regain my composure and recall my train of thought, my hips began to convulse, and I realized that I had become Attorney Elvis.

At this point, I longed for a dark cave to hide in. Unfortunately, I had the undivided attention of everyone in the courtroom. The jurors and the previously slumbering courtroom bystanders were now leaning forward, some of them amused, others wide-eyed with amazement at this startling spectacle. The bailiff was ready to pounce and administer cardiopulmonary resuscitation. The judge was scowling, noticeably annoyed at what he considered a transparent play for the jury's sympathy. My client was stunned, his mouth agape in disbelief. I suspected that he was muttering a prayer that the previous settlement offer—at which I had scoffed in disdain—was still available.

Nonetheless, I pressed on. In order to avoid collapsing, I began wobbling back and forth in front of the jury box. My arms were flailing, my hands were shaking, and my voice was cracking as if I were reentering puberty. My brain turned to mush, and whatever I said over the next 15 minutes remains a mystery. All I recall making were incoherent guttural sounds.

I hoped that my plight was not as bad as it seemed, and it wasn't—it was worse. And juror four confirmed that assessment when he leaned over to juror five and commented, in a voice that I imagined could be heard throughout several neighboring counties, "Hey, what's up with Jell-O Boy?" As a trial attorney, hearing that commentary about your presentations never boosts your confidence.

I continued to stagger about for what seemed an eternity, then lamely whimpered a conclusion. This humiliating fiasco was hardly the triumphant debut I had imagined, and for years I dodged the courtroom whenever possible. Instead, I devoured self-help books, struggling to restore a speck of my dignity. Joining a monastery seemed appealing. I have never forgotten that day although I have desperately tried to do so.

Over the years, I have come to realize that my experience was not unique. Most people—and far too many business executives—have harrowing speaking tales of their own. If they were fortunate, they merely watched from the comfort of their seats as a speaker unraveled on the other side of the lectern. ("He just melted into a puddle; it was so sad.") If they were less fortunate, *they* were the pathetic souls withering under the sympathetic, puzzled, or perhaps annoyed gaze of the audience members. ("I blathered on like a nitwit and sweated like a plow horse.")

ᨒ

Everything is funny as long as it is happening to somebody else.

—Will Rogers

ᨒ

Either experience only reinforces the widely held perception that public speaking is something that should be avoided at all costs. And so most people do avoid it. Many executives we have coached over the years have gone to extraordinary lengths to avoid speaking as they climbed the corporate ladder, until, one day, they found themselves confronted with a speaking situation that could truly make or break their careers. And they realized that they were woefully ill prepared.

The result of avoiding the speaking arena at all costs is that most people are mediocre speakers, but not all. Some are lousy, and some are perfectly dreadful. Few understand how to use their verbal and nonverbal tools to clarify their messages and to inspire or persuade their listeners. How could they? The incentive for many people when they speak is not to excel, but merely to survive.

Since my courtroom calamity, I have learned that anyone can become a confident communicator, and some can become brilliant. "Not me," you think? Yes, even you. How do I know this? Because I have witnessed it thousands of times as an executive presentation skills coach who has had the privilege of coaching and training some of the most prominent business leaders in Fortune 500 companies around the globe.

Ironically, several years after my Jell-O Boy fiasco, I began working as an adjunct professor of communications at Oglethorpe University in Atlanta. (I somehow forgot to mention the Jell-O Boy episode to the faculty committee during the hiring interview.) I have taught beginning and advanced public speaking for more than 20 years, and whenever any of my students cower at the prospect of standing before an audience to speak, I see my reflection in their eyes. I remember that wobbly-kneed attorney who shook so uncontrollably that he could hardly squeak out a word. I understand their fear, and I empathize.

But with a bit of gentle nudging ("Speak or fail—your choice") and lavish encouragement ("I swear that not one of my students has ever died from acute stage fright when speaking"), I have seen these shy and fearful speakers undergo remarkable transformations. Students who, on the first night of class, could not string together two coherent sentences have, at the end of the semester, stepped onto the auditorium stage for their final speech and mesmerized hundreds of fellow students, faculty, and parents by speaking with passion and conviction.

"So what?" you might think. What does that mean to me in the world of corporate America? Simply this: if young, inexperienced, terrified college students can captivate an audience when they speak, you can do so too. But you have to have what my ninth-grade football coach, Roger Hengin, used to call "fire in the belly." You have to have a burning desire to improve and a willingness to commit the time and effort. You have to be prepared to roll up your sleeves and go to work—and it is work—on enhancing your presentation skills. The payoff? It is an invaluable investment in your future, both personally and professionally.

There is nothing mysterious about learning to speak with confidence. It is a craft that anyone—even you steely naysayers—can master with initiative, tenacity, and this step-by-step blueprint for success.

I have also learned that the notion of someone being a "born speaker" is a myth. Not even the most renowned speakers—Barack Obama, Ronald Reagan, Bill Clinton—fit into that category. Gifted speakers make it look effortless, but it never is. Speaking is an art that you develop and constantly hone. Anyone who tells you otherwise is peddling snake oil. There is no magic wand that anyone can wave over your head, no elixir that you can drink, no pill that you can swallow that will make you excel as a speaker. Reading about speaking will guide you, but you will learn to speak skillfully only by actually speaking.

The real problem is that busy executives devote too little time to drafting, polishing, and practicing their presentations. They give their speeches very little thought, or they delegate the tasks of preparing both their presentations and their visual support to others. Some wait to prepare until the last minute, when their anxiety is soaring and the time to present is barreling toward them. As a result, these executives undermine their effectiveness in many ways. They ramble on without any apparent direction or purpose. They drone on monotonously and hypnotically as their listeners doze. They listlessly read, word for word, speeches that they—or someone else—have written out. They blur their points and frustrate the audience by packing their presentations with jargon, clichés, acronyms, and "eses" of all types (business-ese, academ-ese, official-ese, and legalese).

Other executives overwhelm their audiences with a tsunami of facts and minute details. Rather than making three points that stick and resonate with the audience, they attempt to make a dozen. As a result, all the points are lost on the dazed audience. And if they don't confound you with their words, they baffle you with cluttered PowerPoint presentations. Their messages are lost in a dark thicket of random and cluttered ideas. Does any of this sound familiar?

These speakers have shown no mercy for the audience. When a speaker commits any of these sins, everyone (except, sadly, the speaker) can see that the listeners have lost interest and have wandered off toward the nearest mental exit. Communication has failed.

◆

If all my possessions were taken from me with one exception, I would choose to keep the power of speech, for by it I would regain all the rest.

—Daniel Webster

◆

Regardless of where you are on your speaking journey—a neophyte or a seasoned business executive who is well on the way up the corporate ladder—I hope to inspire you to do something that right now may seem unthinkable: to *embrace every speaking opportunity that comes your way.* I can hear you protesting, "Say what? I don't think so!" Just hear me out. You should do this for three reasons.

First, with your words, you have the power to leave a lasting impression on people. I have seen trembling college students, aspiring executives, and those who already occupy the C-suite offices mesmerize listeners with their poignant messages. But that will not happen if you dodge every opportunity to communicate or if your speeches are remarkably bad.

Second, when you connect with an audience—when you catch a spark in the eyes of your listeners, notice their heads nodding in agreement, or see them sitting spellbound, hanging on your next word—the feeling is empowering. Nothing else can duplicate that euphoria.

Finally, and perhaps most important, taking advantage of every speaking opportunity will benefit you enormously in your professional life. Business executives who can stand and deliver their messages with power, passion, and persuasion, regardless of their profession, are invariably more successful in attaining their objectives: to educate, to inspire, to close a deal, or to sell a product or service. Dynamic and engaging speakers typically produce excellent *results.*

The purpose of this book is simple: to show you how to speak with utter confidence and conviction. This book contains the best lessons I have learned after 25 years of working in the speaking arena as a professional speaker, a speechwriter, a university professor, and an executive presentation skills consultant, trainer, and coach. I learned many of these lessons the hard way—*painfully* hard—but by using this book, you won't have to. It will dramatically accelerate your learning.

   Some of the principles in this book may seem obvious, and some may surprise you, but all of them are battle tested, and all will benefit you when you make a presentation. The book contains hundreds of secrets and insights that will significantly enhance your communication skills. It will show you how to become a much better speaker than you are now. Indeed, it will show you how to communicate in a way that will cause you to truly *stand out* every time you speak, a skill that will propel you up the corporate ladder.

   Study this book and practice these principles, and you absolutely will begin to communicate with unflappable confidence. You will be far wiser about what it takes to speak persuasively, clearly, and concisely—to sweep away an audience with your words and attain the results you seek from your presentations. This transformation will not happen overnight, but it will happen. And I guarantee this: if you practice these principles, you will never hear an audience member say, "Hey, what's up with Jell-O Boy?"

PART I

MASTER THE MENTAL

So, you want to speak with confidence? Let's start with your noggin (I promise, there will be no psychological mumbo jumbo). First and foremost, you have to believe that you can speak with confidence, and envision yourself doing exactly that. You should visualize every detail of a successful presentation: a self-assured demeanor, a compelling message, a receptive audience, a forceful delivery, a rip-roaring round of applause, and, of course, closing that huge deal after your amazing presentation.

Use your imagination not to scare yourself to death, but to inspire yourself to life.

—Adele Brookman

This type of visualization is often easier said than done, because insidious doubt and indecision can creep into your thoughts and erode your confidence. If unchecked, they can cause you to tremble, freeze, or mumble to yourself. Some of this speaking phobia stems from inexperience (your ducking every speaking opportunity will not help). Some of it might stem from a nightmarish speaking experience from your childhood (say, the time your classmates mocked you as a "scaredy-cat" when you shook so wildly that your speech rattled in your hands as you solicited their votes to become the hall monitor). Or perhaps some of it stems from that wretched speech when your key client doodled and yawned incessantly as you spoke. All such insecurities can combine, as if to plot your undoing. At best, they can severely handicap you as a speaker. At worst, they can virtually paralyze you.

Part I strips away the shroud of mystery surrounding stage fright and provides a blueprint for mentally preparing yourself to speak with confidence and conviction—without your needing to hypnotize or medicate yourself to calm your jitters.

1

Channel Your Stage Fright

The human brain is a wonderful thing. It operates from the moment you're born until the moment you get up to make a speech.

—Anonymous

People who profess that public speaking does not cause them anxiety cannot be trusted. Let's be honest: speaking is scary. An audience of strangers—or even friends—can be daunting. You are alone up there, free to dazzle or to flop, free to convince your listeners that you are a genius or a buffoon. And your successes—or your failures—are as public as possible. Those are pretty high stakes.

Many people go to extraordinary lengths to diligently, creatively—even maniacally, in some cases—avoid every opportunity to speak, because speaking terrifies them. And here's the proof (sorry, this proof business is a lawyer's obsession). A 1999 study commissioned by the National Communication Association found that only 24 percent of Americans are very comfortable giving a speech or a formal presentation.[1] In a survey that appeared in *The Book of Lists*, 3,000 people were asked, "What are you most afraid of?" and the number-one response was "speaking before a group." It ranked higher than the fear of heights, insects, and even death.[2] In another study, 2,500 people were asked to list their greatest fear, and the largest percentage of respondents listed public speaking.[3] A 1996 study revealed that we fear public speaking more than we fear a job interview, a blind date, being the victim of a practical joke, or being asked personal questions in public.[4] It seems that quite a few people belong to the Stage Fright Club.

Even those who appear to be very comfortable when they speak admit to experiencing presentation phobia at times. Garrison Keillor, host of Minnesota Public Radio's *A Prairie Home Companion*, fought a fear of speaking as a youngster:

> I was terrified of everything [in high school], so afraid of being embarrassed in front of other people, afraid to speak up in class, afraid that I might have the wrong answer to a question that everybody else had the right answer to. . . . I was able to get up in speech class only because I could take off my glasses, and when I did, I could no longer see faces. It was just kind of an Impressionist tapestry.[5]

Actress Carol Burnett confessed, "The idea of making a speech does more than make me a nervous wreck; it terrifies me. . . . I'd rather scrub floors—without kneepads."[6]

Oscar-winning actress Meryl Streep said, "It is odd: I have a career that spans continents, but the pathetic thing is that I can't get up in front of people and speak. I get really nervous."[7]

Every speaker suffers some degree of stage fright, the mild-to-intense feeling of anxiety that you experience when you are asked to make a presentation. You are nervous, and your body produces adrenaline in response. That process is what causes your mouth to feel as dry as the Sahara and your heart to pound so wildly that it seems as if it will explode. In severe cases, you might become incapable of focusing on anything but your imminent demise. The paradox is that this stress, if you channel it properly, is enormously beneficial—Scout's honor. It infuses your speech with energy. The key is learning how to harness the stress to your advantage rather than allowing it to cripple you.

Six Stage-Fright Secrets

Let's whittle this Stage Fright Bully down to size. When wrestling with speaking anxiety, keep the following six secrets in mind:

1. **It is perfectly natural to be anxious.** If speaking or the mere prospect of speaking scares you, you are in the majority. As you can see from the previous comments, speaking in public often intimidates even professional speakers and actors who make their living onstage. If pros with thousands of hours of speaking experience, whose very livelihood depends on speaking confidently, become nervous, then it is certainly natural for someone who speaks infrequently to experience anxiety. You just do not want your anxiety to impair your speech or to become so severe that it drives you bonkers.

   ❧

   The best speakers know enough to be scared. Stage fright is the sweat of perfection. The only difference between the pros and the novices is that the pros have trained the butterflies to fly in formation.

   —Edward R. Murrow

   ⚜

2. **Your worst fears rarely materialize.** Your imagination can be ludicrously wild when you are preparing to speak. You might visualize the worst occurring: your knees knock, you hyperventilate, you babble incoherently, you faint, and you are publicly humiliated. Such fears are imaginary, as these results rarely materialize, so stop cringing, breathe deeply, and get a grip on yourself. There are no known deaths attributed to stage fright, so the odds favor you.

3. **It always seems worse to the speaker.** Immediately after making a presentation, many of the speakers I coach swear that they had never been so nervous in their lives, that their hands had never before shaken that way, and that their knees had never before wobbled like that. But I videotape every

speech, and we immediately review it together. Typically, they are surprised to discover that they appeared far more poised than they felt.

When you are speaking, with hundreds of eyes focused on you, you often feel intimidated, and your anxiety is naturally heightened. You can become your harshest critic. But rest assured: though you may be scared stiff, your audience generally has no clue—unless you look wild-eyed, ghastly pale, or ramrod rigid.

❧

Courage is resistance to fear, mastery of fear—not absence of fear.

—Mark Twain

❧

4. **Your audience empathizes with you.** Every member of your audience has felt some level of anxiety when it has been his own turn to speak. Anyone who denies it is fibbing. As a result, many of them are looking at you with admiration and awe for having the courage to stand and speak; others are simply thinking, "There, but for the grace of God, go I!" They feel your pain.

5. **Your audience wants you to succeed.** The members of your audience have come to hear you speak for a variety of reasons: to be informed, to be entertained, or perhaps to be inspired. They regard you as the expert, and they want their expectations fulfilled. Your listeners want you to succeed, for the simple reason that your success will benefit them. It is a collaborative effort: you want to give a good speech, and they want to hear one. Dispel the notion that your audience is lying in wait, ready to pounce on any mistake.

6. **Your audience has never heard your presentation.** Speakers often scowl and scold themselves (or even let a few invectives fly) when they forget a word, a line, or a point. But remember: your audience has never heard your speech before. No one is

monitoring what you say, line by line, word for word. No one will shout, "Hey, Bonehead, you forgot something!" In fact, listeners rarely know that you flubbed a line or dropped a thought. You can deliver an exceptional speech that only you realize is less than perfect—and you don't have to tell anyone.

Audience members do not know what you planned to say; they know only what you said. That knowledge should reduce your stress, because it affords you the freedom to omit something with very little risk. Of course, if you wince, curse, or mutter, "Dadgumit—I blew it," you will highlight the gaffe for your audience. Fight the urge to be honest in these situations (your mother will understand).

❧

No passion so effectually robs the mind of all its powers of acting and reasoning as fear.

—Edmund Burke

❧

It is possible that my revealing the preceding six stage-fright secrets to you has not assuaged your presentation anxiety. If your anxiety is acute—if the mere thought of public speaking makes you nauseous, if you are wringing your hands and perspiring as you read this book, if you have changed jobs 18 times to avoid speaking—then you should pore over the books included for this chapter in the list of recommended resources at the end of this book.

Learn to positively channel your anxiety, because the speaking game is often won or lost at this stage. If you want to speak with confidence, you have to believe that you can. Rein in your fertile imagination. Learn to transform your anxiety into an asset, and you will take gigantic strides in the right direction. In the meantime, if you are frantic, try to relax, for goodness' sake—and stay away from sharp objects.

2

Visualize Speaking Success

There is nothing either good or bad,
but thinking makes it so.

—William Shakespeare

Think like a champion! That message was painted above the door in my high school locker room. Over the years, the paint had chipped and faded, and thousands of football players had smudged those words of inspiration, slapping them as they raced onto the field of battle. But the message permeated our thinking—four powerful words that the coaches never let us forget, and we never did.

I can think of no better advice for speakers: *think like a champion!* Before every presentation, visualize every speaking triumph you've ever had, in precise detail. Don't limit this to the presentation that was a monumental success. Visualize every victory, large and small: the day you weaned yourself off your script, the time you focused on the audience and really connected, or the time you first ventured away from the lectern, even if only a few steps.

I have participated in more than 100 public-speaking contests throughout the United States. I won a few and lost plenty. Although many of these contests occurred years ago, I can recall everything about those that I won: the lavish applause, the stories I shared, even hoisting the heavy glass and marble trophies. Why? Because those vivid images enhance my confidence whenever I speak. I ingrain my successes into my mind. So should you.

❧

Vision is the art of seeing things invisible.
—Jonathan Swift

❧

Actors, athletes, musicians, politicians, business executives, and anyone else who appears in the public arena visualize success. This visualization bolsters their confidence and helps them mentally prepare to prevail. Former Olympic athlete Vicki Huber describes her visualization:

> Right before a big race, I'll picture myself running, and I will try to put all the other competitors in the race into my mind. Then I will try and imagine every possible situation I might find myself in . . . behind someone, being boxed in, pushed, shoved, or cajoled, different positions on the track, laps to go, and, of course, the final stretch. And I always picture myself winning the race, no matter what happens during the event.[1]

Notice that while Huber includes realistic, difficult elements in her vision, she always focuses on success. This type of mental preparation is enormously helpful for speakers as well. Imagine yourself confidently standing before an audience; envision the smiling faces and the nodding heads of your listeners; hear the hearty congratulations for a job well done. Rather than fretting, "This sure seems like a cranky audience" (and trust me, you will encounter audiences that are packed with sourpusses), substitute a positive thought: "This audience is gonna love me like my dog does! I will own the stage and close this deal!" Feel free to replace the "dog" image with one of your own liking, but you understand the point: visualize your successful presentation in detail.

❧

Obstacles are those frightful things you see when you take your eyes off your goal.
—Henry Ford

❧

Dr. Wayne W. Dyer is the author of numerous bestselling books, including *Excuses Begone!*; *Change Your Thoughts, Change Your Life*; and *You'll See It When You Believe It*. He is also a very successful speaker, and he often addresses audiences of several thousand people. His visualization ritual before speaking is precise and calming:

> I create the speech in my mind before I go on stage. In other words, I meditate on it. I see the whole thing working. I see every little detail, from my arriving, to where I go in, what the room looks like, how the people are going to react to my speech, what I'm going to say when I walk out there, how I'm going to dress, how the lights are going to be. I play the whole thing out in my mind in the meditation, hours before I speak. I get very, very peaceful with that. It's a very comfortable, joyful, kind of blissful experience.[2]

Now, don't delude yourself that visualization will substitute for preparation and practice, because it won't. That is just wishful thinking. If you are unprepared, no amount of visualization—not about your speaking triumphs, not about your platform pizzazz, not even about your audience shouting hosannas—will help. And to make matters worse, if you are unprepared, your audience *really will* be cranky—and rightfully so. No matter how convincing your visualization may be, it is only one of many tools in your speaking arsenal. To transform your vision into reality, you must prepare for your moment in the limelight.

Eight Tips to Boost Your Confidence

You must aggressively battle the fear of speaking, because it is wickedly persistent. It will flourish if you give it room. Here are eight ways to begin developing unshakable confidence when you speak:

1. **Seize every opportunity to speak.** "I don't think so!" I can hear you protesting at this utterly preposterous recommendation. Work with me here, because this is the truth: the more frequently you speak, the more confident you will become. As with any learned skill, you improve with practice. At the

senior prom, you would not walk across the room and ask that little freckle-faced cutie-pie to dance if you had never danced before, would you? Okay, maybe you would, but for most of us klutzes, that is way too much pressure.

Don't wait until that critical presentation (the one, for instance, that will determine whether you will spend the balance of your career in the boardroom or in the mailroom) to develop your speaking skills. Practice speaking in such nonthreatening venues as church meetings, service organizations like Kiwanis or Rotary, or your child's grade school class. Refine your speaking skills in these forgiving environments, not when the stakes are colossal. This practice will produce a rich collection of successful speaking experiences from which you can draw confidence.

2. **Prepare early and thoroughly.** Unless you *know* that you can devote ample time to preparing your speech, don't agree to speak. Even if you are asked to "just say a few words," decline if you cannot prepare. Those "few words" will haunt you if you misspeak, ramble, or fall to pieces. For many, just saying a few words causes the same intense anxiety as delivering a prepared presentation.

   Does it really matter if you are prepared? Absolutely. Preparation can reduce your stage fright by as much as 75 percent.[3] That is a heap of worry and torment that you can avoid by preparing. Simply put, there is no better way to reduce your anxiety and bolster your confidence. So pass if you can't find the time to prepare.

3. **Use positive self-talk.** Psychologists almost universally agree that positive self-talk enhances your confidence. You must believe that you will succeed and that the audience is on your side. Talk yourself into success and disavow the possibility of failure. Tell yourself, "I am confident, because I know my topic better than anyone else. I am an expert, and the audience will see me that way." Just be careful to conduct your pep talk in private, or people may think you are slightly loony.

ॠ

Bless your uneasiness as a sign that there is still life in you.

—Dag Hammarskjöld

✺

4. **Loosen up.** For many speakers, their physical appearance alone eliminates any doubt that they are nervous: they have taut, solemn expressions; their knuckles are white from clutching the lectern; their arms are tightly crossed; and their movements are robotic. Their body language sends a glaring nonverbal message that they are anxious, and everyone immediately senses it. They are downright scary to watch.

   No audience will believe that you are confident as long as rigor mortis seems imminent. Instead, project a self-assured demeanor. Walk to the lectern confidently, not tentatively; act as though you are excited to be speaking, not as though you were marching to the gallows; pause before you begin; plant your feet firmly and stand erect; look at your audience; and smile (principle 30). This will help you appear and feel more confident. The audience wants to see a relaxed speaker, not a somber, starchy one.

5. **Remember that very few speakers are flawless.** We often place unrealistic expectations upon ourselves ("I have to be flawless, or my career is kaput and my life is ruined!"). We seldom live up to those intimidating standards, so don't yank your hair out trying. Professional speakers, who have devoted their lives to perfecting their craft, will tell you that they are constantly refining and honing their presentation skills, and that some of their earlier presentations were putrid.

   Recognize that despite your best efforts, you will not excel in every presentation. Sometimes you will get rattled, sometimes your audience will not be receptive, and sometimes those blasted planets are misaligned. It happens. We do not have to be perfect, and we rarely are. Just remember: there will be another speech, another day. No speech is fatal (although if you bomb, you may spend a few years in the mailroom).

&

Progress has not followed a straight ascending line, but a spiral with rhythm of progress and regression, of evolution and dissolution.

—Johann Wolfgang von Goethe

&

6. **Meditate, or engage in relaxation activities.** If they are unchecked, your prespeech jitters can immobilize you. Whether you meditate, listen to music, chant, or sing (preferably in the shower) before you speak, engage in some activity that helps calm you. Try all of the following relaxation techniques:
   - *Breathe.* Inhale deeply through your nose, drawing air into your diaphragm. Hold it for several seconds, and then exhale slowly through your mouth.
   - *Stretch.* Stretching will help relieve the tension in your head, shoulders, and back. Before your speech, retreat to another room to relax and stretch. To ease the tension, gently roll your head and shoulders clockwise and counterclockwise repeatedly. Finally, to loosen the muscles in your face, open your mouth as wide as possible and move your lower jaw around. Avoid doing this with small children present.
   - *Move around.* Release nervous energy by taking a short walk to collect your thoughts and warm up your muscles before you speak. Just don't work yourself into a sweating lather or wander off—you still have to speak.
7. **Eat sensibly.** Okay, so what does eating have to do with visualization? Well, you are not going to visualize *anything* positive if your body is rebelling. On the day you speak, avoid all dairy products (which create mucus), carbonated beverages (which can result in embarrassing belching), and caffeine (which can make you jittery). Eat only a light snack before you speak. Sip room-temperature water constantly throughout the day to hydrate your vocal cords, and always have a glass of water (no ice) available while you speak. Don't guzzle water like a camel, however, or you may need to bolt from the stage midway through your speech—never a confidence booster.

ৡ

Before thou engagest, ask thyself, What if my Design miscarr[ies]?

—Thomas Fuller

✌

8. **Mentally prepare for the unexpected.** Sometimes, the best of plans go awry. In *What to Say . . . When You're Dying on the Platform*, professional speaker Lilly Walters writes:

> Nothing is more terrifying than standing up in front of a group and finding that something is going VERY WRONG! Like, "I'm dying up here!" . . . How many times have you . . . [w]ished you'd "remained silent and been thought a fool" instead of opening your mouth and proving them right?[4]

You may encounter various problems while speaking, such as a bungled introduction, a microphone meltdown, a pesky questioner, a lost train of thought, and a few other snafus described in principle 40. Mentally preparing to address these challenges will reduce your anxiety.

ৡ

The greatest mistake you can make in life is to be continually fearing you will make one.

—Elbert Hubbard

✌

Enhance your confidence every time you speak by visualizing an ideal outcome and reliving previous successes. You must "think like a champion!" to speak like one. Tape those words onto your computer, write them at the top of every speech, and most important—sear them into your mind. Make them your creed.

3

Park Your Ego at the Door

[O]ne who does less than he can is a thief.
—Mohandas K. Gandhi

There is no household repair or improvement project so simple that I cannot botch it. A hammer, a saw, a screwdriver, and, heaven forbid, any power tool—they all haunt me.

After I purchased my first house more than two decades ago, a 1940s-era handyman special, I spent many weekends at The Home Depot, eager to tackle dozens of challenges. I would wander the cavernous aisles with my list in hand, intrigued by the seemingly endless number of ways in which I could improve my house.

I would load my mammoth orange cart with a glut of supplies and tools for projects that I had not even considered before I entered the store. As I rolled along, I bonded and swapped how-to stories with other customers in The Home Depot fraternity. Although I was a bungler with tools, I rationalized, "Surely, with gritty determination, I can master any task that my fellow shoppers can. Bring it on!"

I was wrong. I accomplished only the simplest tasks, abandoning most of the projects out of sheer frustration. I had mistakenly assumed that because I had a law degree, home improvements would be a breeze. After repeatedly smashing my fingers, scraping my knuckles, and uttering more profane words than Sister Mary Margaret Rainey would ever have imagined were in her former pupil's vocabulary, I had to admit it: there was no correlation between being well educated and grasping the nuances of spackling a wall, mitering a joint, or caulking a bathtub (and don't even get me started on cutting tile). It was a humbling admission.

My frustration grew when I realized that my building brethren— even the ones who seemed to have the same intellectual capacity as the two-by-fours they were buying—were effortlessly completing projects far more difficult than mine. Embarrassed by my failures, I avoided The Home Depot, fearing a chance encounter with someone who might ask how one of my many forsaken projects was progressing.

I have come to an equally startling realization about speaking: there is no correlation between your level of education and your ability to speak with power, passion, and persuasion. Some dunderheads are exceptional speakers, and some brilliant people are absolute bumblers when you give them a microphone.

❧

You can have brilliant ideas, but if you can't get them across,
your brains won't get you anywhere.

—Lee Iacocca

❧

It is no sign of weakness that your speaking skills are deficient, or even woefully inadequate, if you have never learned these skills. If I were to strap on a pair of skates, grab a hockey stick, slide onto the ice, and attempt to whack the puck around, it would be an ugly spectacle. I have never played hockey, so I would spend more time picking my fanny up off the ice than I would gliding effortlessly about dazzling everyone. I would have to learn and develop my skating skills. Speaking is no different.

The most difficult step on the path to becoming a more proficient, confident speaker may be the first: a willingness to park your ego at the door and recognize that there is always room for improvement. This is often an enormous challenge, especially for highly successful people. For many high achievers, acknowledging any shortcoming is tantamount to failure. They have risen to the pinnacle of their professions by resilience, focus, and determination; they resolve most problems through thinking and reasoning. But these virtues do not help with public speaking—it is a learned skill, and one in which most professionals have had little or no training. If they develop any speaking skills, it is often done by hit-or-miss—and most miss. Typically, either they ramble aimlessly while their audience yearns deeply for some direction, or they drone on and on while their audience waits vainly for some sign that it is a human being who is speaking.

❧

Creativity is constantly in danger of being destroyed by success.
The more effectively the environment is mastered, the greater
is the temptation to rest on one's oars.

—Henry A. Kissinger

➳

Attitude Is Everything

If you want to become a better speaker, you must not let pride stand in your way. No harm will be done and the sky will not fall if you admit that maybe, just maybe, you can and should improve. Here is the glaring truth: we can all become better speakers (yes, even you). But you must approach the challenge with a positive attitude.

Over the years, I have delivered more than 1,000 presentations and conducted hundreds of executive presentation skills workshops. It is only natural that, with so many opportunities, I have occasionally blundered and made some really dumb comments. When that happened in the early years of my speaking journey, my instinctive reaction was always the same: to avoid speaking. I concocted some amazingly creative excuses: "I would love to speak, but I have this darn recurring laryngitis." Or "I'm sorry, I have to attend *another* wedding at 9:00 a.m. on Tuesday." My rationale was simple: if I didn't speak, I couldn't fail.

But I soon realized that unless I was prepared to blaze a path as the mute trial attorney or be forever known as Jell-O Boy, I had to become a much better speaker. (Besides, the Tuesday morning wedding excuse was raising a few eyebrows.) I also realized that my attitude was critical to my success. I needed to glean whatever kernel of insight each speaking experience taught me and push myself to excel.

❧

The only way to be absolutely safe is never to try anything for the first time.

—Magnus Pyke

❧

You need to do that, too. You need to recognize that your speaking skills will improve only if you practice and approach every presentation with a willingness to learn. Don't let a false sense of pride restrain you. Honestly analyze each presentation and ask yourself difficult questions: "Am I *really* always prepared to speak?" "Do I understand the issues facing my audience?" "Is my message muddled or my organization chaotic?" "Am I genuinely passionate about my topic?"

Videotape and critique every presentation (principle 21), and constantly challenge yourself. Seek blunt and honest feedback from people whose opinions you trust—and who have the qualifications and experience to evaluate your speeches constructively. Their input may be humbling, and sometimes dismaying, but it will invariably be revealing and helpful. Evaluate their suggestions objectively, not defensively (stop bristling). Your ego may be bruised, but your presentations will get better, and that should be your ultimate goal.

❧

What I have learned bears no other fruit than to make me realize how much I have to learn.

—Michel de Montaigne

❧

Even the Best Can Get Better

You will learn to speak with authority and confidence by consistently practicing and refining your craft. I have coached and trained thousands of C-level and senior executives around the world, and I have never encountered any speakers, regardless of their skill level, who could not improve provided they were willing to constantly challenge themselves and set uncompromising standards.

Anthony Robbins, an electrifying professional speaker, built his career by demanding more from himself as a speaker than anyone else could possibly expect. How did he develop his speaking talent? In his words:

> I became an excellent public speaker, because, rather than once a week, I booked myself to speak three times a day to anyone who would listen. . . . My associates talked about how "lucky" I was to have been born with such an "innate" talent. . . . [But] mastery takes as long as you want it to take. . . . Were all my speeches great? Far from it! But I did make sure that I learned from every experience and that I somehow improved until very soon I could enter a room of any size and be able to reach people from virtually all walks of life.[1]

Les Brown is another prominent professional speaker who understands the importance of constantly improving. His simple philosophy:

> I know speakers who have given the same speech for thirty years and never changed and have no intention of changing. They have gone back to the same audiences and given the same speech several times. . . . [But speakers] interested in mastering the art of communication . . . [should] always [ask]: "What new things can I incorporate into my presentation that can take it to another level, that will have a greater impact on the audience?" . . .
>
> When you approach [speaking] from a growing perspective, as opposed to doing the same thing over and over again, the possibilities are unlimited. . . . [N]ever be satisfied with yourself. Realize that you haven't given your best speech yet, and there's more within you. And learn from as many sources as you possibly can.[2]

Excellent speakers are always looking for techniques they can use to enhance their effectiveness. Their pride does not hinder their growth. They always strive to improve. What about you? Do you have the desire, the fire in your belly, to be your best every time you speak?

Some speakers, for a variety of reasons—fear, pride, denial—will never leave their speaking comfort zones. They delude themselves by thinking that their expertise is all that really matters.

If you refuse to honestly critique your presentations, or if you reside in the world of delusions and rationalizations, your prospects for truly effective communication will plummet. Ask yourself one simple question every time you speak: "Is this the very best I can do?" If yes, congratulations—to all three of you in the world. If no, park your ego at the door. Plunk yourself down, roll up your sleeves, and get to work.

PART II

PREPARE TO PRESENT

Here is a profundity: whatever your audience, whatever your topic, and whatever your purpose in speaking, if you fail to prepare, be prepared to fail. (All right, maybe it's not a profundity, but it's certainly a truism.) There is no substitute for preparation—not your knowledge, not your fearlessness, not even your lucky rabbit's foot. Exceptional speakers are fanatical about preparation. They leave nothing to chance. They understand their audience, and, like skilled craftsmen, they meticulously build their presentations brick by brick.

ào

I'm a great believer in luck, and I find that the harder
I work, the more I have of it.

—Thomas Jefferson

às

If your speech begins to implode because you are unprepared, your confidence will evaporate. You may be able to blunder along and stagger to a conclusion, but you'll do little more than that. Even if the speech does not flop entirely, it will certainly disappoint your audience and fall short of the ideal mark. And if it really begins to crumble as you are babbling away, you will silently pray for the earth to open up and swallow you—and your audience may well join in that prayer. Part II addresses the preliminary steps you should take to avoid that fate.

4

Build a Speech Foundation

The unluckiest insolvent in the world is the man whose expenditure of speech is too great for his income of ideas.

—Christopher Morley

Polished delivery will never compensate for a speech that lacks substance. A frothy speech leaves the audience feeling empty and cheated. Your speech should be built on a solid foundation of facts, details, examples, and anecdotes. A presentation that is packed with substance enhances your credibility and clarifies your message so that it is understandable, informative, and memorable for your audience.

Where can you find material for your presentations? Search anywhere and everywhere, and not just in the obvious places. Nose around in unusual crannies for your speech content: graffiti, cereal boxes, billboards, voice mail messages, idle musings, political babble—it is all useful grist. Collect any information that you find interesting or appealing. If it amuses or impresses you, chances are pretty good that it will amuse or impress your listeners as well. Relentlessly clip or copy articles related to your topic, even if you are unsure how you might incorporate them into your speech. I hope it is not sacrilegious to say this, but rip articles out of the magazines in your doctor's waiting room if necessary—I am positive that is what they are there for. All that accumulated information will result in a richer, more colorful speech. Anecdotes, examples, quotes, and smidgens of humor can make a dry topic sparkle.

But—and this is important—you must snatch the ideas immediately, because they will disappear in a flash. Poof! And those brilliant insights will be gone forever. Scribble them in a journal, store them on your computer, write them on your hand if necessary—just capture them. Hoard your ideas like a miser. Avoid wasting valuable time later, ransacking your porous memory for the pithy quote or provocative thought that you were sure you would remember.

❧

My little [note] books were beginnings—they were the ground into which I dropped the seed. . . . I would work this way when I was out in the crowds, then put the stuff together at home.

—Walt Whitman

❧

Become a data pack rat. Better yet, if you feel especially industrious, become an organized pack rat and categorize those nuggets somehow as you gather them. If that seems too ambitious, just jam them in a shoebox, but secure the shoebox.

Don't wait until the evening before you plan to speak to gather material. At that point, it is too late. And don't expect the ideas to come cascading out of your head and leap onto your notepad. Fickle Mr. Inspiration seldom shows up on your schedule; he is pigheaded that way. That ticktock sound will grow deafeningly loud as you stare at the blank computer screen and the fateful moment to speak draws near. You are not likely to produce your best work with your head in the deadline guillotine.

Five Speech Resources

Here are a few suggestions for the types of materials you might incorporate into your presentation to make it more persuasive, entertaining, and informative, but don't limit yourself to these. Be creative. Stockpile anything that might give your talk a little zing, even if right now you do not know exactly how you will use it. Principle 5 will share some ideas about where to search for your material:

1. **Personal stories.** Everyone loves a juicy story—the juicier, the better (principle 13). The best speakers are typically masterful storytellers. They capitalize on this skill in their presentations. Why? Because a compelling story will rivet an audience and make any message unforgettable. Tell them a tale, and they will lend you their ears (or something like that).

❧

A man would do well to carry a pencil in his pocket and write down the thoughts of the moment. Those that come unsought are commonly the most valuable and should be secured because they seldom return.

—Francis Bacon

❧

2. **Examples.** Let's face it: some material is so darn complex or abstract that it baffles even the most intellectual audience. Examples can clarify the complex or abstract. They can make minute details understandable. For example (smooth segue, right?), instead of simply saying that the interest payments on the federal debt are a gazillion dollars a day (they are actually two gazillion, but let's not nitpick), describe your fact in a more understandable context: "How much does this deficit cost taxpayers every day? Imagine a football field, end zone to end zone, with every square inch tightly packed with 10-foot-high stacks of crisp $100 bills. That is what taxpayers shell out, every day, in interest on the federal debt." That example should make the idea easier to grasp than a "gazillion," I hope. The point: use examples to make obscure, complex, or abstract points clear.

3. **Quotations.** Relevant quotations enliven your message and enhance your credibility, particularly if the source of the quotation is a well-known and respected figure, such as

Mohandas Gandhi, Rosa Parks, or Theodore Roosevelt (principle 15). On the other hand, a quote from "Vinny the tollbooth operator" or from "Bart Simpson," although interesting and perhaps entertaining, will have little persuasive impact (sorry, Bart). The quote must be relevant to your point and from a recognizable and credible figure.

4. **Comparisons and contrasts.** To clarify your points, compare and contrast situations and positions. Apt comparisons make your topic more understandable and persuasive. For example, former president Ronald Reagan repeatedly asked voters to consider one simple question: "Are you better off today than you were four years ago?" The answer to that provocative comparison for the voters was a resounding "no," and that resulted in a decisive victory for Reagan.

Contrasts can help listeners distinguish between alternative positions. Politicians often draw a stark contrast between themselves and their opponents: "My opponent trusts big government. I trust you." Advertisers also frequently rely on contrasts: "Chuck says, 'Tastes great.' I say, 'Less filling.'" To be effective, however, contrasts must be clear and accurate. If they are confusing, exaggerated, or misleading, they are seldom helpful.

❧

My task which I am trying to achieve is, by the power of the
written word to make you hear, to make you feel—it is, above all,
to make you see. That—and no more, and it is everything.

—Joseph Conrad

❧

5. **Statistics.** Statistics are a double-edged sword. The line between statistics that enlighten and those that confound is incredibly fine. Your statistics must be simple and understandable: "In a blind taste test given to 1,000 New Yorkers, 75 percent preferred Death by Chocolate Brownies over Mama's Finest Brownies (notwithstanding Mama's protests of a fix)." If your statistics are

complex and confusing, or if you overuse them, they quickly become a liability. You will bog your listeners down in the swampy wasteland of incomprehensible complexity: "In fact, 67.4 percent of the top 3 percent of the 510 ridiculously rich muckety-mucks who reside in the tony section of Manhattan prefer Mama's Finest Brownies." Many accountants and computer geeks live in that treacherous land of complex statistics and speak its occult language; you, however, should stay away from there when you speak.

A speech consisting solely of your impressions and opinions is seldom as valuable or as persuasive as one that is grounded in concrete, clear facts—unless, of course, you are Bill Gates, Warren Buffett, or some other notable visionary (and if you are, why are you reading this book, anyway?). The rest of us mere mortals must do our homework and build our speeches on a solid bedrock of substance.

5

Use Presentation Building Blocks

He who resolves never to ransack any mind but his own
will soon be reduced from mere barrenness to the poorest of
all imitations; he will be obliged to imitate himself and to
repeat what he has before often repeated.

—Sir Joshua Reynolds

So, you are a little light on substance? (Don't get touchy—I'm referring to the speech, not you.) You have come to the right spot. Limitless resources are available for speakers to use to support, embellish, and enliven their presentations. The larger challenge may be sifting through the mounds of information you will dredge up in order to discover the precious nuggets of substance. Within seconds, you can access the world's largest library, the World Wide Web, and conduct research that not long ago would have taken you weeks or even months. Now, with the use of technology, you are able to tap into formerly unimaginable sources.

Thirteen Sources for Speech Content

The following are just a few teasers on where to begin your search, but keep in mind that the possibilities are infinite. Follow your imagination (just don't go exploring places you would not be willing to take your mother).

Before you plunge in, my apologies. This section gets a bit bookish. It's useful, I hope, but slightly tedious. Try digesting it in bite-size morsels. Plod through it one section at a time (pinch yourself periodically if that helps you to stay alert) and revisit it whenever the spirit moves you—or when you become absolutely desperate for ideas. I promise you, it's valuable, so steel yourself and forge ahead.

1. **Newspapers.** Newspapers are an excellent source for current facts, statistics, and anecdotes for your presentations. Newspapers such as *Investor's Business Daily*, the *New York Times*, the *Wall Street Journal*, and the *Washington Post* offer current, in-depth coverage of events affecting the world. The writing is typically lively, the perspectives are diverse, and the range of topics addressed is very broad.

   Many newspapers are available online; for example, the URLs for those mentioned in the preceding paragraph are, respectively, www.investors.com, www.nytimes.com, www.wsj .com, and www.washingtonpost.com. These publications will automatically e-mail you breaking news. This helps ensure that you have the most current information on your presentation topic. Here are a couple of exceptional news-related Web sites:

   - LexisNexis (www.lexis.com) is an online service that indexes more than 700 full-text databases, including a significant number of U.S. and international newspapers and up-to-the-minute information from such news wire services as Reuters and the Associated Press. Heed the warnings that a fee is involved, however; with a minimum of puttering around, you can incur hundreds or thousands of dollars in fees. That's a pretty hefty price for very little fun and no party favors.

- The Newsroom (www.auburn.edu/~vestmon/gif/news.html) links to most leading newspapers and broadcast news organizations and contains excellent business and financial information.

2. **Magazines.** Magazines such as *BusinessWeek, Forbes, Fortune, Harper's, Harvard Business Review, The New Republic, The New Yorker,* and *Time* explore diverse topics in great depth, making them rich resources of thought-provoking material that you can weave into your presentations. You can research many magazines on the Web. See, for example:
   - *BusinessWeek* (www.businessweek.com)
   - *Computerworld* (www.computerworld.com)
   - *IngentaConnect* (www.ingenta.com), which indexes more than 26,000 scholarly journals and magazines
   - *Newsweek* (www.newsweek.com)
   - *Scientific American* (www.scientificamerican.com)
   - *Time* (www.time.com)

3. **Television.** Television can be a rich source of data, if you ignore such rubbish as inane reality shows and insipid sitcoms. Transcripts from investigative reports (for example, *Dateline NBC*, CBS's *60 Minutes*, and ABC's *20/20*) and other excellent television broadcasts (the Discovery Channel, the History Channel) are frequently available online, sometimes without charge. Morningside Partners (www.fdch.com), formerly the Federal Document Clearing House, has many transcripts, audiotapes, and videotapes available for free. Other useful television Web sites include these:
   - www.abcnews.go.com
   - www.cbs.com
   - www.cnn.com
   - www.c-span.org
   - www.foxnews.com
   - www.msnbc.com
   - www.pbs.org

4. **Books.** Books are a valuable source of ideas and issues that every audience member confronts: personal responsibility, courage, dealing with change, life's passages, and—most important—the trendiest diets. Consider such a classic book as Napoleon Hill's *Think and Grow Rich*; such popular business books as *Good to Great* by James C. Collins, *Made to Stick* by Chip Heath and Dan Heath, *Outliers* by Malcolm Gladwell, and *The 7 Habits of Highly Effective People* by Stephen R. Covey; or such favorites with simple but poignant messages as *The Prayer of Jabez* by Bruce Wilkinson, *The Five People You Meet in Heaven* by Mitch Albom, or *It's Not About the Bike: My Journey Back to Life* by Lance Armstrong and Sally Jenkins. And for simple lessons that will spark the interest of every audience, peruse children's books, such as those by Dr. Seuss, *Sesame Street*, or Mister Rogers.

   You can find hundreds of thousands of books at local bookstores or online at Amazon (www.amazon.com) or Barnes & Noble (www.bn.com).

❧

What one knows best is . . . what one has learned not from books but as a result of books, through the reflections to which they have given rise.

—Sébastien Chamfort

❧

5. **Encyclopedias.** Encyclopedias offer a wealth of information to beef up any presentation. Many encyclopedias are readily available online, free or by subscription, such as *Encyclopaedia Britannica Online* (www.eb.com). In addition to such general encyclopedias, there are many on specialized subjects, including the following:
   - *Asian American Encyclopedia*
   - *Encyclopedia of Medical History*
   - *Encyclopedia of Philosophy*
   - *Encyclopedia of Religion*

- *Encyclopedia of World Art*
- *Encyclopedia of World Crime*
- *Food and Nutrition Encyclopedia*
- *Latino Encyclopedia*
- *McGraw-Hill Encyclopedia of Science and Technology*

6. **Dictionaries.** You should always have an excellent dictionary at your fingertips when you prepare any speech. The *American Heritage Dictionary*, *Merriam-Webster's Collegiate Dictionary*, and the *Oxford English Dictionary* are all respected general-purpose dictionaries. Many have downloadable software to expedite your search. Such specialized dictionaries as *Black's Law Dictionary*, the *Computer Dictionary*, and *Word and Phrase Origins* are also very helpful.

   There are dictionaries about virtually every subject: dictionaries of slang, bad manners, dates, symbols, statistics, feminism, business, economics, biographical information, and foreign languages. The best Web site to begin your search is one with links to over 800 dictionaries in 160 languages, found at www.yourdictionary.com. OneLook Dictionary Search (www.onelook.com) allows you to type in a word and then search the Internet for dictionaries containing the word. This site indexes approximately six million words—that ought to be enough to get you started.

ॐ

Consider not so much who speaks as what is spoken.

—Thomas Fuller

❧

7. **Almanacs.** Almanacs are an excellent source of information on a diverse range of topics, including education, law, politics, sports, and dates and events in history. Many almanacs are found on the Internet. The Infoplease site (www.infoplease .com) contains about 70 almanacs grouped by categories, and Refdesk (www.refdesk.com) links to more than 20 almanacs.

8. **Internet search engines.** You can find a wealth of information on the Web to aid you in preparing any presentation. This is both a blessing and a curse, since your search for a particular topic may generate several hundred thousand entries.

   To avoid getting smothered with information, master the rudimentary skills of Internet research. If you do not have those skills (or a child in grade school who can teach you), consider taking a class at a local college or university, or buy *How to Use the Internet* by Rogers Cadenhead; *The Internet for Dummies* by John R. Levine, et al.; or a similar how-to book. These books will save you countless hours of frustration.

   ❧

   Knowledge is the food of the soul.

   —Plato

   ❧

   Learn how to refine your searches so that an inquiry does not unearth thousands of marginally related sites. You can use a wide variety of search engines, such as the following, to find the information you need:
   - AltaVista (www.altavista.com)
   - Bing (www.bing.com)
   - Excite (www.excite.com)
   - Google (www.google.com)
   - Northern Light (www.northernlight.com)
   - WebCrawler (www.webcrawler.com)
   - Yahoo! (www.yahoo.com)

   Also try several metasearch engines, such as Dogpile (www.dogpile.com) and Metacrawler (www.metacrawler.com). These Web sites send your information request to numerous search engines at one time. One particularly useful site, where you can simply type in a question rather than a keyword, is Ask (www.ask.com). For example, if you were looking for information on bungee jumping, you would simply type in, "Where do I find information on bungee jumping?" Click the

Search button, and presto! Hundreds if not thousands of Web sites would appear that address your question (including several that might suggest a saliva test to gauge your sanity for even considering bungee jumping—but I digress).

9. **Internet reference sites.** The Internet has many excellent reference sites:

   • NewsLink (newslink.org) is a great source for radio and television broadcast information.

   • Refdesk (www.refdesk.com), already mentioned under the "Almanacs" source, provides hundreds of links to other reference sources, such as dictionaries, thesauri, news media, and magazines.

   • UCI Libraries Research (www.lib.uci.edu) contains useful references with links to encyclopedias, dictionaries, and historical documents.

10. **The public library.** My younger readers are scratching their heads and asking: "What's a library?" Yes, libraries still exist, and they are excellent resources for information on virtually any subject. Rummage around and you will discover a wealth of ideas. Moreover, they usually have reference librarians (who are occasionally grumpy and sometimes scary, but harmless), who can help steer your research in the right direction. Endear yourself to them (calling them "grumpy" probably will not help your cause), because these experts can save you countless hours of digging for information, and they often come up with ideas and sources that you might not have considered.

    In the library—and online in many cases—you will find all the sources already identified, as well as other valuable research tools, including the following:

    • *Bartlett's Familiar Quotations*
    • *Biography Index*
    • *The Guinness Book of World Records*
    • *Information Please Almanac*
    • *The New York Times Index*
    • *The Reader's Guide to Periodical Literature*

❧

*Some [people] regard the library as a sinner regards church—as a place
to be entered in the most desperate circumstances.*

—Stephen E. Lucas

❧

11. **Organizations.** The library and the Blue and Yellow Pages of
the telephone book provide listings of many civic, historical,
trade, and government organizations that are delighted to
provide you with valuable background information and
literature, and, of course, a membership application. Start
your investigation by looking under key words, such as
"business associations," "organizations," "fraternities," "clubs,"
and "Chambers of Commerce," and you will discover many
promising leads.

12. **A speaker's library.** Build a personal library filled with
research tools that you can use when drafting and revising
your speech. While some of these reference tools are found on
the Internet, sometimes the selection online is more limited.
Recommended reference sources for your personal library
include the following:

   - *Bartlett's Familiar Quotations* by John Bartlett
   - *The Chicago Manual of Style,* fifteenth edition
   - *The Elements of Style,* fiftieth anniversary edition, by
     William Strunk Jr., and E. B. White
   - *Garner's Modern American Usage* by Bryan A. Garner
   - *Merriam-Webster's Manual for Writers and Editors*
   - *The New Dictionary of Cultural Literacy: What Every
     American Needs to Know,* edited by James Trefil, Joseph F.
     Kett, and E. D. Hirsch
   - *The Oxford Dictionary of Quotations,* edited by Elizabeth
     Knowles
   - *Random House Webster's Quotationary,* edited by Leonard
     Roy Frank
   - *Roget's International Thesaurus,* sixth revised edition, edited
     by Barbara Ann Kipfer, Ph.D.

You should also own several books of great speeches, which you can find in the business or speaking sections of any bookstore. All these books will generate ideas as well as illustrate how exceptional speeches are crafted.

13. **Government resources.** If you are searching for obscure or esoteric information from the government, such as studies, reports, bulletins, trivia, and miscellaneous gobbledygook, poke around on the following Web sites. Beware, however: don't venture into these dreary sites without first gulping a triple jolt of java:

- The Federal Web Locator (www.lib.auburn.edu/madd/docs/fedloc.html) links to all major U.S. government Web sites, including the sites for Congress, the FBI, the Department of Education, the Food and Drug Administration, the Centers for Disease Control, and the Environmental Protection Agency.
- FedStats (www.fedstats.gov) provides statistics from more than 100 U.S. federal agencies.
- FedWorld (www.fedworld.gov) contains useful federal government information.
- State and Local Government on the Net (www.statelocalgov.net) links to all 50 state governments, as well as to selected cities and towns.
- *The Statistical Abstract of the United States* (www.census.gov/compendia/statab) provides tables, statistics, and other information about life in the United States.
- *The World Factbook* (www.cia.gov/library/publications/the-world-factbook/), published annually by the U.S. Central Intelligence Agency, provides information about people, governments, economies, communication, and transportation from every country in the world.

Breathe! You made it through principle 5 without dozing off, although your eyes do look a little bleary. You might end up using only a fraction of what you discover while ransacking for information, but the range and depth of knowledge that you will gain during your quest will broaden your perspective, prepare you to answer questions, and enhance your confidence and credibility. Start sleuthing.

6

Analyze Your Audience Before You Speak

*A speech is a solemn responsibility. The man who makes a bad
30-minute speech to 200 people wastes only a half hour of his own time.
But he wastes 100 hours of the audience's time—more than four
days—which should be a hanging offense.*

—Jenkin Lloyd Jones

Why is it important that you research your audience before you speak? (It had better be important, to warrant devoting an entire principle to it, right?) Here's why: your typical audience member today has a microscopic attention span, about 30 seconds—45 on a really good day. I hate to burst your bubble if you cling to the romantic notion that your listeners are riveted to your every word. Sorry, they are not.

But you can't blame them, because the competition for their attention is stiff. The lives of most of your audience members are stretched paper-thin; they are juggling tight schedules, with crushing personal and professional demands on their time. While listening to you, each of them is simultaneously thinking about a variety of issues unrelated to your speech: "Will wispy Joey *finally* make the peewee football team (the sixth time is the charm, after all), or will his dreams be dashed once again?"

"Will I have to spend hours trapped in horrendous rush-hour traffic, listening to sappy elevator music?" "Will the tyrants at Weight Watchers somehow bless the triple-butter biscuit I just gobbled down?" And if the idea of all that chatter and hubbub competing for their attention is not enough, the following assertion will really dismay you: many people in your audience could probably point out numerous places that they would rather be, and a dozen things that they would rather be doing, than sitting in their uncomfortable seats listening to you.

So what does all that mean for you as the speaker? You had better know the members of your audience and what they want to hear. And you had better give them exactly that—and give it to them quickly, too. Otherwise, they may hang around for a while during your talk, but not for long; by the forty-sixth second, they will be off and away, thinking about far more pressing personal matters.

This principle examines *why* you need to know your audience and *what* you need to know about them; principle 7 will give you some techniques on *how* to get to know your audience.

Why You Need to Know Your Audience

Look at it from your listeners' perspective: as they sit there, they are giving you their most precious commodity—their time. You waste that time at your peril. An audience resents a speaker who knows nothing about her listeners, who is unprepared, who rambles aimlessly, who doesn't appreciate the gift of time that she has been given, and who brazenly squanders that gift. A speaker who commits these transgressions sends a clear message to everyone who is listening: "I'm important, but you and your time are not. Deal with it." Do that too often, and your speaking prospects will shrivel up—fast.

Suppose you are advocating a zoning variance at a neighborhood planning meeting. You are the big enchilada of Boffo Builders, and you need the variance so that you can begin construction of your dream project: a sewage treatment facility (some people have peculiar dreams). Your crack attorney has pondered and churned this issue for weeks and has finally advised you, for a legal fee that would purchase a small yacht, that, by golly, you are legally entitled to the variance.

Still, you have no desire for a nasty, costly dispute with the proactive neighborhood group, which—surprise!—prefers that you build the sewage plant anywhere else (for instance, in your lawyer's neighborhood). You prefer to resolve this amicably, by engendering goodwill with the neighbors (well, as much goodwill as anyone plunking down a sewage plant in the neighbors' backyard can expect).

ঽ▲

There are some who speak one moment before they think.

—Jean de la Bruyère

◢§

Unfortunately, rather than studying and understanding your audience's perspective, you, being the wily advocate that you are, decide to rely solely on the strength of your legal arguments when addressing the neighborhood zoning board. You spout legal mumbo jumbo: "The legal precedent for unfettered construction of sewage plants on every street corner was first set in 1876 in the case . . . *blah, blah, yammer, yammer.*" But something promptly goes amiss, and your listeners become surly. They shake their heads in disagreement, lock their jaws, and glare menacingly. You begin to fear for your safety. Round one in the titanic sewage plant struggle goes to the homeowners. Why?

You did not know your audience. If you had bothered to nose around before you spoke, you would have discovered that the planners were wary because a previous builder had lied to them. You might also have learned that it was just one or two instigators from the neighborhood who were fueling the flames of discontent (and they own a porta-potty company). Perhaps you could have earned the zoning board members' confidence if you had addressed their concerns, defused or neutralized some of their hostility, or focused your talk on the advantages of a sewage facility (increased tax revenue, more jobs, surplus yard fertilizer—okay, I'm grasping here).

A presentation based on law and logic might have been entirely appropriate for a different, more receptive, less emotional group. But your legal and technical arguments were doomed to fail with these audience members, because of their peculiar circumstances: the previous deceitful builder and the couple of instigators in the audience with their own hidden agenda. Unfortunately, you needed to uncover those critical details *before* the presentation, not after it. Once you are in the midst of the maelstrom, with your agitated listeners spewing invectives and hurling books and drinks at you, it's too late. At that point, you can only duck and pray.

❧

In a conversation, keep in mind that you're more interested in what you have to say than anyone else is.

—Andrew S. Rooney

❧

The bottom line is simple: know your audience. No one can *make* them listen to you, and if you don't lure them in, they won't listen. It is up to you to make them *want* to listen. If you are only guessing about their backgrounds, experiences, interests, and concerns, you are simply rolling the dice. And the chances are excellent that you will guess wrong. Before you can tailor your presentation to your listeners' interests, you must get to know them by answering the following questions.

What You Need to Know about Your Audience

All right, you think that maybe you ought to get to know the members of your audience a little better. What do you want to know about them? Everything—but since knowing "everything" might be somewhat over-whelming (not to mention intrusive), let's use the tips in principle 7 to focus on finding the answers to a few demographic, philosophical, and psychological questions, such as the following:

- What is the size of your audience? The dynamics of speaking at an intimate gathering in a conference room are far different from those of speaking in a civic center that's jammed to the rafters with bodies.

- What is the ethnicity of your listeners? Do they share a collective heritage and a sense of ethnic pride? Do they share customs, culture, language, or history?
- What is the economic status of your listeners? Are they living in poverty, comfort, or luxury? Listeners will be more receptive to a message that demonstrates an understanding of and sensitivity to their economic conditions. For example, college students sustaining themselves on compressed mystery meat in a can and KooKoo cupcakes will not relate to some filthy-rich windbag huffing and puffing about his stock portfolio and his "cottage" in the Hamptons.
- Are your listeners there voluntarily, because they are genuinely interested in your topic, or are they required to attend your presentation by the bigwigs? That makes a huge difference.
- What group affiliations do your listeners have, such as social, golf, or tennis clubs; university alumni clubs; political parties; sororities or fraternities; civic organizations; professional associations; or religious affiliations? Members of the Sierra Club would react far differently to a presentation on increasing oil exploration in wilderness regions than would a group of petroleum executives.
- Do your listeners share common values and beliefs that are consistent with your message, or will your speech challenge or threaten their values and beliefs?
- What is your audience's attitude toward you and your topic: receptive or hostile, interested or indifferent? Do audience members have inflexible opinions that will prevent them from really listening to you?
- Do members of your audience have a hidden agenda?
- Will your message rankle anyone in your audience because of its controversial, religious, or political content? The mere mention of such words as *abortion* or *gun control* (or maybe *sewage plants*) will cause some people to bristle.
- Have previous speakers addressed your topic? If so, does your slant support or contradict the position of those speakers? Does your presentation offer a new perspective?

- What do your listeners *expect* to hear? What do they *want* to hear? What do they *need* to hear?
- What is the average age of your listeners? Why is that important? Because if your message is centered on a historical event that occurred before your listeners were born (the Cuban missile crisis or Captain Kangaroo's exploits, for instance), you will need to explain that event in more detail. Conversely, your message involving the latest rage in body piercing and tattooing might be lost on your audience of senior citizens unless you give them some background. If you don't consider your listeners' average age, expect looks of bewilderment.
- Are your listeners familiar with the issues you will be addressing? Don't waste time belaboring what they already know, and, conversely, don't talk about some esoteric issue that will whiz right over their heads.
- Will your listeners understand the industry-specific, scientific, or technical terminology you may be using? Don't try to impress them with pretentious terms, because that is just as likely to baffle them. And ask yourself, for the sake of simple clarity, if you *really* need to use jargon, acronyms, euphemisms, or pompous language even if they do understand it?
- Finally, what are the real-life experiences and concerns of your listeners?

Once you have all this information—and principle 7 will provide tools to help you find it—you can decide what is important to your listeners, what motivates them, and how you might persuade them. Then you can tailor your talk in the most productive way. Does this mean that you should skirt controversial issues or kowtow to your listeners? No, but it does mean that you had better be well prepared. Anticipate their reactions and craft your presentation with all the potential risks and benefits in mind.

I once heard an abominable speech by a pasty civil servant in which he droned on for an hour (though it seemed like an eternity plus a day to every unfortunate soul in his audience) about the proper way to complete a 25-page procurement proposal for a government contract. Beyond being dreadfully boring, the speech was crammed with dense terminology and obscure acronyms that few people in his audience understood, and few were up for the challenge of trying to understand. His audience was composed of predominantly ambitious Internet entrepreneurs who had zero interest in listening to his irrelevant topic.

It was apparent that his listeners were detached and stupefied. I am sure I heard someone from the back of the room plead, "Please, please make him stop!" Many were texting on cell phones, others were reading *Fast Company* or the *Wall Street Journal*, and still others were surfing the Internet on their BlackBerrys. Meanwhile, up at the podium, the hack trudged along, but no one was listening. His mistake? He had failed to assess his audience before speaking, and it seemed clear that he knew nothing—or cared nothing—about them. He was probably still humming along when they shut off the lights; I didn't stick around to find out.

❧

Every fact depends for its value on how much we already know.

—Ralph Waldo Emerson

✖

I know what you're thinking: "Gosh, this sounds like a lot of work!" It is, but it makes a bloody big difference. When you tailor your presentation to your audience, you are far more likely to be persuasive and achieve the results you desire, and your audience members are far less likely to vote with their feet and bolt for the exits during your talk. Invest the time necessary to get to know your audience and reap the enormous benefits.

7

Use These Tools to Get to
Know Your Audience

I keep six honest serving-men
(They taught me all I knew);
Their names are What and Why and When
And How and Where and Who.

—Rudyard Kipling

As a speaker, you want your listeners to go where you want them to go, to see what you want them to see, and ultimately to agree with or, at the very least, thoughtfully consider your conclusions. But that is not always easily accomplished. Why? Because your listeners may not be hearing or processing the information the way you would like them to. They may not get it the way you intended. And bludgeoning them with your message, grousing that they are buffoons, or even holding your breath until you turn blue will not help.

You are dealing with human beings with preconceptions; they hear your message through the filters of their experiences and expectations. This means that they typically hear only what they want to hear, and disregard the rest. So they are very likely to veer off the course you have charted for them:

> [People] usually want to hear about things that are meaningful to them. People are *egocentric*. They pay closest attention to messages that affect their own values, their own beliefs, their own well-being. Listeners typically approach speeches with one question uppermost in mind. "Why is this important to *me?*"[1]

Determining what is important to an audience can be daunting, because each audience is different. But determining what is important is your task, so keep it in mind at all times. If you talk only about what matters to *you* and focus only on *your* perspective, you cannot expect your audience to concur with your conclusions or even tag along as you make your points. To be an effective speaker, you need to anticipate your listeners' interests, likes, dislikes, ambitions—the whole shebang. Let them know that you understand their perspective and their concerns. Sharpen your focus, and tailor every presentation to your listeners. It will make a huge difference.

Eight Tips on Researching Your Audience

Instead of wailing and gnashing your teeth about this challenge ("Gee, more work?"), or blindly throwing darts and hoping that something you say might be pertinent, act like a private investigator (all right, strap on a cap gun and pin on a badge if you must), and start researching. Before you begin crafting your speech, you need to find answers to the questions posed in principle 6. The following profitable tips will help you find those answers:

1. **Send a prepresentation questionnaire.** Here is a novel concept: if you want to know what is important to your listeners, ask them. Insightful, right? Months before the event, send a prepresentation questionnaire to the company, organization, or association where you will be speaking. Tailor your questions to the purpose of your talk. Ask prospective audience members to complete the questionnaire and return

it to you. Make it easy for them by allowing them to complete and submit the information by e-mail. Assure them that their responses will be kept anonymous if you want to enhance participation.

Not everyone will respond, so don't get your feelings hurt. But any kernel of insight can help you gauge your listeners' knowledge, interests, and expectations regarding the presentation. That is a huge step on the road to understanding them.

2. **Explore the organization's Web site.** Most organizations and associations have a Web site that is a gold mine of information. It typically contains a flowery letter from the CEO or president, a mission statement, the company's vision, current company news, press releases, and other valuable tidbits that you can blend into your speech. Just as important, you might discover the political quagmires you should skirt in your speech — company downsizing, pending federal investigations, or setbacks for the company's golf team.

3. **Search the Internet.** Thanks to the World Wide Web, precious information is at your fingertips, including many recent newspaper and magazine articles and press releases (principle 5). Explore away on Google, Yahoo!, or your Internet search engine of choice. LexisNexis (www.lexisnexis .com) provides background information on literally millions of individuals and companies globally. Hoover's Online (www.hoovers.com) has current and historical information on thousands of companies. The Internet Public Library's *Census Data and Demographics Reference* (www.ipl.org/div/subject/ browse/ref24.00.00/) gives demographic profiles of people based on their country, state, county, city, and zip code. The U.S. Census Bureau *Gazetteer* (www.census.gov/cgi-bin/ gazetteer) makes it easy for you to customize a search for demographic information based on zip codes. Finally, the Better Business Bureau Web site (www.bbb.org) contains profitable historical information on more than 2 million businesses and charities.

ᴥ

Every great work is the fruit of patience, perseverance, and
concentration.

—Santiago Ramón y Cajal

ᴥ

4. **Review company literature.** Obtain copies of programs or handouts from any recent meetings that may be available (brochures from an annual meeting are a great starting point), as well as a preliminary draft of the agenda for the event at which you will speak. If the organization has a newsletter or an e-zine, request copies of the past few issues. Some of these materials may be available on the company's Web site. These sources will provide current, relevant information that you can use fruitfully in your presentation.

5. **Analyze shareholder reports.** Quarterly and annual shareholder reports contain the lowdown about a company's philosophy and culture. You may doze off as you pore over portions of this mind-numbing information, but try to stay alert, because it can be valuable digging. And a word of caution: these reports are often written euphemistically, to paint a rosy picture. There is probably an untold story between the lines, so review this information with a skeptical eye.

6. **Inspect public records.** There is a prodigious—some might even say frightening—amount of information on many individuals and most organizations in the public records: news articles; reports filed with government agencies, including filings with the Securities and Exchange Commission; pending litigation; or outstanding judgments. Root around to identify current developments, the influential representatives of the organization (CEO, president, chief financial officer), and the company's position on various issues. You can find much of this information online, in the county courthouse records, in the public library, and in the Library of Congress.

7. **Interview your host.** Buy your host, or some knowledgeable insider with the organization or association where you will speak, a bagel, a cup of coffee, or a scoop of cookie-dough ice cream, and interview him. Many corporations and associations have a public relations coordinator, who can provide you with a wealth of information. Start there.

   Be focused and precise in your inquiries. Don't start racking your brain for questions while your interviewee is fidgeting before you, drumming his fingers, rolling his eyes, and anxiously anticipating the end of the meeting. Be prepared, with a tight agenda and specific questions.

   Emphasize how important this information is to the success of your presentation. Typically, the person you interview has a vested interest in providing you with this information, since your presentation will also be a reflection on her. Subtly mention: "If I flop, we both flop" (or something perhaps a tad more diplomatic, but you get the point).

*He is considered the most graceful speaker who can
say nothing in [the] most words.*

—Samuel Butler

8. **Interview audience members.** If possible, talk to some of the influential audience members (the chairman, a director, a member of the management team, or the true oracle of most organizations: the receptionist). Interview them using the questions in principle 6. Ask them about the most important issues facing the company, such as what the company could do to improve employee loyalty or morale, what the employees like most about working for the company, and how the company differs from its competitors. This information will not only help you customize your speech, but it will also bestow upon you the added cachet of being an insider and a member of the team.

Be careful not to use information that might embarrass or offend anyone. When in doubt, take it out. If you use it sensibly, however, the information you gather in this interviewing process will add interest, credibility, and perhaps a splash of humor to your speech.

So, there is the task and the starting point. Completing the task will require some plain old hard work and a dollop of gumption, but rest assured that your listeners will be flattered that you have customized your comments for them. Get into their heads and answer their critical question: "What is in this for me?" Listeners are remarkably perceptive, and they will quickly spot, and appreciate, a prepared speaker. Make sure that this is the conclusion they form about you.

8

Adopt from the Best Speakers

Example, the surest measure of instruction.

—Pliny the Younger

Here is a bit of advice that may sound like pure heresy: disregard what you learned as a child and become a relentless copycat. Steal (okay, stop squirming; "imitate" if that eases your conscience) techniques from the best speakers and make them yours. Don't just do this occasionally; do it constantly, shamelessly, and proudly. Look for anything you can use to sharpen your speaking skills, from minor tweaks to sweeping changes. It is perfectly acceptable to do this. Alarms will not sound, and even your clergy would approve.

Why copy? To dramatically accelerate your progress. Emulate, and not only will you enhance your skills as a speaker, but, just as important, you will avoid many speaking snafus, those painful goofs that can bruise your fragile speaking psyche. If you are resisting the idea of copying because you are intoxicated with your speaking prowess, sober up (and review principle 3). Even exceptional speakers can get better; they constantly work to improve their presentations, and you should, too.

Brian Tracy, a prominent professional speaker, credits much of his speaking success to studying others:

> The key to success is to learn from the experts. Study and copy the very best people in your field. Do what they do, day after day, until it becomes second nature. And then, Surprise! Surprise! You will begin to get the same results.[1]

Your ultimate goal is to develop a speaking style that fits you now and that will evolve with you over the years, a style that makes you the most effective, authentic, and compelling speaker you can be.

Don't wring your hands about borrowing from others, because no two speakers are alike, and there is no one perfect speaking template that applies to every speaker. Even if you adopt *every* technique that a certain speaker uses, you will never be able to exactly replicate that speaker's style. Virtually every aspect of your delivery—the cadence, timing, pausing, intonation, vocal energy, movement, body language—will be different. Not only that, but certain techniques that work for others may fail miserably for you.

❧

Better be wise by the misfortunes of others than by your own.

—Aesop

❧

For example, consider two exceptional professional speakers, Paul Harvey and Anthony Robbins. It would be hard to find two people with more diverse speaking styles. Mr. Harvey cajoles and soothes, while Mr. Robbins thunders and rants. Mr. Harvey would hardly seem genuine, and would probably look absurd, if he were to bound around the stage like a whirling dervish, thumping his chest, exhorting the audience to jump about wildly, and slapping hands with perfect strangers. In fact, he might hurt himself if he tried. But that is Mr. Robbins's unique style. At the same time, Mr. Robbins would not seem authentic if he were planted in one spot, relying on Mr. Harvey's easy, folksy manner, replete with dramatic pauses, titillating stories, and frequent surprises. His audiences would suspect that he had been sedated. Each speaker, however, excels with what works for him. Experiment using some of their techniques — just be careful not to bruise yourself.

Study other speakers and ask probing questions about them and their speeches:

- Does the speaker seem to be authentic, or does she seem phony?
- Does he project confidence, or does he exude fear?
- Does she talk *to* you, or does she simply talk *at* you?
- Does he move fluidly, or does he seem as stiff as one of NASA's robots?
- Is her delivery natural, or is it disjointed and choppy?
- Is he speaking so quickly that he jabbers, or so slowly that he drags?
- Are her words precise and vivid, or is the speech riddled with jargon and pretentious language?
- Are his descriptions and stories fresh and engaging, or are they hackneyed and lackluster?
- Are the theme and points clear and concise, or is the speech just a big blob of random words and thoughts?
- Is her organization tight, or does it veer around like a yo-yo?
- Does he smoothly segue from point to point, or does he lurch along?
- Does she seem passionate, or does she seem indifferent?
- Does he sound pleasing, or does he sound strident, shrill, and unnatural?
- Does she engage you, or does she bore you?

Eight Powerful Speaking Techniques

If you want to emulate the best, begin by studying a speech that many experts consider to be one of the finest of all time: "I Have a Dream," by Dr. Martin Luther King Jr. He delivered it from the steps of the Lincoln Memorial in Washington, D.C., on August 28, 1963, to more than 200,000 people.[2] The speech is packed with outstanding lessons.

It is a masterpiece both because of the way it was crafted and because of the manner in which Dr. King delivered it. To fully appreciate the artistry of this speech, you should study a tape of it. Simply reading the words, though instructive, fails to do justice to Dr. King's eloquent delivery. His speech illustrates at least eight exceptional speaking techniques:

1. **Imagery.** Dr. King used descriptive phrases, such as "a great beacon light of hope," "flames of withering injustice," and "crippled by the manacles of segregation and the chains of discrimination." He created vivid pictures that each audience member could clearly visualize, and precise images make any speech more memorable.

ᴥ

Genius . . . is the child of imitation.

—Sir Joshua Reynolds

ᴥ

2. **Metaphor.** Dr. King relied on metaphors throughout his speech. Expressions such as "down in Alabama, with its vicious racists, with its governor having his lips dripping with the words of interposition and nullification" and a "lonely island of poverty in the midst of a vast ocean of material prosperity" breathed heart and soul into the speech. These graphic metaphors intensified his message by providing physical examples of the raw emotions he was expressing.
3. **Alliteration.** Through the adroit use of repeated consonant sounds, such phrases as "the bank of justice is bankrupt," "marvelous new militancy," and "they will not be judged by the color of their skin, but by the content of their character" made the message rhythmic and poetic.
4. **Vocal energy.** Listen to a recording of the speech, and study how Dr. King used his voice—the inflection, the vitality, the variation in his highs and lows—to convey his emotions and engage his listeners. He used his voice masterfully to express

his passion and conviction about his topic. Unquestionably, this heightened the impact of his words.

5. **Repetition.** To further heighten the impact, Dr. King repeated such phrases as "now is the time," "let freedom ring," and, of course, "I have a dream." These phrases forcefully emphasized the theme of his speech, especially as the intensity of his delivery built with each repetition.

❦

All great speakers were bad speakers at first.

—Ralph Waldo Emerson

❦

6. **Rhythm.** The carefully selected language in the speech created a rhythm of expression. The following selections are prime examples of this: "We cannot be satisfied as long as a Negro in Mississippi cannot vote and a Negro in New York believes he has nothing for which to vote" and "we will be able to work together, to pray together, to struggle together, to go to jail together, to stand up for freedom together . . ."

7. **Pauses.** Dr. King paused repeatedly throughout the speech— when he delivered key passages, when he made transitions from point to point, and when the crowd was applauding. This focused the attention of his listeners on the point that he was about to make or had just made. It also allowed the listeners time to process the message.

8. **Audience connection.** To forge a strong connection with his audience, Dr. King used the word *we* throughout the speech. Such phrases as "we have come to this hallowed spot," "we can never be satisfied," and "when we let freedom ring" created a sense of inclusiveness between Dr. King and his audience.

❦

We are, in truth, more than half what we are by imitation. The great point is, to choose good models and to study them with care.

—Lord Chesterfield

❦

To find great speeches, rummage around the Internet as well as in your local library, bookstore, or video store. Analyze videos, ranging from the basics on how to make a persuasive speech to the greatest speeches of all time.

Surf the Web, and you will discover a variety of exceptional speeches on an array of topics, both historical and current. To watch these videos, you need software such as RealPlayer or Apple's QuickTime, which you can download free. Go to the Web site Rhapsody & RealPlayer (www .real.com) or Apple-QuickTime-Download (www.apple.com/quicktime/ download/win.html), and follow the prompts for downloading. The History Channel speech archive (www.historychannel.com/speeches) has the speeches of such prominent figures as Amelia Earhart, Winston Churchill, John F. Kennedy, and Malcolm X. FedNet (www.fednet.net) provides real-time as well as archived presentations.

Watch the television evangelists on Sunday morning. Analyze their body language, gesturing, storytelling, vocal variety, pacing, and dramatic pausing (but be careful not to get seduced into a tithing frenzy). Study the man standing on the park bench, raging about our decadent lifestyles, as well as the candidate, wheedling voters with grandiose promises. The world is your speaking laboratory, and you just never know where you will find inspiration.

❧

Keep company with those who make you better.

—English proverb

❧

Be a shameless copycat. You will not turn into a pillar of stone if you "emulate," "copy," "borrow from," or "mimic" exceptional speakers. Become a critic and a sponge, absorbing techniques from every speaker you hear; be constantly vigilant for anything that will help you improve. Cultivate role models. There are all kinds of speakers and all kinds of techniques. Fiddle endlessly until you find the style that works for you. Do you want to become your best? Then adopt from the best.

PART III

BUILD WITH A BLUEPRINT

If you are a procrastinator who is stimulated by a deadline—that is, if you budget about eight minutes to draft your speech in the car on the way to your speaking engagement—this truism may jolt you: exceptional speeches are *never* created in a single draft—*never*. Sorry, but even the finest speakers wrestle with their texts. More likely than not, your initial stab at the speech will be plagued with faults: tortured logic, circular construction, cluttered language, and obscure jargon . . . and that is on a good day.

ﻉﺍ

> *You've got to be very careful if you don't know where you are going,*
> *because you might not get there.*
>
> —Yogi Berra

ﺍﻉ

Exceptional speeches don't just tumble out of your head or come up and bite you on the bottom. They are carefully planned, meticulously drafted, and repeatedly refined. They share one common characteristic: uncompromising attention to detail. Excellent speeches are constructed with solid building blocks, which include a clear theme, logical organization, a captivating opening, precise sentences, vivid imagery, colorful language, engaging stories, and a dynamic closing.

As you craft and edit your speech, decide whether you are saying what you want to say in the most compelling manner. Ask yourself one simple question at every stage: "Will my listeners *want* to listen to this?" Be brutally honest. If the answer is no, grab your editing pen, because you will not get a second chance to make a favorable impression. Part III provides the blueprint for building a memorable presentation.

9

State Your Purpose

He is one of those orators of whom it is well said, "Before they get up, they do not know what they are going to say; when they are speaking, they do not know what they are saying; when they sit down, they do not know what they have said."

—Winston Churchill

The caffeine is flowing through your veins, and you are ready to write your speech. You have read Part II (you didn't skip ahead, did you?) and carefully followed the guidelines. Your shoebox of speech material is brimming with clippings, notes, random thoughts, and insightful snippets that you have squirreled away for this speech, and you are sure you know the audience like you do a good friend. Even better, the ideas are floating around in your noodle, and you are raring to go. But, before you draft your first word, answer this one pressing question:

What's your point?

You muse: "To write a speech?" "To make a report?" "To please my boss, who actually expects me to say something meaningful?" All true, perhaps, but dig deeper. Never lose sight of the reason why you are speaking—a simple rule that mediocre speakers regularly flout. You should always be able to state in one concise sentence: "My purpose in speaking is _____" (this is the part where you fill in the blank). If you cannot state your purpose so succinctly that you could write it on the back of a business card, then maybe, just maybe, you don't know the point of your talk. And, rest assured, your evident failure to know it *will not* please either your boss or your audience.

If you don't know your point, watch out, because you are sliding down the slippery slope of Murky Thinking, plunging head first toward Utter Confusion. You will barrage your listeners with minute details, or you will ramble aimlessly from topic to topic, creating a hodgepodge of random thoughts. The befuddled audience members will impatiently mutter, "Sheesh, where in the world is this going?" At best, your message will be severely diluted; at worst, it will be utterly ineffective.

❧

What's the point of coming to the point when you don't have a point?

—John R. Trimble

❧

Cavett Robert, an exceptional speaker and the founder of the National Speakers Association, used a wonderful expression that precisely summarizes the importance of making your purpose clear: "If it's foggy in the pulpit, it's foggy in the pews." If the message is not clear to you, it will not be clear to your audience. Sometimes the fogginess is so maddening that your listeners just want to leap from their seats and shout, "My kingdom for a point . . . any point!" When that happens—and, with many speakers, it happens far too frequently—the audience members will straggle off in search of another speaker, one who can be clear. And they will not be easily lured back.

Why are so many speakers unfocused? There are several plausible— but unacceptable—explanations.

Perhaps the speaker is attempting to establish his expertise by smothering his listeners with information. Such a strategy is never productive, because his listeners cannot and will not process an avalanche of words. They will just shut down. Too many details are just as confusing as too few; an effective, focused speaker provides the pertinent facts but not every tiny factoid.

Perhaps the speaker is unprepared, and she has deluded herself into thinking that she can dazzle her listeners by speaking "off the cuff." That's doubtful. She would have to be amazingly good to do that, and most of us are not amazingly good when speaking off the cuff. You seldom hit your target with this haphazard approach. You typically lose your bearings early in the speech, and then you soon notice—if you are looking, that is—the puzzled looks of your listeners.

Sometimes a speaker is unclear because he has failed to clarify his purpose in his own mind; he just doesn't know what he wants to say. He hopes that if he yammers long enough, his listeners may grope around until *they* somehow understand the purpose. As a result, what should be clear, informative, and persuasive is often jumbled, obscure, and disappointing.

Finally, there is the speaker who is intentionally vague in order to defuse opposition or to mask her position. If she could honestly explain it to you, she might say, "Being vague is the only refuge I have—my smoke screen. . . . Vagueness lets me get by with sort-of-understanding, and it disarms you a bit, since you'll have difficulty knowing where you disagree with me."[1]

✦

I love talking about nothing, Father. It is the only thing
I know anything about.

—Oscar Wilde

✦

One of the senior partners at my first law firm used to listen to each of the neophyte attorneys advocate a position. I can still remember the pensive pause at the end of one of my dismal, meandering presentations. Finally, after clearing his throat, he began his critique. His scathing words wilted me and to this day still send shivers down my spine: "I've just heard a lot of fuzzy-headed thinking in this room." This is an apt litmus test for any speaker. Ask yourself: "Am I fuzzy-headed about my reason for speaking?"

How can you enhance the prospect that your audience will grasp your message? Simple: be clear. Not to be flippant, but it really is not much more complicated than that. Make your theme clear from the outset. Give your audience direction. In the first minute of your presentation, tell your listeners what you intend to accomplish. Help them understand; don't make them guess (because they will usually guess wrong) or work too hard to decipher your meaning (because they usually won't work at all).

Say you lived in Orlando and wanted to drive to Des Moines, but you had never driven there before. (All right, choose a different destination if Des Moines doesn't get your juices flowing.) Would you simply pack the car, cross your fingers, and head off into the great unknown ("Maybe I will drive due west for a bit, then I will head north for a while . . .")? Would you stubbornly press forward even if your path were leading you directly to the middle of nowhere? I hope not. And if you did, most of the passengers in your traveling party would be worried about your adventuresome approach; they would prefer to know that you had a precise plan, or maybe even a map to guide you.

Audiences are no different from your passengers (in fact, they *are* your passengers): they want to know where you are headed, and they want to know it quickly. You need to provide your listeners with direction.

❧

Men of few words are the best men.

—William Shakespeare

❧

Limit Your Points

After you have clarified your purpose, distill your message to just those points that are essential for supporting your theme.

One aspiring politician began a campaign speech with this startling pronouncement: "There are *20* reasons why I deserve your vote." The audience laughed awkwardly, no doubt hoping that he was simply engaging in hyperbole. He was not. Thirty minutes into the presentation, after he had covered the fifth reason, it was obvious that he intended to discuss all 20 reasons in excruciating detail. He lost the audience that day, and he ultimately lost the election—probably because the voters feared that they would have to listen to another one of his rambling speeches.

There are no categorical rules on how many points you should include to support your primary theme. That depends on such factors as the amount of time you have to speak, the relative importance of each point, and your audience's level of interest in and knowledge of your topic. Clearly, 20 points are far too many; no audience will stay focused for the time it would take to develop so many ideas. Keep this thought in mind: in the entire history of speaking, only a handful of audiences have ever complained that a presentation was too short. Let that be your ultimate guide.

ᴥ

Don't drown yourself in details.

—Ferdinand Foch

♣

Just because you know everything about your topic does not mean that you should bore your listeners with every detail. Tell them only what they need to know, that which affects them, and eliminate the rest. And don't try to squeeze in more information by simply talking faster. That strategy undermines your professional image and credibility.

Never lose sight of your purpose in speaking as you draft and revise your speech. Weed out any cluttered thinking or random thoughts—even the witty ones if they sidetrack you. Know exactly what you want to accomplish with your speech. Eliminate all "fuzzy-headed thinking," so that when you step up to the lectern, you will be clear.

10

Organize for Coherence

Order and simplification are the first steps toward mastery of a subject.

—Thomas Mann

The rules of speaking are constantly evolving; what was forbidden yester-day is acceptable today. There are simply very few immutable maxims. Nevertheless, here is one: *be organized.* Your stories might be interesting, your delivery might be energetic, and you might just be an unbelievably charming person (stop puffing out your chest)—but if your speech is disorganized, you will not be effective.

This rule may cause a hissy fit among some speakers and outright conniptions among others, those who like to just "wing it," confident that they are "at their best when they just talk." Sorry, they are not. With *rare* exceptions, a disorganized presentation is typically mediocre and some-times appallingly bad. As the speaker staggers around in a mental fog, the audience is more often baffled than enlightened. It is not enough just to be an expert on your topic; you must be able to convey your expertise in an understandable fashion. Allow me to illustrate.

During a jury trial, one of the lawyers was woefully disorganized; every one of his presentations was a labyrinthine tangle of random thoughts.

Ironically, he knew the facts and the law better than anyone else in the courtroom, but his inability to convey that information in a coherent fashion to both the judge and the jury undercut his case.

As he shuffled documents and fitfully zigzagged from point to point, he repeatedly apologized for his lack of organization. Where the goal should have been clarity, confusion reigned. For a while, the jurors struggled mightily to comprehend his points (his floundering aroused their sympathy, if nothing else), but their struggle was all in vain. They remained bewildered. Frustrated, they eventually stopped listening; they began doodling on their pads, counting ceiling tiles, and inspecting their fingernails to pass the time. The results were awful for his client (though excellent for mine).

❦

Half the world is composed of people who have something to say and can't, and the other half who have nothing to say and keep on saying it.

—Robert Frost

❦

All right, we might as well get it out in the open: You must be organized, *and* this is a difficult task for many of us. It requires plain hard work:

> [Organization is not] the part where you roll right along, humming a merry tune as the words tumble over one another in their eagerness to get on the page. Writers seldom shout, "Boy, this outline is really cookin'!" . . . What's more, the effort that goes into organization is largely invisible. You'll never hear a reader say, "My, this (essay/letter/novel/report) is beautifully organized." The job may be a pain in the butt but it's thankless too.[1]

I know, I know: the "wing it" school of thought is looking better every second. Don't despair. Becoming organized is much easier if you have a plan, and—look!—there are a few plans given here. Mush on.

Eight Ways to Organize Your Speech

So, how do you go about structuring your speech? There are many options, and you do not need to be ridiculously rigid about your organization

("I have five major points, each containing three subpoints, and four sub-subpoints . . ."). The touchstone is always the same: "Is my message clear?" Here are a few excellent plans for organizing a speech:

1. **Tell 'em, tell 'em, tell 'em.** Sister Teresa's words still ring in my ears: "Tell 'em, tell 'em, tell 'em!" (Perhaps my ears are also still ringing from her perpetually tugging on them as she dragged me to the time-out corner.) Anyway, she was right, as usual. Her rule is an excellent way to organize any speech. The opening of the speech is an introduction that tells the audience members what you will be telling them, the body actually tells them, and the closing is a summary that tells them what you have just told them—a simple, concise, and clear format. This is a proven method for structuring your thoughts.

❧

[A person] who forms a judgment on any point but cannot explain it might do well never to have thought at all on the subject.

—Pericles

❧

2. **Topical organization.** With topical organization, you address issues in a logical fashion based solely on—surprise!—the topic. For example, if you were describing a camping adventure at Jellystone Park, you might break your talk into three topics: packing ordeals, the costs, and your exploits wrestling bears (go ahead and embellish). Lump all the relevant details into each appropriate major topic, discuss that topic, and then proceed to the next. Be careful not to bounce back and forth between and among topics (from packing your sleeping bag, to your fearless encounter with the bears, and then back to the chagrin you felt when you realized that you had forgotten to pack your deodorant), or you will confuse your listeners.
3. **Problem and solution.** As you might have guessed (and if you haven't, I am worried about you), in this method, you first explain the problem and then propose a solution. For example, if you

were addressing the traffic congestion in your city, you would first denounce the problems (clogged roadways, accidents, loss of productivity, pollution, rampant hand signals being flashed among drivers) and then propose the solutions (carpooling, telecommuting, mass transportation, bicycle paths, prayers).

4. **Cause and effect.** Illustrate how an effect was created by the cause (or how the cause created the effect, for you active-voice purists). For instance, in explaining the decrease in Girl Scout cookie sales over the past few years, you could list all the contributing factors (stiff competition from the Cub Scouts, an appalling shortage of Thin Mints, less aggressive sales tactics) before ultimately explaining the effect (canceling the Girl Scout Jamboree, firing the Girl Scout troop leader).

⚫

Any man may speak truly; but to speak with order, wisely and competently, of that, few men are capable.

—Michel de Montaigne

⚫

5. **Advantages versus disadvantages.** This is a simple way to clarify your message. In essence, you draw a line down the middle of the paper and list the pros and cons of a particular decision. Either you list all the advantages first, followed by all the disadvantages, or you alternate back and forth, pairing each advantage with its corresponding disadvantage. Objectivity helps with this method: if you skew the facts excessively to favor your position, or if you ignore obvious alternatives, you undercut your credibility. (Shameless fact spinning usually backfires, unless you are a politician.)

6. **Acronym.** Constructing an easy-to-remember acronym from the initial letters of a group of words in your speech is an effective way both for you to organize your points and for your listeners to recall them. For example, Mr. Big Honcho, the CEO of a behemoth company, was addressing more than 10,000 company troops assembled at an annual meeting. Attempting to inspire

them (in lieu of cash bonuses, apparently), he challenged them to exceed their accomplishments of the previous year by making "BHAG" their mantra for the upcoming year: "Big Hairy Audacious Goals." (This is the PG version of the letter A, but you get the point.) Using this road map, he proceeded to outline what he meant by big (a 20 percent increase in sales), hairy (thinking creatively), audacious (securing dozens of new clients), and goals (achieving personal, departmental, and company goals). While his message was clear, it was obvious that the employees would have preferred a "BHAB": "Big Hairy Audacious Bonus."

7. **Chronological organization.** With this method of organization, you convey details in the sequence in which the events occurred. Storytellers frequently use sequential order to tell a story from start to finish (principle 13). This is also the way we generally communicate, so it is easy for the audience to follow along as the speaker moves from point to point.

   The following story illustrates chronological organization: "Little Davey Joe was determined to finally see Santa that year, so he devised a plan. At 6:00 p.m. on Christmas Eve, he set the sugar cookies and chocolate milk at the base of the Christmas tree, slid behind the sofa, and began the stakeout. At 7:00 p.m., no sign. At 8:00 p.m., nothing—no reindeer, no Santa, no elves. He was sleepy but determined. At 8:30 p.m., he waged a fierce battle with his mother and fought off her attempts to coax him to bed. At 9:00 p.m.: it was just a matter of time, he thought, as he nodded off." I still believe in Santa.

8. **Numbering and grouping points.** Keep your listeners focused by telling them how many points you will be making. You might say, for example, "There are four reasons that this proposition should be rejected: first, the cost; second, the safety issues; third, the inherent unreliability of the proposition; and finally, the better alternative—mine. Let's begin with reason one, the cost." Numbering also provides your listeners with signposts ("The *third* issue, inherent unreliability, is illustrated by . . ."), so that they know which point you are addressing.

❧

I take the view . . . that if you cannot say what you have to say in 20 minutes, you should go away and write a book about it.

—Lord Brabazon of Tara

❧

Don't expect your audience to struggle to understand your message. Organize every speech so that your message flows logically and coherently. Guide your listeners from point to point with painstaking precision. A disorganized speech is built on a flimsy foundation. You can adorn such a speech with colorful words and lively stories, and even deliver it with heartfelt conviction, but your adornment and delivery will never remedy the speech's fundamental flaws. Get organized—it's the law.

11

Open with a Hook

Unless a speaker can interest his audience at once,
his effort will be a failure.

—Clarence Darrow

I ran track in high school. Our team was bad, and I was the worst. I have forgotten most of what I learned from this unpleasant period, but I do recall one nugget of wisdom. Crusty Coach Hengin would bellow and growl incessantly: "Explode out of the starting blocks, you sissies!" Sometimes we were "weenies," "wimps," or "weaklings" (or a few choice descriptions unfit for print), but his dictate never changed: "Explode!"

That is also your challenge as a speaker: to draft an opening that will cause you to explode out of the starting blocks and instantly create a thrilling buzz in your audience. Your opening is the most important part of your speech. A feeble one can contaminate your presentation, and a rotten one can ruin it. How about that for a little pressure? You have mere seconds to persuade your audience that you have an excellent message that warrants its fickle attention, so don't futz around.

With your first words, say something that snaps your listeners to attention and compels them to literally perch on the edge of their seats and think: "*Wow!* This is going to be exceptional!" Let your opening surprise, delight, and intrigue your listeners—and occasionally even make them gasp—and they will stay with you for the rest of the journey. An exceptional opening will enhance the likelihood that they will not only *listen* to your message, but also—and this is critical—*hear* it.

I can hear you musing, "*Surely* the listeners will tag along until I make a few points, right?" *Surely they won't.* Your opening determines whether your audience will stampede toward the mental exits (or, worse, the real exits). If your opening does not entice your listeners, they will be off and away. And an audience is a terrible thing to waste.

If the opening is crucial, why are so many openings as bland as oatmeal? They feel like a moist, limp handshake to the audience (no one enjoys that, do they?). Some are tired. Some are pure rubbish. And sometimes there is no opening at all: the speaker just starts droning or jabbering, plunking his listeners down somewhere on the winding speech trail, never giving them a clue about where they are going and how they will get there. Everyone, including the speaker, is discombobulated.

Immediately give your audience a compelling reason to listen—period.

❧

I think the end is implicit in the beginning. It must be. If that isn't there in the beginning, you don't know what you're working toward. You should have a sense of a story's shape and form and its destination.

—Eudora Welty

❧

Eight Openings to Avoid

Before I identify some top-notch openings, I have to caution you about a few openings that are just real yawners—unimaginative, stale, and counterproductive. Here is a list of the usual suspects. If you feel an urge to begin your speech in any of the following ways, fight it:

1. **An admission.** Never admit that you are unprepared, because it alerts your listeners that your talk may be a waste of their time. Few things gut a speech more quickly. Save your confessions for the confessional. If you are not prepared to speak, do the best you can under the circumstances—then go to your room without supper.

2. **An apology.** Bite your lip if you have the urge to apologize for your lack of speaking experience ("Who knows why they asked me to speak"), your anxiety ("Sorry, but speaking gives me the heebie-jeebies"), or the length of your speech ("Better get comfortable, folks, because this bombast is going to drag on for a while"). Your apology will seldom generate sympathy, understanding, or goodwill, so don't handicap yourself.

3. **A prolonged opening.** Some speakers spend a maddening amount of time *preparing* to speak *after* they are introduced (were they surprised that they would be speaking?). They adjust the lectern light; bang on the microphone and ask, "Is this on?"; methodically arrange and rearrange their notes; guzzle water; groom themselves; smooth their clothing; and check the time. Finally, they begin. Those moaning and hissing sounds are coming from the audience.

   Your audience is evaluating you from the moment it first sees you, so be ready to speak within seconds after you are introduced. Adjust, test, arrange, gulp, preen, smooth, and check long before you stand to speak.

4. **Insincere flattery.** I once attended a black-tie banquet that was a disaster. For no apparent reason, the event began one hour late. The room was too hot, and the lights were too dim. The microphone regularly emitted shrill feedback, and the food was greasy, cold, and inedible. Nonetheless, the keynote speaker began, just as he had planned, by fawning over the host: "Hasn't Jill done a marvelous job planning this

special event?" His audience, of course, was prepared to bury Jill (alive), not praise her.

Jill might have appreciated the speaker's comments, but the miserable audience members concluded that the speaker was disingenuous. Insincere flattery erodes your credibility and alienates your audience. Don't go there.

☙

Once a word has been allowed to escape, it cannot be recalled.

—Horace

❧

5. **A cliché.** Clichés tell the audience that your talk will be dreary and that you are not too finicky about how you express your ideas. Clichés are nothing more than convenient crutches for speakers. Such vapid, trite phrases as "comparing apples and oranges," "crystal clear," "it is what it is," "fast and loose," "to make a long story short," and "pulled no punches" make hackneyed openings (for that matter, they gum up any part of the speech). There is nothing creative or captivating about them, so prune them from your presentations. They are the "kiss of death," "if you catch my drift."

6. **A joke.** Unless your joke is *very* brief, *utterly* hilarious, and *directly* related to your topic (and most jokes pass none of those tests), save it for the next dinner party. The opening of your speech is not the time to hone your clunky skills as a stand-up comedian.

Why? A joke is way too risky. Maybe it's funny, but maybe it's not. Many jokes bomb and are greeted with throat-clearing silence or perplexed looks (the types of painfully awkward moments that will make you question your sanity for ever having agreed to speak). And it may confuse a few of the dullards ("Huh? I don't get it!"); you definitely don't want to have to explain it. Worst of all, your joke may offend someone (and audiences today have the thinnest of skins). Avoid these pitfalls.

Humor can add a little zing to most speeches, but there are better ways to be humorous than to stick a risky joke into the opening of your speech. To learn about injecting humor into your speech as a whole, see principle 14.

⚜

There is all the difference in the world between having something to say, and having to say something.

—John Dewey

⚜

7. **An embarrassing statement or act.** Some speakers have intentionally stumbled as they approached the lectern, and then opened with a ridiculous comment: "I sure had a nice trip up here!" Some engage in pure nonsense, such as shooting a squirt gun or hurling confetti or foam balls into the crowd. These are excellent openings—in the circus. Leave them there.

8. **A shocking act.** Here is the booby prize for the worst opening ever in the history of speaking. I would not have believed this, except that I was actually there (and no, I was not the speaker). The speaker's talk was to be about his experience running the Boston Marathon. Apparently he wondered: "What can I do to re-create the feel and excitement of the race?" Then he stumbled upon what he believed was an ingenious idea.

After being introduced, he walked to the front of the room, reached into the lectern, and abruptly hoisted above his head a starter's pistol—which looks and sounds like a real gun—and fired a blank. (If you've learned from this principle the importance of starting your presentation with a bang, please understand that this lamebrained opening is *not* what I meant.) At first the audience members were stunned and frightened, and then they were furious. This dimwit had nearly re-created the feel and excitement of an angry lynch mob. If you choose to shock the audience in the opening, use a smidgen of common sense.

❧

A good beginning hath a good ending.

—James Howell

❧

Four Proven Openings

So, now that we have examined and spurned several disastrous openings—from wimpy apologies to bombing jokes to circus pratfalls and idiotic stunts—let's explore some openings that are more likely to captivate an audience. You need to hunt for one that is fresh, lively, and intriguing. Remember, you have only seconds to prove yourself worthy of your listeners' attention. To open your speech, use the same formula that exceptional writers employ.

> If, at the very outset, a writer seems bored, unwilling to use his imagination, indifferent to his reader, and unclear in his thinking, he's apt to remain that way. But if his opener reveals passion, a clear perceptive mind, and a flair for drawing in the reader, the odds are he will stay true to form. . . . It's like a good comedy situation: it ignites.[1]

Where can you find an opening like that? Well, don't expect trumpets to magically blare, with the town crier heralding the arrival of the perfect opening for you: "The opening is here, the opening is here—long live the opening!" Like most inspirations, these brainstorms will typically come moseying along when you least expect them—when you are jogging, driving, or even showering. Reflect on your topic and be ever vigilant. Ask yourself one question when drafting the opening of your speech: "Will this intrigue my audience?" Here are four proven openings:

1. **Open with a quote.** Why open with a quote? Because a pertinent, succinct quote will seize the attention of your audience and add sparkle to your talk.

    One savvy speaker opened a poignant presentation about risk taking by quoting that inimitable *Sesame Street* sage, Big Bird: "The tragedy in life, Oscar, is not that it ends; it's that we wait too long to begin it."

Big Bird's discerning wisdom charmed this speaker's audience; his listeners began recalling times in their lives when they had procrastinated and missed opportunities. The speaker had hooked the audience. Read more about the power of quotations in principle 15.

2. **Open with an intriguing statement.** Entice your listeners by saying something interesting or fascinating. Try something that will make them smile. I am easily amused, so a pithy opening like the following works for me: "I've often wondered what goes into a hot dog. Now I know and I wish I didn't."[2]

   Peruse literary classics for ideas, because exceptional writers are adept at snagging their readers' attention immediately. For example, consider what George Orwell wrote in the opening line from *1984*: "It was a bright cold day in April, and the clocks were striking thirteen."

   One of my law school professors (a humorless woman and an alumna of the World Wrestling Entertainment, I am pretty sure) opened her first lecture of the semester in this memorable way: "My name is Helga [name changed for the author's protection]. Look at the person sitting on your right. Now look at the person sitting on your left. One of them is going to fail my class." By opening with these terrorizing words, she had our undivided attention for the entire semester.

   ❧

   Begin with something interesting in your first sentence.
   Not the second. Not the third. The First! F–I–R–S–T! First!

   —Dale Carnegie

   ❧

3. **Open with an anecdote.** Narrative works because we love stories (principle 13). Here is an example: "When I was three, my father died suddenly. We lived with my Grandmother Valasek for several years while my mother found her way in life. Grandma was a stern woman, who kept a thick leather belt hanging behind the refrigerator to enforce the peace.

She wasn't bashful about using it, either. This iron-willed lady taught me three valuable lessons."

Crisp, concise, and relevant anecdotes will engage your audience and set the tone for your presentation. But be brief. Avoid long or convoluted stories, because by the time you get to the point, your audience won't know, and won't care, what your point is.

4. **Open with a question.** Opening with a thoughtful question is a great way to captivate your listeners immediately as well as establish the theme of your speech. "If you could do it all over again, what would you change?" "How many of you would rather swallow worms than give a speech?" "Where do you stand on the great cookie debate: Snickerdoodle or oatmeal?" Your listeners will begin to contemplate the question and formulate their answers.

But when you ask your question, remember to pause and allow your audience to process it. I repeat: *be sure to pause.* If you ask a question and then dash ahead without pausing, your listeners will necessarily conclude that you really don't care what they think, and they will ignore the question.

Create an opening that will propel you forward. Be selective. Never settle for something that just "works"—*explode* at the outset. Capture the hearts and minds of your audience with creativity, surprise, and suspense, and you will set the tone for a successful speech. But leave the starter's pistol at home.

12

Revise, Revise, Revise

Modern English, especially written English, is full of bad habits which spread by imitation and which can be avoided if one is willing to take the necessary trouble.

—George Orwell

I can hear you grousing (or are you whining?): "Ugh, this is going to be grimy, grunt work. Maybe I will just skip ahead to the next principle and peek at this later." Hold on.

Okay, I will be honest: revising is hard work. It can actually drive you loony. At times, as words and ideas fail you, you will wince, tug your hair, and grind your teeth. Your lucid moments may be rare. And during the darkest hours, when you see no glimmer of light at the end of the tunnel, you will want to capitulate and just settle for a serviceable but mediocre speech.

Why should you bother revising? Because it will make a colossal difference in your speech. Because it will distinguish your speech from the thousands and thousands of pedestrian to remarkably bad speeches thrust upon us every day by indifferent speakers who don't bother.

And because it will send an unmistakable message to your audience: this is a speaker who cares—this is a speaker who deserves my attention.

Unfortunately, exceptional speeches *never* just leap out of your head on the initial draft. The first draft of your speech will probably be a messy blob of tangled words and thoughts. It may be mired in the muck of tortured logic, convoluted organization, hazy ideas, and anemic language. Your elusive gem may not even begin to surface until the sixth or seventh draft. And you'd better sit down for the following distressing bit of news: sometimes your first stab at a speech may be so bad that you will not be able to resuscitate it; a swift burial may serve you best. That is okay; you are not sinning by doing that.

❧

I am an obsessive rewriter, doing one draft and then another and another, usually five. In a way, I have nothing to say but a great deal to add.

—Gore Vidal

❧

Don't dismay. Even the best writers (a very select club, which most of us don't belong to) struggle at this stage, but they understand the importance of revising and honing their work:

> Revising is part of writing. Few writers are so expert that they can produce what they are after on the first try. Quite often you will discover, on examining the completed work, that there are serious flaws in the arrangement of the material. . . . [D]o not be afraid to experiment with what you have written. . . . Remember, it is no sign of weakness or defeat that your manuscript ends up in need of major surgery. This is a common occurrence in all writing, and among the best writers.[1]

Twelve Rules for Revising Your Speech

Good, you are still with me, and hopefully you are no longer whimpering. I suggest that you pour yourself a cup of coffee (extra strong) and, with a red pen in your hand or with your fingers poised on the keyboard, begin to revise. Here is how.

Set your initial draft aside for a few days and then revisit it with a fresh perspective. Obviously, you need to budget some time for this (more bad news for you procrastinators). What seemed so logical and persuasive initially may now seem verbose and muddled. Ask yourself some tough questions (no fudging here—no one will see your answers):

- "Is my speech organized logically, or is it hopelessly disjointed?"
- "Does it make sense, or am even *I* scratching my head?"
- "Are my points clear and concise, or *are* there any points?"
- "Is my opening captivating, or does it meander?"
- "Is my theme precise, or is it jumbled?"
- "Is my language crisp and colorful, or is it stale and tepid?"
- "Do my descriptions launch floating word pictures, or do they lull listeners into dozing?"
- "Does my closing solidify my message, or does my speech end with a resounding thud?"

So, you have a little work to do? Begin ruthlessly revising every point, sentence, and paragraph. Slash away without compunction or hesitation. Cut, paste, juggle, and tinker with everything. Lop off entire sections if necessary.

Here are several useful revising guidelines. (You didn't think I would send you into battle ill prepared, did you?)

1. **Use the first person.** Build rapport with your listeners by using the first person ("I," "we," "us"). The first person is inclusive; it involves your listeners in the presentation and makes you one of them. Constantly referring to "you" or "they" creates a buffer between you and the audience. It seems as if you are lecturing to your listeners or pointing an accusatory finger at them (and it is never polite to point, remember?).
2. **Use the active voice.** Wimps hide behind the passive voice ("mistakes were made," "the doughnuts were eaten") so that they do not have to take a position. This kind of obscure evasion of responsibility begs the question about who did what

(*Who* made the mistakes? *Who* ate the doughnuts?). Nike's slogan, "Just Do It!," is precise and motivating; "It Should Just Be Done by You!" inspires us only to reach for another doughnut. Whenever possible, eliminate the passive voice from your speech. Instead, be clear and forthright with the active voice: "I made mistakes" (be bold and accountable); "I devoured the doughnuts" (or better yet, blame someone else).

❧

Simple speech is the best and truest eloquence.

—Martin Luther

❧

3. **Eliminate qualifiers.** Stop hedging your points and qualifying your words: "assuming that this occurs," "perhaps this might explain," "it might be said that, all things considered, some scholars feel that in certain circumstances there might be occasional instances of similar behavior on the part of likely participants — possibly." One speaker vacillates out of fear that she will alienate her listeners; another speaker has no idea how he really feels about what he is saying, so he flops around, groping for clarity in his confused mind.

❧

Embarrassed, obscure, and feeble sentences are generally, if not always, the result of embarrassed, obscure, or feeble thought.

—Hugh Blair

❧

If you equivocate, your listeners will conclude that you are unconvinced of your own position, that you are a milquetoast, or that you are untrustworthy. Such conclusions will obviously sap your credibility and persuasiveness. Say what you think, even if your listeners disagree (just abandon any dreams of becoming a lawyer).

4. **Avoid hyperbole.** In an effort to be more persuasive, a speaker may exaggerate ("clearly," "undoubtedly," "unquestionably," or

"indisputably"). She might be embellishing out of an attempt to prop up her flimsy arguments, or maybe she is really intoxicated with her own passionate conviction. Some hyperboles sound downright silly: "The pancakes were stacked a mile high on my plate," or "This is the most despicable act any person has ever committed in the history of mankind!" Unlikely.

Overstatements actually weaken your point and undermine your credibility. Listeners will become suspicious of everything else you say (or waste time imagining a mile-high stack of pancakes). Weed hyperbole out of your speech.

ও.

*You mustn't exaggerate, young man. That's always
a sign that your argument is weak.*

—Bertrand Russell

ঙ্গ

5. **Eliminate offensive language.** Eliminate all potentially sexist, biased, or offensive language ("you guys"; "lady boss"; "those people"). Audiences today are attuned and sensitive to these gaffes. Be aware of what you say. If you are unsure whether your choice of words or ideas might offend someone in the audience, purge them.

   In the 2004 presidential campaign, Democratic candidate Howard Dean constantly handicapped himself with flippant comments. For example, he tried to win Southern votes by blustering that he wanted to be the candidate for "guys with Confederate flags on their pickup trucks." He backpedaled from that comment for weeks with implausible explanations, all to no avail. Several similar speaking blunders doomed his campaign. Choose your words carefully.

6. **Eliminate needless words.** Always choose a single word if it can do the work of two or three. Ruthlessly prune the verbal clutter that creeps into your presentations: "at the present time" (now); "he is the man that" (he); "owing to the fact that"

(since); "during such time as" (while); "notwithstanding the fact that" (although). Verbal clutter only begets presentations that are mystifying and lifeless. They are mystifying, because it is hard for a listener to parse through all the clutter. They are lifeless, because there is no net gain from the clutter: the effort to parse produces exhaustion. And eliminate redundant words ("free gift"; "mix together"; "new recruit"; "actual fact"; "regress back"; "mutual agreement"; "learned, educated person"; "future plans"; "a hot, steamy, torrid day").

❧

Let thy speech be short, comprehending much in a few words;
be as one that knoweth and yet holdeth his tongue.

—Ecclesiasticus

❧

Also, a speaker may draft a speech that is chock-full of clauses, riddled with prepositional diversions, and garnished with parenthetical thoughts. Such flowery prose might work well in a book (I certainly hope so, since I've practiced it in this book), but it has no place in speeches. Have mercy on your listeners. By the time you finish delivering your convoluted utterance, even you cannot decipher who did what to whom, or when or where it was done. Rest assured, your audience has already started searching for another speaker, one who can be clear.

Verbosity smothers the message. Lean, succinct sentences have the most impact. Strip every sentence down to the bare essentials:

A sentence should contain no unnecessary words, a paragraph no unnecessary sentences, for the same reason that a drawing should have no unnecessary lines and a machine no unnecessary parts. This requires not that the writer make all sentences short, or avoid all detail and treat subjects only in outline, but that every word tell.[2]

7. **Avoid jargon.** Resist any temptation to camouflage your points with authoritative-sounding twaddle or obscure, pretentious

language: "B2B" (business to business); "portfolio optimization" (profit); "suffering from the hyperingestion of ethanol" (drunk).

Avoid euphemisms, legalese, technical gobbledygook, clotted language, doublespeak, verbal sludge, pompous acronyms, and other mumbo jumbo (that ought to cover the gamut), which merely conceal your message and cause listeners' eyeballs to roll. Most listeners are confused rather than impressed by obscure expressions. Let it rain, not precipitate.

♣

The chief virtue that language can have is clearness, and nothing detracts from it so much as the use of unfamiliar words.

—Hippocrates

♣

8. **Be clear.** Your audience is not clairvoyant (thank goodness for us speakers!), so be brave enough to be clear. That advice can be simply gut-wrenching to the legions of speakers who hide behind ambiguity. If you are vague, your listeners will get stuck as they attempt to understand what you said or what you meant. They may also conclude that you are sneaky, so don't pussyfoot around. If you express yourself obscurely ("If we do not see a precipitous increase in performance and return on expenditures, the pointed expressions of concern from the board of directors may escalate"), your audience will most likely think, "Huh?" Be clear: "If we don't do a better job, the board of directors will fire us."

9. **Be specific.** Drab, toothless descriptions such as "car" or "fruit" dilute your message. Select descriptive words, such as "canary-yellow Volkswagen Beetle" and "shiny Red Delicious apple." Give your speech zing; make it glitter with precise and vivid words:

Prefer the specific to the general, the definite to the vague, the concrete to the abstract. . . . The greatest writers—Homer, Dante, Shakespeare—are effective largely because they deal in particulars and report the details that matter. Their words call up pictures.[3]

Dull and dreary words result in a dull and dreary presentation. Rather than simply stating that it was a "beautiful morning at the beach," describe the "dazzling sun and powder-white sand, the waves gently folding over themselves, and the sea oats swaying in the mild breeze." Transport your audience with lively details.

❧

Words have weight, sound, and appearance; it is only
by considering these that you can write a sentence that
is good to look at and good to listen to.

—W. Somerset Maugham

❧

10. **Create imagery.** Make your text breathe and spring to life so that your listeners will experience your message, not just hear your words. Set images floating in their minds with your words.

An excellent example of a speech that painted vivid word pictures effectively was the moving eulogy that President Ronald Reagan delivered after the space shuttle *Challenger* tragically exploded on liftoff from Cape Canaveral, Florida, in 1986. All seven astronauts, including the first civilian on a space flight, were killed. Millions of Americans witnessed this horrifying space disaster. Reagan's nationally televised eulogy included the following poignant language:

There's a coincidence today. On this day 390 years ago, the great explorer Sir Francis Drake died aboard a ship off the coast of Panama. In his lifetime the great frontiers were the oceans, and a historian later said: "He lived by the sea, died on it, was buried in it." Well, today we can say of the *Challenger* crew: Their dedication was, like Drake's, complete.

The crew of the space shuttle *Challenger* honored us by the manner in which they lived their lives. We will never forget them, nor the last time we saw them, this morning, as they prepared for their journey and waved good-bye and "slipped the surly bonds of earth" to "touch the face of God."[4]

11. **Make your message conversational.** Choose plain English and conversational language over rigid and pedantic prose. Make your speech friendly and inviting. You don't want to sound like a pompous windbag. Talk *to* the audience, not *at* the audience. Draft your presentation as if you were speaking to a friend rather than to hundreds of strangers. Imagine that you are talking to them in your living room (all right, imagine you have a humongous living room if that helps).

ᨠ

Words are, of course, the most powerful drug used by mankind.

—Rudyard Kipling

ᨠ

12. **Write your speech to be spoken.** "Write my speech to be spoken? Duh!" You think? Well, this is a little trickier than it sounds, unless you keep in mind the differences between that which we read and that which we hear. (And there are some differences other than our ability simply to toss aside a boring book, something that is often tempting, but much more difficult to do, with a boring speaker.) Let's review three of the distinctions.

    First, your listeners can absorb only a limited amount of information. At some point, they will think, "Enough already!" and shut down. When a writer covers 10 or more points, readers can review and process those points at their own leisurely pace, but listeners cannot do that. They may hear each of your points only once or twice, and—if you are really lucky—they might recall a few of the more memorable ones: "Read my lips: No new taxes!" "If it doesn't fit, you must acquit!"

    Second, written material often has headings set in italic or boldface type, making it much easier for readers to see the transitions from point to point. They know where they are all the time, and they can reread passages to clarify any questions they may have. In contrast, your listeners are relying on you, the speaker, to be their guide, so you need to point out the critical facts on the sightseeing tour: "The *first* of three distinctions, that old impediment, the price. . . ."

•

Put the argument into a concrete shape, into an image—some hard phrase, round and solid as a ball, which they can see and handle and carry home with them—and the cause is half won.

—Ralph Waldo Emerson

•

Finally, we typically read in the solitude of our office, bedroom, or secret hideaway in a cranny of our home, but when we listen to speeches, we are surrounded by many distractions (inconsiderate yakkers, a baby wailing, the sick-as-a-dog person at the next table hacking, industrious waiters banging dishes). Your listeners can be easily sidetracked.

You need to keep these inherent differences between writing and speaking in mind. If you want to hold your listeners' attention, write your speech using crisp, concise sentences; limit your points; and signal when you are moving to the next topic.

Review some of the classic works on the basics of cogent, precise writing listed in the recommended resources at the end of this book. Most of the books listed there are relatively short and easy to read. They are excellent refreshers on the rules of grammar, diction, punctuation, and style—the hallmarks of effective writing.

In addition, several useful Web sites can help you determine if your sentences or words are redundant or hackneyed. Deadwood Phrases (www.klariti.com/technical-writing/Deadwood%20Phrases.shtml) is a compilation of abused and overused expressions that are frequently included in speeches; each expression is accompanied by a suggested alternative. Common Errors in English (www.wsu.edu/~brians/errors) identifies frequently misused words and phrases. Finally, Merriam-Webster Online (www.m-w.com) provides a dictionary, a thesaurus, and valuable links to other language-related sites.

Author Truman Capote summarized in four words what it has taken me multiple pages to say:

> Good writing is rewriting.

Yes, it is time-consuming, and at times frustrating, but it makes an unmistakable difference. It will make your speech distinctive. Diligently revise your speech, and you will take a gigantic step toward separating yourself from the bloated ranks of average speakers.

13

Harness the Power of Stories

The best orator is one who can make men see with their ears.

—Arab saying

We all love a roaring-good yarn. As kids, we pleaded: "Tell me'nuther story, Grandpa!" "Daddy, read me 'bout the lil' enjun' train that could!" We couldn't wait for story time in preschool, and, as adults, we are captivated by stories on television and in the newspaper.

Excellent speakers are invariably excellent storytellers. Tell your listeners a story—or merely mention the word *story*—and you will grab their attention. Perfect this skill and you can enthrall them. A story that is packed with vivid images and told with passion will infuse life into any speech and make your message reverberate with your listeners. Look at each story not merely as a vehicle to clarify your points, but as a means to connect with your listeners intellectually and emotionally.

ə.

Imagination is more important than knowledge.

—Albert Einstein

ə$

A courtroom drama often involves all the key elements of a gripping story: a whodunit, seeking to unravel who, what, when, where, and why. To illustrate the power of storytelling, let's dissect a story describing an automobile accident.

Consider several ways in which a lawyer might describe the event. For example, she could simply convey the facts to the jury: "Mr. Gleason was severely injured in a terrible automobile accident when the defendant's SUV crashed broadside into his car. He was paralyzed, and his life has been dramatically altered."

That's accurate, yes, but it's pretty feeble. This might engage the jurors intellectually (they understand the facts), but it would not engage them emotionally (they feel no connection with Mr. Gleason). Moreover, this description uses vague words such as *severely* and *dramatically*, which have different meanings to listeners, depending on their life experiences and a host of other factors that skew their perceptions.

But what if the attorney shared the events using the techniques of a gifted storyteller, painting vivid pictures with details?

At 8:45 a.m., Sunday, September 25, Albert Gleason, the manager of the Ace Hardware store in midtown, was enjoying a morning drive with his seven-year-old son, Justin. They both cherished these Sunday mornings, because Albert's job required long hours, and this was their precious time together.

They were traveling south on Peachtree Street near the Brookhaven train station, enjoying the beautiful, sunny day, when Justin suddenly screamed, "Dad, look out!" Albert reacted instinctively and immediately jammed on the brakes. And out of the corner of his eye he caught a glimpse of a gigantic black Hummer barreling through the red light.

Albert swerved, but he was too late. He recalls the horrific sounds of metal ripping and glass shattering as that mountain of steel slammed broadside into the Gleasons' tiny green Toyota Corolla. The violent impact whipped him about like a rag doll. The air bag exploded with so much force, Albert's head snapped back and his glasses cracked. He soon felt warm blood trickling down his forehead and into his eyes, but when he tried to wipe it away, he couldn't . . . because he had no feeling in his arms. He was paralyzed, his neck shattered. And he was terrified, because he was unable to help his only son, who was screaming. He cried out to him, "Justin! . . . Justin! . . . Justin!" This is the last image Albert remembers before he blacked out.

The facts remain the same, but the second story will resonate with the jurors. Why? It is gripping. It humanizes the characters and conveys the details in a personal way (a father and son bonding). We relive the accident with the Gleasons, and we feel as if we are in their car, because the story is so vivid. This version precisely describes the vehicles, and uses descriptive words: *barreling, slammed, metal ripping,* and *glass shattering.* We empathize with Mr. Gleason, because we understand the fear that a parent experiences when his child is in danger, and we can visualize the horror of a huge sport utility vehicle smashing into a much smaller passenger car. We can imagine the terror of being trapped in crumpled wreckage, helpless and paralyzed.

❧

Let thy speech be better than silence, or be silent.

—Dionysius the Elder

✧

Seven Keys to Powerful Storytelling

All right, let's shuttle the lawyer off the stage (*It's about time!*) and get back to the business at hand. What are the secrets of the master storytellers? Here are several techniques used by the best:

1. **Constantly gather stories.** Exceptional speakers are always searching for ideas that they can weave into a story. You should, too (principles 4 and 5). Save ideas and articles that amuse you (the lowbrow Redneck Olympics, involving such events as toilet-lid tossing, bobbing for pigs' feet, or the mud-pit belly flop—I am easily tickled), infuriate you (the egomaniacal athlete making $15 million for playing baseball six months a year, who complains about his "stressful job"), or inspire you (a heroic pilot safely landing a commercial airplane on the Hudson River). Stockpile these stories, because you just never know how or when you might be able

to knit them into a speech. You have to capture these stories immediately, however, because those fickle thoughts will evaporate in a flash if you don't.

2. **Strive for universal appeal.** Search for stories that have universal appeal. What lesson did you learn about perseverance by continuing to try out for the swim team or the cheerleading squad despite repeatedly being cut? What lessons about optimism does your disabled child teach you? What lessons of loyalty can you learn from Jethro, your golden retriever? What lesson did you learn about commitment as you watched your grandparents renew their wedding vows after being married for 70 years? Everyone has real-life experiences that can become the vehicle for a universal message that will move and teach any audience.

❧

What comes from the heart, goes to the heart.

—Samuel Taylor Coleridge

❧

3. **Make your stories relevant.** Select stories that are relevant to your talk, stories that clarify, not cloud, your purpose. For example, imagine that you are making a sales presentation, unveiling a revolutionary new product, "Chicken Paste." Rather than plunging, as you should, right into your talk by highlighting all the benefits of congealed chicken parts in a handy tube ("My children love this more than they do Pop Tarts and Cocoa Puffs; the Chicken Paste package fits in your purse; Chicken Paste has a shelf life of 200 years"), you begin instead with your hilarious but irrelevant airline story ("It was a nine-hour flight from London, I was shoehorned in the middle seat between two sumo wrestlers adjacent to the latrine . . . *blather, blather*").

Your flight debacle might amuse your listeners, but you will have diverted their attention from Chicken Paste. They will be contemplating your airline predicament rather than focusing on the advantages of a meal in a tube. Make your stories relevant, or you will only confuse your audience and dilute your message. Ask yourself, "Does this story support and illustrate my point?" If the answer is no, discard it.

4. **Describe people, not concepts.** People are always fascinated with human-interest stories. *People* magazine, *Entertainment Tonight,* and the *Oprah Winfrey Show* succeed because they involve people. Your audience will not relate to abstract concepts such as "courage" and "heroism." Instead, tell your audience about the courageous athlete who repeatedly failed but refused to quit or the teacher who sacrificed lucrative business opportunities because of his love for teaching. Your listeners care about real people and real events.

ひ

Rattling good stories . . . contain characters so filled with the breath of life that [you] can no more forget them than [you] could forget [your] most intimate friend.

—William Lyon Phelps

◆§

5. **Deliver the details.** Provide precise, meaty descriptions. If you rely on bland, commonplace words rather than fresh, colorful ideas, you will dull the senses of your listeners. For example, if you merely mention a "car" and leave it at that, your listeners will filter that word through their individual perceptions. To some, the word signifies a Ford minivan; to others, a compact Honda sedan; to still others, a Porsche 911 Turbo. But if you instead describe a "fire-engine-red Corvette," you will conjure up an exact picture.

To help your listeners visualize exactly what you want them to see, provide details. Choose words that are whimsical, offbeat, arresting, or vivid—for good reason:

Words can reveal thoughts, conceal pain, paint dreams, correct errors, and pass along dearly bought lessons to the latest generation. . . . Words can build walls between people, or bridges. Words can tear down or build up, wound or heal, tarnish or cleanse.[1]

❧

We think in generalities, we live in detail.

—Alfred North Whitehead

❧

6. **Display emotions.** You need to share your story in a way that is congruent with the message. If you tell a tale indifferently, then indifference is exactly the response you will get from your audience. The very best stories crackle with powerful emotions such as love, fear, antipathy, and anger.

Let's say that you are disgusted with your cellular phone service provider (all seven of you in the world who are not disgusted may skip ahead). If you were merely to share, meekly and dispassionately, the relevant facts concerning the company's abysmal service ("Gosh, Simple Cellular disappointed me again"), you would evoke little more than gaping yawns and a so-what-else-is-new response from your listeners.

On the other hand, suppose you were to select concrete words and deliver your story with fire and passion: "Let me be blunt: Simple Cellular stinks! The service is atrocious, the charges excessive, and the billing nightmarish. And I defy you to ever get a human being rather than a recording maze when you call. Simple Cellular epitomizes all that is wrong with businesses that focus only on the bottom line and that could care less about customer service!"

Pound your fist, wag your finger, rumble and thunder—heck, toss in some salty language if it's appropriate. Your voice, body language, and facial expressions must depict the emotion and convey the anger that you feel. Don't blow a gasket, but you get the point. To really engage your audience in your stories, create drama.

❧

[The passions] are the winds that fill the ship's sails. Sometimes they submerge the ship, but without them the ship could not sail.

—Voltaire

❧

7. **Titillate the senses.** A mesmerizing story engages the senses, emotions, and intellect of your listeners. Infuse life into your stories by delivering them using vocal energy, diverse pacing, timely pauses, expansive gestures, and wide-eyed excitement.

In the same way that your dad might have eerily described the slimy, green monster lurking under the bed (and why was there always one under every child's bed?), ready to snatch your ankles if you dared to get up, you need to share vivid, lifelike details with excitement and passion. Make your listeners experience your story by taking them on a journey and describing the events in a way that will touch their senses. If you can get beyond your listeners' minds and into their hearts, you will elevate your message from the merely interesting to the unforgettable.

Enhance your storytelling skills by poring over the list of recommended resources at the end of this book.

We always hope that our listeners will cling to our words and recall them forever, but typically, they don't. Most audiences forget most of what speakers say—quickly. It's disheartening, but it's true. If your listeners remember what you said even a week after your speech, you are ahead of most speakers. But your listeners seldom forget a story that moves, surprises, or enchants them. Do you want your messages to be remembered? Then forget what you learned in grade school—go ahead and tell stories.

14

Make 'Em Laugh

Why doesn't the fellow who says, "I'm no speechmaker," let it go at that instead of giving a demonstration?

—Kin Hubbard

Do you wring your hands at the very thought of using humor in your speeches because—horrors!—it might flop? Do you always stick to the facts, the facts, and nothing but the facts? Does the title of this principle make you cringe or break out in a cold sweat? If so, don't even think about skipping ahead.

If your presentations are a tad boring—or, worse, real snoozers—humor will add some pizzazz. Do I hear howls of protest? "I'm not funny!" "That's not my style!" "I'm a corporate bigwig who must be taken seriously!" Take a breath. You don't have to morph into a stand-up comedian, be sidesplitting hilarious, or engage in shenanigans (slinging confetti, banging gongs, or rattling off jokes incessantly). Acting foolish would undermine your professional image and destroy your credibility. Just consider adding a few zany twists or snappy tidbits to punch up your talk and evoke a smile from the audience.

There are several excellent reasons to try incorporating humor into your speeches. First, you engage your audience. Audiences today are bombarded with a seemingly endless parade of tiresome speakers. If it is drudgery to listen, your listeners will mentally check out. They will hear a humming sound as you drone on ("So our quarterly projections for the eastern region . . . *yammer, yammer*"), but they are not listening; you might as well be speaking Hungarian.

❧

Many times what cannot be refuted by arguments
can be parried by laughter.

—Desiderius Erasmus

❧

Second, audiences need to relax periodically, to smile and breathe, especially when you are addressing a serious, complex, or statistics-laden topic. Some of the greatest speakers in history—Winston Churchill, John F. Kennedy, and Ronald Reagan—dealt with topics of enormous importance, yet they often made their points with humor. Even if your talk has gargantuan implications for your audience (which is unlikely in most cases), loosen up.

Finally, humor humanizes you, and that will make your listeners far more receptive to your ideas. It also alerts them that you are confident and willing to take a risk. Your humor may not always work, but the potential rewards more than justify the risks.

❧

Humor can turn the serious into the bearable, the humiliating
into the humbling, the mundane into the unique.

—Lian Dolan

❧

Ten Tips for Adding Humor to Your Talks

All right, so you want to make your talks more entertaining. How can you do that without undermining your professional image and without taking inordinate risks?

Well, don't just start lobbing one-liners willy-nilly and hoping for the best. That haphazard approach is likely to come crashing down around you. Use the following plan to add a little mirth to your talks:

1. **Study others.** Study and emulate entertainers who incorporate humor into their performances successfully. Comedians such as Jim Carrey, Eddie Murphy, and Jerry Seinfeld each use humor differently, but they are all very entertaining. Furthermore, there is no humor template that applies to every speaker, so experiment and develop your own style.

   Analyze entertaining speakers and ask what makes them funny. Is it the topics they discuss, their animated delivery, or perhaps the unexpected twists they intersperse in their presentations? Watch their body language, gestures, and facial expressions as they speak. Listen to their timing and their use of pauses. Study how they recover when something bombs. (At some point in your speaking life, that will come in really handy — trust me.) Learn from the best, but be selective. Resist the urge to smash watermelons, blare air horns, or jump around like a raving loony (see tip 7, "Don't go bonkers") — there are limits.

   ❧

   All the wit in the world is lost upon him who has none.

   —Jean de La Bruyère

   ❧

2. **Remain vigilant.** Entertaining material for your speeches is floating around everywhere: current events; personal exploits; the lessons of eternal optimism that your mutt, Shep, has taught you. Everything has potential if you are attuned and creative. Study how such comedians as Jay Leno, David Letterman, Dennis Miller, and Conan O'Brien twist ordinary events into extraordinarily funny observations. Often the best ideas come from our own embarrassing experiences (see tip 5, "Take aim at yourself").

If it amuses you, it will probably delight your audience, so try it. And if it bombs, it will not be fatal (I have a rich history of bombing, yet I live to bomb another day). If no one laughs, it may be because your audience is riddled with killjoys. Some sourpusses in your audiences have seldom smiled, have never laughed, and basically have no sense of humor. Although it is difficult, you just have to endure them.

3. **Capture your thoughts.** When you see or hear something that amuses you, snatch it immediately, because those pearls of wit and wisdom will vanish in an instant, and our memories are notoriously unreliable. I don't know about you, but inspiration seldom shows up on my schedule.

   Write down your mirthful observations or that zany story, or create a repository of humor on your computer, titled "Really Funny Stuff" (or "*Potentially* Really Funny Stuff"). Stockpile this material; you can never have too much, and you can never anticipate how it might come in handy.

4. **Make it creative and relevant.** Don't aim for a laugh at any price. Avoid irrelevant, inane, or predictable humor that reeks from the outset: "You meet ol' Saint Peter at the Pearly Gates, and he seems a little annoyed as he reviews your life's records . . ." or "Two fat ducks waddle into a bar in Boston. . . ."

   Please spare everyone. That type of humor wears the hackneyed brand. You may get a laugh, but it is just as likely to bomb and be greeted with rolling eyes and rampant groans—a reaction that will erode your confidence.

   But the real downside of stale humor is that it diverts your audience's attention if it does not relate to your talk (and Pearly Gates and fat-duck humor are seldom related to any talk). Once the fickle attention of your audience has vanished, it may never return. That is a very steep price to pay for a chance at a laugh.

5. **Take aim at yourself.** Does anyone enjoy listening to a somber windbag? You are giving a speech, not resolving world hunger. Ease up and add a dollop of self-deprecating humor to your talk.

Disarm your listeners by showing them that you do not take yourself too seriously.

Describe a thorny predicament that you experienced, or perhaps recount a humbling speaking gaffe (I know—there are so many to choose from). Let your listeners know that underneath that sober patina, a likable human being resides. Do that, and you are far more likely to connect with your listeners.

❧

To make other people laugh is no great feat so long as one does not mind whether they are laughing at our wit or at ourselves.

—Georg Christoph Lichtenberg

❧

6. **Consider using visual aids.** Visual aids can have a greater impact on your audience than anything entertaining you might say during your speech. So consider using such visual aids as photographs or drawings to add a little snap, crackle, and pop to your speech. Principles 36, 37, and 38 delve into all the ways in which you can weave visual aids into your presentations, but be careful: you need to be comfortable incorporating this added layer of complexity, and the timing and use of the visual aid must be strategically planned.

7. **Don't go bonkers.** Don't go wild, injecting snappy banter every other line. Aim for well-timed humor rather than an endless succession of bon mots or anecdotes. Incorporate humorous material sparingly until you get a better sense of what works for you.

    Your purpose in speaking will dictate the amount of humor you mix into a presentation. For example, if you are making a toast, talking at a roast, or speaking after dinner, sprinkle entertaining stories, parodies, or satire liberally into your talk. But if the mood is more serious, and you are simply attempting to ease the tension or provide a brief interlude from a weighty or complex message, just add an occasional quip or a brief entertaining story. During the memorial service for President

Ronald Reagan, President George Herbert Walker Bush spoke of his memories of Reagan's quick wit by sharing a conversation he once had with him: "Mr. President, how did your meeting go with Desmond Tutu?" he asked. "So-so," Reagan responded. The congregation laughed, and that eased the tension.

8. **Use discretion.** Use only humor that is appropriate for your listeners. Research your audience, and tailor the humor to the group (principle 6). What works when you speak at the Real Manly Men's Club may flop when you speak at the Southern Baptist Ladies' Auxiliary. When in doubt, err on the side of caution and leave it out.

   It sometimes works to direct your pithy comments toward someone in the audience who is well known. This approach can make your presentation seem more customized to that audience. Just be careful not to aim your jest at a humorless target—your boss, for example—unless you enjoy scouring the help-wanted ads.

   ❧

   Laughter is wine for the soul.

   —Sean O'Casey

   ❧

9. **Critically analyze your humor.** Ruthlessly slash any humor that has even the slightest sexist, ethnic, or racial connotation. Never use offensive humor or language in a speech. Even if some people laugh, others may become defensive and resentful toward you. It is unlikely that audience members who are seething with resentment will be receptive to whatever else you might say. Your talk could be doomed, and you may not even know it.

10. **Practice.** Here is the big fat secret about humor: two words, timing and delivery. They count as much as, if not more than, your material itself. Factors such as pausing, pacing, body language, facial expressions, and tone of voice are all critical. If your timing is off, if your body language or facial expressions

are incongruent with your words, or if the tone of your voice is lifeless, the humor will fizzle.

So, before you deliver your ripsnorting funny speech (or the one you at least fancy will be ripsnorting funny) to your intended audience, you had better test it out. Gather family members or friends—even strangers at the bus stop, if you are really desperate for an audience—and deliver your humdinger. Then perform an objective assessment: "Did they laugh, or at least smile, or did they react with icy silence?" "Did they understand my humor, or did they stare at me with inane grins and puzzled looks?"

Don't despair if your humor didn't work as well as you had expected. You may only need to tweak the wording or hone your comedic timing. Often slight adjustments will make a dramatic difference. Even speakers who regularly use humor in their presentations constantly refine their material and rehearse their delivery. Don't expect perfection immediately. If it were easy, everyone would be doing it successfully.

ॐ

I'd like to begin today by quoting Homer from the *Odyssey*. . . .
In the Eleventh Book of the *Odyssey*, he writes, "There is a time
for many words, and there's also a time for sleep." That's true.
I just hope my remarks won't be a time for both.

—Olympia Snowe

ॐ

If you need to add zing to your speeches—and most of us do— review the recommended resources at the end of the book, and sleuth around on the Web (just avoid risqué humor sites that your grandmother would disapprove of). Here are a couple of places to start mining for funny material:

- Comedy Zone (www.comedy-zone.net), which offers a broad range of humorous ideas
- Murphy's Laws and Corollaries (www.roso.epfl.ch/dm/murphy .html), which contains a wide variety of clean humor

If you really want to connect with today's audiences, make your presentations distinctive and entertaining. You don't need a walloping stand-up comedy routine, and you don't need to repeatedly blow up paper bags and pop them to engage the audience. Just add a surprising tweak or a juicy quip that will add a little sparkle. If you flub, you'll survive. And if it works, it will be magical, and your chest will swell with confidence. Be brave—try it.

15

Quote for Credibility

I often quote myself; it adds spice to my conversation.
—George Bernard Shaw

Let's start with an embarrassingly easy pop quiz (I said an *easy* quiz, so no carping): would you like to add a smattering of wit to your speech, perhaps a poignant observation that causes the members of your audience to reflect or that stirs their imagination? If you answered yes, step forward to accept your gold star (all right, two gold stars) and begin hunting for the perfect quote.

Speakers can embellish their presentations by sprinkling in quotations from a variety of sources: scripture, poetry, literature, politics, and writings of virtually any type. An apt quotation will add pizzazz to a tepid presentation, charm or surprise your audience, enhance your credibility, and perhaps persuade skeptics where your words alone may fail. To make your speech distinctive (and who among us would not like to deliver a more distinctive speech?), intersperse a few quotations.

Seven Questions to Ask Your Quotations

Excited by the possibility of making your speech distinctive, with a wild glint in your eyes, you dash out lickety-split, searching for quotations. You are not too particular in your hunt, because any handy quotation will work, right? No. And you will miss the mark if you simply begin cramming quotes into your speech, hoping that somehow one of them might resonate with your audience.

Let's adopt a few rules before you go bananas quoting. Become judicious and selective (bordering on obsessive) about whom you quote and where you plug your quotes into your speech. Don't just settle for any motley quote that comes sauntering to your doorstep. Inspect all potential quote candidates and choose among them carefully (because, as we know, "Many are called, but few are chosen").

Turn the hot spotlight onto each quotation and subject it to the following seven-question inquisition. For your quotation to pass muster, you want the first four answers to be yes, and the last three to be no.

1. **Are you short?** Limit the length of your quotations. Most audiences will not be able to—or want to—focus on and process lengthy quotations. Shorter, punchy quotes are typically more compelling and memorable. You also appear to be well prepared when you recite a quotation from memory, a task that is much easier to accomplish with a short quote.

‰

Every quotation contributes something to the
stability or enlargement of the language.

—Samuel Johnson

‰

2. **Are you the right fit?** Regardless of how pithy or inspirational the quotation may be, it must be appropriate for the speech. Does it intrigue your listeners? Does it cause the speech to ripple with emotional energy? Does it add a smidgen of comic relief? Sometimes a wonderful quotation just may not fit the mood or

tone of your speech. For instance, a playful quotation at the wrong moment in a serious message may perplex your audience. They will not know whether to laugh or to remain stoic.

You may be loath to say good-bye to a snappy quotation, but if the quotation does not enhance your speech or support your point, reject it. Don't let it lurk around, because you can become emotionally attached to it ("But I just *love* that saying") and be tempted to sneak it into your speech. Root around until you find the right candidate for the job. Be fastidious.

3. **Are you clear?** Will your audience members immediately understand why you interjected the quotation? Will they readily grasp the point of the quote, or will the quotation shroud your message in obscurity?

    You do not want it to create a mental logjam, leaving your audience wondering, "Where on earth is she going with that point?" If you do that, your audience will be left behind, pondering the meaning of the quotation while you proceed with your presentation. Most audiences will not work hard, and they will shut you off in a flash. Avoid that by carefully selecting quotations that support and clarify your point.

❦

That is always the grand challenge of good writing, isn't it: to bring people around—to teach them, amuse them, inspire them, goad them, charm them, awaken them, convince them.

—John R. Trimble

❦

4. **Do you pack a punch?** Quotations from well-recognized sources have impact; those from obscure sources do not. Quoting such respected and highly acclaimed people as Mother Teresa or the Reverend Billy Graham enhances your credibility. On the other hand, however much Ralph, the attendant in the locker room, is a recognized authority on gym politics and protocol, he is still unknown to the general public.

Citing Ralph is likely to cause your listeners to puzzle, "Who?" rather than to concur: "Absolutely!" Unless you are addressing your locker room buddies, dig deeper for your quotations.

5. **Are you highbrow?** Try this quote: "'Now lat us ryde, and herkneth what I seye.' And with that word we ryden forth oure weye." This quote from Chaucer sounds so stuffy that, unless you are speaking to a group of Middle English scholars, it does not entice your listeners to "ryden" any further on the journey with you or to "herkneth" to anything else you have to say.

    Don't try to dazzle your audience with esoteric or pretentious quotations, because if the meaning of the quote zips right over their heads, they will be neither impressed nor persuaded. Instead, they are likely to conclude that you are pompous. Highbrow quotations label you as someone who is intent on impressing, rather than reaching, your audience.

6. **Are you tainted?** Does the person you are quoting dogmatically advocate only one point of view? For example, political talk-show hosts typically see the world and its many issues in black and white, never in subtle shades of gray, and they frequently spin the facts to suit their purposes. Some of them cavalierly disparage opposing viewpoints without any factual or logical basis for doing so, thus undermining their own credibility. Listeners are rightly suspicious of such sources, so avoid quoting someone whose credibility is tarnished by a narrow-minded agenda.

7. **Are you a lightning rod?** Will the quotation inflame the audience for the wrong reason? Some quotes may be right on point but all wrong for your speech. For instance, quotes from such celebrities as Congresswoman Nancy Pelosi, Reverend Al Sharpton, imprisoned investor Bernard Madoff, or developer Donald Trump are likely to be counterproductive. These sources are so controversial to many people that merely mentioning their names evokes strong negative reactions (bulging veins, flaring nostrils, hyperventilation).

By citing such provocative sources, you risk polarizing some of your listeners: they will react emotionally rather than logically, and they will discount anything you say regardless of its merit. Always know your audience (principles 6 and 7) and weigh the potential ramifications when quoting controversial figures. If you are unsure, opt for the safe choices (Big Bird, Winnie the Pooh, and Elmo spring to mind).

Almost every wise saying has an opposite one,
no less wise, to balance it.

—George Santayana

To trigger ideas for your presentation, leaf through a book of quotations. There are hundreds available, but the best is *Bartlett's Familiar Quotations*, which contains more than 20,000 gems of wisdom from historical and contemporary figures. For example, if you are looking for an insightful saying on "truth," you will find nearly 300 entries under that topic. You can easily draw from such sources as William Shakespeare, Blaise Pascal, Victor Hugo, and John Lennon (and you cannot get much more eclectic than that).

Bartlett's is an invaluable friend when you are drafting a speech and hunting for the ideal quote. It belongs in every speaker's library, so splurge for your own copy, or put it on your birthday wish list. You will find other excellent sources for quotations in principle 5 and in the recommended resources at the end of this book.

Decorate your talks with quotations. Use them to create frivolity, profundity, and drama. They can make your presentation shine. Don't settle for a merely adequate quote—find an exceptional one. You may have to interrogate hundreds of candidates before you settle on the right ones, and, yes (ugh), the interrogation will require an investment of time. But those little pearls of sagacity and inspiration can help to dramatically differentiate your speech from the mundane. Most important, you will earn a few extra gold stars with the audience—guaranteed.

16

Close with a Bang

I love a finished speaker, I really, truly do. I don't mean one who's polished, I just mean one who's through.

—Richard Armour

Assume that the closing of every speech is critical. (It is, so work with me, all you doubting Thomases.) How should you close your speech? Which of the following should you be?

- A *packer*, who mumbles her final words while staring at the lectern and simultaneously gathering up her notes and accessories
- A *randomizer*, who has no prepared closing, as he is never quite sure what the closing will bring and simply goes where the fickle spirit of the moment moves him
- A *rigid reader*, who reads her closing because she fears ever varying from the exact words on her script
- A *skedaddler*, who is anxious to dart away, just darn thankful that he survived the speech with a speck of dignity

The answer? None of the above. (Yes, I know that was not a choice.) If you ever learned that any of those methods is the right way to close your speech, unlearn it now. From all indications in the speaking world, quite a few speakers should start unlearning.

How important is the closing, you ask? It's crucial, because most audiences will remember what you said first in the speech, followed by what you said last, and, if you are really lucky, they might recall something that you sandwiched in the middle. This statement may dismay you, but numerous studies support it. Your closing is your final opportunity to make a lasting impression with your audience, so capitalize on it.

The closing is not the time to pack, shuffle, organize, mutter, ramble, waffle, ponder, read, or skedaddle (that ought to cover the spectrum of closing sins). End on a high note, with your audience wishing that you would continue, not celebrating your exit.

Five Closings to Shun

If the closing is so blasted important, why are so many baffling or anemic? Often the audience is stupefied, dozing during the grand finale, or left scratching their heads and wondering, "What'd he say?"—hardly a monumental ending. Let's banish the worst villains from your closing repertoire. With apologies to David Letterman: "From the home office in Wahoo, Nebraska, David Dempsey's Top Five Dreadful Closings":

1. **The abrupt closing.** If your listeners are not sure that you have closed until you start walking away from the lectern ("What, it's over? That's it?"), you have left them dangling. Your audience should never be surprised that you have closed. Plan your closing precisely. Ease into the closing, and alert the audience that the journey is concluding: "In closing, . . ." or "My final words to you today are . . ." Never close abruptly, in the middle of a thought. Close your speech emphatically.

2. **The whimpering closing.** Don't cower in the closing like the Cowardly Lion from *The Wizard of Oz*. If your position is controversial, even if you risk alienating some people in your audience, stick your neck out: look them in the eye and have the courage to speak with clarity and conviction. Your audience members may not like what you have to say, they may even glare, hiss, and flat-out reject your conclusion, but they will certainly remember it, so don't be a wussy.

❧

Better never to begin than never to make an end.

—John Clarke

❧

3. **The endless closing.** You have rounded the closing corner, and you are barreling toward the finish line. Never tease an audience by promising to close ("In closing, let me just say . . .") and then droning on . . . and on . . . *and on.*

Audiences become grouchy, and their grouchiness quickly morphs into hostility if speakers continue to yak after signaling that they are going to close. This invariably seems to happen with the most excruciating presentations (those that are too long, too boring, too disorganized, or—horrors!—all of these). When the speaker finally stops yapping, the audience applauds not in appreciation of the speech, but in relief that it's over. Adhere to the advice of Franklin D. Roosevelt: "Be brief, be sincere, be seated."

You delude yourself if you think that your listeners are enraptured with the sound of your voice and are always eager to hear more from you. They are not. Listeners *rarely* complain that a speech was too short, but when a speaker exceeds the time allotted, the restless listeners are not just looking at their watches—they are tapping them to see if they are still working. Wrap it up and get out while the gettin's good.

4. **The "and another thing . . ." closing.** Sometimes during the closing, a lightbulb will go off above a speaker's head, and she will recall something that she had planned to discuss earlier in the speech but forgot ("Oh, yes, now I remember what I wanted to say . . ."). Or she might spontaneously interject new ideas in the closing ("And another issue that deserves mentioning . . ."). It's too late. Those thoughts might have deserved mentioning in the body of the speech, but they are unwelcome intruders in any closing.

   Do not introduce new topics when closing. You will not have time to develop these points, and they may obscure the points that you have already addressed. Know your purpose and remain focused and organized; this is not the time to improvise. Save your unexpressed ideas for the next presentation.

❧

Good to begin well, better to end well.

—John Ray

❧

5. **The read closing.** Among the vast multitude of wretched closings, there may be one that is worse than a closing that is read—but I doubt it. You might as well pass out a script of the closing to your audience, exit stage left, and just let them read it at their leisure.

   Barbara Bush delivered a commencement address at Wellesley College that was drafted with a wonderful mix of personal stories, humorous anecdotes, and inspiring quotations, and, miraculously, it was a true rarity for a commencement address—it was short. But it was apparent that Mrs. Bush had spent no time reviewing or practicing the speech, so she awkwardly read the closing. She concluded with a resounding thud (I don't think it caused her husband to lose the presidential election, but you never know).

   Most read closings suffer a similar fate. The closing is the climax of a speech, and it should be practiced repeatedly until you can deliver it confidently and emphatically. Never read your closing—ever.

Six Dynamic Closings

You have mulled it over, and you have decided that you would prefer to close to roaring applause rather than to jeers and yawns. Wise decision. So how do you craft a closing that will do that? Look for ways to close that are fresh, surprising, and unforgettable. Here are six exceptional ways to close a presentation, but don't be afraid to experiment.

1. **Close with a quotation or a poem.** Apt quotations or poetry, practiced and delivered with confidence, can add the perfect crescendo to any presentation. Constantly gather quotations or short poems that resonate with you and save them in a notebook, a computer file, or a shoebox for future use. In principles 5 and 15, and in the recommended resources at the end of the book, you will find lists of sources, including Web sites, that can aid you in your search for the perfect quotation or poem to end your presentation.

2. **Close with a story.** Conclude with a relevant story to captivate your audience (principle 13). Dramatic, humorous, surprising, or allegorical stories leave a lasting impression. You can also use the closing to complete a story that you began in your opening or in the body of your presentation. Renowned radio announcer Paul Harvey skillfully used this technique with his signature closing, "And now you know the rest of the story." He engaged his audience with his intriguing tales that slowly unfolded until the mystery was solved in the conclusion.

   But don't interject just any story; be discriminating. Don't trot out an irrelevant story, no matter how titillating and entertaining you think it might be. That will only befuddle your audience. Make your story brief (no more than two minutes, and ideally less), cogent, applicable, and clear.

❧

Great is the art of beginning, but greater is the art of ending.

—Henry Wadsworth Longfellow

❧

3. **Close with a challenge.** I blush even to mention this next piece of advice, for fear you will think, "Why does he belabor the obvious?" Sadly, since this axiomatic principle is ignored so frequently, I must state it clearly: *if you want the members of your audience to take action, you have to ask them to do so.* The closing is the time to ask. (Glaringly insightful, right?)

   Audience members must clearly understand what you want them to do, so don't waffle. If you have laid out your position convincingly, they will act, but only if you ask. Challenge them to get involved: "Chocoholics, they have banished us from the grade school cafeterias; they scorn us at Weight Watchers conventions; we have even become the scapegoat for society's rampant obesity. It is time that we draw a line in the cookie crumbs, grab our Kit Kats and Ben & Jerry's Chunky Monkey, and proclaim: 'Enough! We are spitting mad, and we are not going to be bullied any more!'" What self-respecting chocoholic would not answer that call to arms?

❧

Tell them you're ending, and they'll be all yours. Even the weakest tip-off, "In conclusion," or one of its bland variations, snaps people awake.

—William Parkhurst

❧

4. **Close by emphasizing an earlier point.** Conclude by answering a question that you asked earlier in the presentation, or by repeating a quotation, statement, or observation that you previously made. This is an excellent way to reinforce your message, because most audiences need to hear a point repeated several times before they retain it.

   For example, if you posed a question in the opening—"If you could ask your grandfather only one question, what would it be?"—answer it in the closing: "I would ask this: 'Grandpa, what is the most valuable lesson you have learned in the past 95 years?'" This closing wraps up your message in a tidy little package for your audience.

5. **Close with a question.** Close with a rhetorical question, or a series of questions, that will cause your audience to pause and reflect. Audiences today want to participate in the speaking experience, and your questions will engage them in your talk. For example: "Let me ask you this, ladies and gentlemen: the Department of Education spent $27 million last year studying whether reality television shows based on dimwits immersing themselves in a mammoth drum brimming with maggots are intellectually stimulating for our children. Now, is that a prudent use of our tax dollars?" The persuasiveness of your presentation should lead your audience to only one answer: the position that you have been advocating (the maggot insanity must stop!).

6. **Close with artistry.** At times, the tone and content of your message may call for an emotional, poignant closing. General Douglas MacArthur's closing in his moving farewell address to the cadets at the U.S. Military Academy illustrates this technique brilliantly:

> In my dreams I hear again the crash of guns, the rattle of musketry, the strange mournful mutter of the battlefield. But in the evening of my memory always I come back to West Point. Always there echoes and re-echoes: duty, honor, country. Today marks my final roll call with you. But I want you to know that when I cross over the river, my last conscious thoughts will be of the Corps and the Corps and the Corps. I bid you farewell.[1]

The closing is your final opportunity to summarize your message for your audience, so craft it carefully. Your goal is to leave your message ringing in the ears of everyone in the room.

Make your final words unforgettable. Don't pray for divine inspiration or assume that your conclusion will magically appear out of thin air as you are caught up in the moment. That rarely happens. Raise your right hand and vow never to be a packer, a randomizer, a rigid reader, or a skedaddler. Know exactly what you will say and say it with absolute confidence. It is your last shot with your audience, so make it your best shot.

PART IV

PRACTICE FOR PERFECTION

You have meticulously researched, drafted, and revised your presentation, and you are raring to speak. Now you just need to fill the seats, pick up a microphone, and—poof!—you are ready to amaze the gathered masses, right? Not quite. Not before you complete another crucial step: focused practice.

&

Practice is the best of all instructors.

—Publilius Syrus

&

Do I hear you protesting, "Wait. I am an expert, and I have mastered my topic, so do I *really* need to practice?" Yes, you do, because to deliver an exceptional presentation without practice, you need to be extraordinarily good, and most of us (even you, most likely) are not extraordinarily good. Even virtuoso speakers, who have delivered thousands of speeches, constantly critique, hone, and practice their delivery. What ultimately distinguishes their speeches from so many forgettable ones? Practice, practice, and (did I mention it?) practice.

Almost everyone can stand before an audience and listlessly share information. If you are lucky, you may even reach an audience on an intellectual level by doing that (assuming that your listeners hang around long enough to hear what you have to say). But you will seldom touch people on an emotional level. If you really want to make a lasting impression, you need to move both the minds *and* the hearts of your listeners. You cannot do that without practice. Part IV provides a game plan on how to practice to attain extraordinary results.

17

Polish with Practice

Excellence is an art won by training and habituation. We are what we repeatedly do. Excellence, therefore, is not an act but a habit.

—Aristotle

Do you recall the valuable lifesaver we attempted to use when we played games as children? If we whiffed with a wild swing, lobbed up an air ball, or emerged from the water, gasping for air, yards short of our underwater goal, we pleaded: "Do-over, do-over, I call a do-over!" Typically, our fellow zealous competitors jeered and howled, "No way, Butterfingers!" or "Too bad, Choker Boy!"

Well, here is a bit of sobering news: many of your former playmates are now in your audience. And here is the harsh reality of speaking: there are no do-overs (or mulligans, for you golf aficionados). You have only one chance to make a favorable impression with every audience. If you whiff, fumble, or choke, you have squandered your opportunity.

Worse, audiences will rarely understand or appreciate—and may not even care about—all the time and effort you devoted to researching, drafting, and preparing your speech. Even if your brain is bursting with insights, that knowledge is useless if you fail to convey your information in a logical, compelling manner. What your listeners care about in exchange for the most valuable commodity they can give you—their time—is what you say and how you say it. Your challenge is to distill all your expertise into a succinct, cogent speech.

So, with all those hurdles to leap, do you think you ought to practice?

Speaking is a learned skill, and as with any learned skill (tennis, hopscotch, tiddlywinks), the truly dramatic improvements result from practice. There is no substitute—not your bravado (even blustering has its limits), not your shamelessness, not even your innate gift for gab. Reading about the skills required to make a dynamic presentation (such as those in the speaking bible you are currently holding) and watching and imitating exceptional speakers (principle 8) will help immensely. But that passive approach will get you only so far; you will master the skills necessary to speak with confidence only through focused practice. Mark Twain said it best: "If you hold a cat by the tail you learn things you cannot learn any other way."

Twelve Practice Pointers

Obviously (at least, I hope it is obvious by now), it is essential that you lay the proper foundation for every speech—thorough research, logical organization, and fastidious drafting and redrafting—because even practice cannot salvage a speech that has fundamental flaws. But assuming that your speech is ready for prime time, how do you prepare to speak with authority and conviction?

❧

Talking and eloquence are not the same: to speak,
and to speak well, are two things.

—Ben Jonson

❧

Since you do not enjoy the do-over option (and wouldn't we all love to have a few of those treasures lying around?), you have resolved to practice.

But how can you ensure that you are practicing effectively? Should you painstakingly memorize the speech until you are mumbling it in your sleep? Should you read it aloud at least 100 times? Should you resort to writing the speech on your hands and arms for easy reference? No, none of those approaches is the answer.

Haphazard practice wastes time, and it will produce, at best, haphazard results. What you need is a plan, and—presto!—here it is. Use these pointers to practice productively. Where noted, several of the tips are covered more extensively in subsequent principles, but they are mentioned here for handy reference:

1. **Make the layout useful.** First, configure the speech into a functional format for practicing. I realize that tree-hugging conservationists might have conniptions at what I am about to say, but start by being extravagant with your paper. Don't try to cram your entire speech into a space the size of a Post-it note; you will go bleary-eyed deciphering it as you practice.

   Triple-space your text; highlight your key concepts in boldface, italics, or underlining to ensure that you address them; and use an 18- to 22-point font so that you can see the text easily. Leave ample space in the margins to write those fleeting, random thoughts that arise as you practice the speech ("This is poppycock!" "Really?" "Say what?"). These spontaneous observations will be very useful as you continue to edit the presentation. More on this in principle 18.

   ৵

   Preparedness heralds opportunity.

   —English proverb

   ৵

2. **Recite the speech repeatedly.** Begin reciting your speech out loud, in a conversational tone (think human being, not robot). Recite it repeatedly until it flows smoothly. At this juncture, you will probably be reading your speech, but that is fine—no

one will punish you for it. You are simply finding out how your speech sounds as you deliver it. Then quiz yourself: Does it sound natural or jerky? Are there any clunky, unwieldy sentences? Is it verbose? You most likely will need to tweak, edit, or maybe whittle down entire sections before you resume your practice.

3. **Mark the text.** Next, grab your red pen (or crayon) and edit your speech by inserting delivery cues in the text. For instance, if you tend to speak faster than an auctioneer, put a slash between words to remind yourself to slow your delivery at certain key junctures; write delivery notes to yourself throughout the speech ("PAUSE," "SLOW," "SMILE," and "BREATHE"—yes, remind yourself to breathe); or draw an eyeball (not too ghoulish) to remind yourself to maintain eye contact with your audience and not focus on your notes.

   Consider color-coding the text to reflect the moods or tones in your delivery: yellow for a lighthearted mood, blue for somber, and red for passionate. But don't go berserk with your color scheme. This is not the time to unleash your suppressed artistic flair. If your color-coded notes resemble a rainbow, you will have defeated the purpose of highlighting for easy reference, and bedlam will ensue as you wonder: "Is that highlighting red or orange?" "Green means faster, doesn't it? Or does it mean slower?" Avoid that, and choose no more than three colors for your notes.

   These cues and the color coding will prompt you not only in what to say, but also in how to say it for greatest impact.

4. **Graduate from the script to prompt words.** Practice your speech many times using the full text, but do not plan on using the complete text when you actually deliver the speech to your audience. Why? Because when you are standing anxiously before your audience, the text becomes an alluring crutch, regardless of how many times you have practiced it. It can become addictive.

When you feel comfortable with your material, reduce the text to an outline and follow the same procedure of making helpful notations. Finally, graduate to using only prompt words to remind you of the topic or the idea you intend to discuss next (for example, "WALDO QUOTE," "BALLOON STORY," "SPANKING LESSON"). Just remember that this weaning from your notes does not happen in one day; it takes time (yet *more* discouraging news for procrastinators!).

Using this technique will ensure that you cover the key points and ideas, and it will help you internalize and solidify the presentation in your mind. Rely less on notes with each recitation. Ultimately, you should be able to deliver the speech fluidly and confidently, looking primarily, if not exclusively, at your audience. Continue practicing until you can deliver your entire speech without fumbling, mispronouncing words, butchering syntax, or losing your train of thought.

ᘛ

We cannot make it rain, but we can see to
it that the rain falls on prepared soil.

—Henri J. M. Nouwen

ᘛ

5. **Practice with distractions.** In the *ideal* speaking world, it would be as quiet as a monastery when you spoke, your audience would be engrossed in your talk, and no one would move until you had concluded. You silly dreamer!

   In the *real* speaking world, it is typically noisy, and sometimes chaotic, when you speak. Distractions are inevitable: people pirouette in and out of the room; buffoons in the audience jabber away, oblivious to you; cell phones shatter the peace; the members of the waitstaff bang and sling trays and dishes as though they were competing in an Olympic sport; hacking, sneezing, and nose blowing are rampant; and that shifty microphone screeches at the most inopportune moment.

Protest the unfairness of it all if that is cathartic for you, but plan on this hubbub.

Practice delivering your speech under tumultuous conditions, such as having your children wrestling at your feet; Skippy, the wonder dog, yapping for your attention; or the television blaring some drivel. Becoming accustomed to dealing with distractions as you practice, and remaining poised throughout, will mentally prepare you to deal with them during your actual presentation. Otherwise, you may unravel with the first disruption, which is never a pretty spectacle.

6. **Do not memorize.** Do not memorize the entire speech—ever. You will sound mechanical and vapid. Worse, you may eventually freeze. When that happens, your brain will degenerate to mush, you will babble like a baby, and death will seem like a welcome relief. Enough said for now, but much more on this topic in principle 19.

7. **Record your practice sessions.** While you are practicing, record and analyze your presentation. Why? Because a video camera never lies, although sometimes you might wish it would. It zeros in on all your idiosyncrasies. But before you whine too loudly, rest assured that the recording is just as likely to bolster your confidence by spotting your speaking strengths. To master this tool, use the guidelines set out in principle 21.

❧

*However much thou art read in theory, if thou
hast no practice, thou art ignorant.*

—Sa'di

❧

8. **Forge ahead while practicing.** As you become more comfortable with your delivery, refrain from stopping or repeating yourself when you flub a line or stumble over a portion of the speech—and you certainly will do both. Why forge ahead? Because in every speech, no matter how much you have practiced, you will surprise yourself by saying

something unexpected ("Where did *that* thought come from?") or expressing a word, phrase, or idea differently from what you had planned. These mental lapses are an unavoidable consequence of speaking, and they actually add spark and vitality to your speech.

But if you constantly stop and scold yourself for your lapse ("You moron!") or start over ("Speech, Take 7, From the Top, Action!"), intent on delivering the speech verbatim, you will have the same Pavlovian response when you are speaking in front of your audience.

Instead of stopping and fussing, just continue speaking until you get back on track. Become accustomed to delivering your presentation based on its ideas and concepts rather than on its exact words. The result will be a more conversational, natural presentation, not merely a precise, mechanical recitation of a script.

&ᴥ.

Chance favors only the prepared mind.

—Louis Pasteur

◆§

9. **Stand, move, and gesture as you speak.** As you practice your speech, stand, move, and gesture (principles 24 and 25). If you practice your delivery only while you are plopped down in your supple leather chair, elbows braced on your desk and holding your text, you will be entering unfamiliar territory when you actually deliver the presentation without these security blankets. You will encounter a much different speaking experience when you step to the lectern and confront a sea of faces.

Create a realistic speaking experience by standing and moving around. Focus on an imaginary audience; glance at your notes only periodically. Replicate as nearly as possible the experience of speaking to an audience. (If you want to simulate the whole shebang, dress up in your Sunday finest when you practice.)

10. **Practice with your visual aids.** Visual aids clarify and reinforce your message, but they can also sabotage your talk in countless ways with lightning speed. If you intend to use any type of visual aid during your presentation, practice with it (see principles 37 and 38). Your visual aid will affect virtually every aspect of the presentation: your movements, timing, positioning, and interaction with the audience. Unless you relish public embarrassment as you blow a fuse battling with (or sometimes cursing at) inanimate objects, practice with these fiendish tools. You will be thankful that you did (and so will your audience).

11. **Monitor the time.** Here are three simple rules. First, when you are in the final stages of rehearsing, time your presentation, and fit it within the prescribed time limits (being mindful that shorter is almost always preferable). Second, if you will be fielding questions during or after the presentation, allow additional time in your planning; if you use all your time speaking without allowing time for questions, you may frustrate your audience. Finally, if you anticipate laughter or applause as you speak (and what speaker does not want both?), budget time for that. Time limits are sacrosanct; exceed them at your peril. More on this pointer in principle 33.

❧

You prepare the ground so that a lucky accident can happen.

—Sidney Lumet

❧

12. **Test your presentation.** You are feeling plucky and a little bullish. You have buffed the speech and fine-tuned your delivery, and now you are thumping your intrepid chest and chanting, "Bring on the audience!" For those *really* significant speeches, however—say, those where either a gazillion dollars or your job hangs in the balance—consider one additional step: test it.

Deliver your speech to a carefully selected focus group. Present it to people whose opinions you trust and who will provide meaningful, constructive feedback. Their insights can be invaluable. Ask them: "Is my message clear?" "Are my stories and examples vivid?" "Is the speech logically organized?" "Should I slash material?" "Do I seem to exude confidence?" "Is my delivery energetic or feeble?" "Were any mannerisms distracting?" and, most important, "How can I improve the presentation?"

Assess the feedback and dismiss such inane comments as "Lose 20 pounds, Tubby" or "Tell some yo'-mama's-so-ugly jokes to punch it up a bit." But if the input is valid, revise your talk and continue practicing. Smooth out the kinks before the live presentation.

There you have it: the quintessential practice plan (am I thumping my swollen chest now?). Start with these practice pointers and experiment to devise a scheme that works best for you. Most important, practice. It may not make you perfect, but it will propel you much closer to the Promised Land: a first-rate presentation.

18

Master Your Notes

Speak as though it were the last sentence allowed you.
—Elias Canetti

In a perfect speaking world, you would stand to speak, and your words would cascade out freely, effortlessly, and eloquently. You would deliver your message from your heart and dazzle your audience without the need for any notes. But then, reality crashes in on your "perfect speaking world" party.

In the real world, that fanciful scenario is unrealistic for most speakers. Why? Because, let's be honest: speaking to any audience can be intimidating. If you are anything like me, facing one without a safety net of notes can nearly immobilize you. You risk losing your train of thought, and in your heightened state of speaking anxiety, your memory can play wicked games. Sometimes you cannot remember what you just said or what you planned to say next; in extreme cases, you might not even be able to remember your name or why you are standing before the audience. Notes can help you maintain your focus and, if you are in dire straits, rescue you from your mental quicksand.

Speakers often struggle to find the perfect formula for using notes. One speaker lugs his entire presentation to the lectern; another transposes his presentation, verbatim, onto note cards and marches to the lectern with a fistful of cards in his hand. Both of these speakers are determined never to venture from their script. They don't, and as a result, their presentations sound mechanical. Worse, even before they begin speaking, the members of their audience are already dreading their presentation. They have concluded that speakers who need the entire speech or a bundle of notes must be unprepared, or that their speeches will be tedious, or both. They are usually right.

Eight Tips on Using Notes Effectively

Since most of us will use notes when we speak, here are some tips on how to use them most profitably:

1. **Shun the verbatim script.** It is tempting to take your entire presentation to the lectern, but resist this temptation. Why? Because invariably, the entire typed script of your speech becomes alluring when you are standing at the lectern, particularly if you flub a line (and you will) or temporarily forget a point (a distinct possibility). The script is like a siren beckoning you toward the jagged rocks ("Look at me, read me, fixate on me!"). A quick glance will deteriorate into a protracted stare, and, before long, you will be drawn into full-blown reading. Within moments after you begin reading, the members of your audience will slip into daydream mode, and jolting them back to reality during your speech will be a challenging task. Even the very best speakers have succumbed to the Script Siren's temptation.

❧

Never underestimate your power to change yourself;
never overestimate your power to change others.

—H. Jackson Brown Jr.

Remember, you are a *speaker*, not a reader. Leave the script at your seat. For some people, that very thought is unthinkable. But if you are prepared to speak, you will not melt into a pathetic puddle without your entire speech, I promise.

2. **Use a concise outline or note cards.** Many speakers prefer to speak from an outline of their presentation so that they can add last-minute notes in the margins, they can easily highlight key words or phrases, and they do not have to deal with the challenges posed by sliding note cards as they speak.

   Other speakers prefer three-by-five-inch note cards, with one or two points per card. If you are a note-card devotee, you can discreetly slide the cards as you speak without alerting your audience that you have notes (see tip 7). Also, your note cards will fit on any lectern. Most important, because each card should contain only key words or concepts, you cannot rely on them excessively, so you will have better eye contact with your audience.

   Experiment with different outline and note card techniques until you find a system that works for you.

3. **Make your notes legible.** "What happened?" you wonder as you squint to read your notes. The words on your note cards were perfectly legible when you reviewed them, sitting at your desk in the solitude of your well-lit office. Now, as you are standing before an audience in a dim banquet room, the words seem microscopic.

   Here is some excellent tactical advice: pray for the best speaking conditions, but plan on the worst. I have had to improvise in some of my presentations when the lectern size was suitable for a munchkin, and when it seemed as though only candles were illuminating the gloomy auditorium. Like a conscientious Boy Scout, be prepared.

   Set your notes in a large font size (at least 18- to 22-point) and use only one side of the paper or note card. If you must handwrite your notes (and you really should avoid that option), print clearly—no cursive, no scrawl—with dark ink, in large letters. Leave wide margins and ample space between the lines. Don't cram words together; this is not the time to fret about trees lost from using excessive paper. The combination of your anxiety, poor lighting, and your need to pick up points quickly will render tiny print useless.

4. **Number your note cards.** Number your note cards, because either they will become disorganized as you review them, or (far more likely) the dreaded Note Gremlin will snatch them out of your hand and scatter them everywhere just as you are about to speak. You will not recall fondly those awkward moments of silence with your audience staring at you as you fumbled to organize your note cards.

   Also, mark any nonessential note cards so that you know what points to skip if you are pressed for time (principle 33). To remind yourself that the point on a particular card is expendable in a time crunch, make a simple note in the corner: "DROP."

❧

The fellow who thinks he knows it all is especially annoying to those of us who do.

—Harold Coffin

❧

5. **Isolate quotes or critical information.** You may occasionally want to share some critical information with your audience, such as a quote, a shocking fact, or a complex statistic. You need to guarantee that you deliver this information precisely, so you should devote a separate note card just to it. If the quote is too long to memorize (see principle 19), you may even want to pick up the card and read from it to alert your audience that the point is important. You are not cheating if you read this type of information.

6. **Practice using your notes.** Pristine outlines or notes sound great in theory, but if you have not practiced using them, you will not know where to glance when you are standing before

your audience. Then you will waste valuable time scanning your notes, groping for the words or ideas that will trigger your next thought. As you stare at your notes during your word hunt, you will soon begin talking simply to break the silence, and, before long, you will be having a monologue moment with your notes. Avoid that.

Practice your presentation with the same notes you plan to use while you are speaking (principle 17). You need to know exactly where the key words or ideas appear on the paper; practice will help you become accustomed to pinpointing that spot immediately, with a single glance.

7. **Slide your note cards.** Ideally, you want to deliver your speech without alerting your audience that you are relying on notes. But some speakers flip their cards with genuine gusto, eliminating any doubt that they are using notes.

Be subtle. Simply slide (don't flip) each card to the side as you finish using it, while maintaining eye contact with your listeners. Practice doing this so that your notes never become a distraction. (And your reliance on notes can be your little secret.)

8. **Talk to your audience, not to your notes.** No matter how you use your notes, remember to always focus on your listeners. If you continue speaking while you are glancing down, all your vocal power will be directed toward the lectern rather than projected out toward the audience. Even worse, if you spend more time talking to your notes than talking to your listeners, they may feel slighted, and soon they will begin to whisper about your peculiar relationship with your notes. Goodness knows where that will lead!

If you need to sneak a peek at your notes, do the following: (1) Pause (in other words, stop speaking); (2) Glance down at your notes; (3) Collect your thoughts; (4) Lift your head; (5) Reestablish eye contact with your listeners; and (6) Then, and only then, resume speaking.

Since you will, in all likelihood, use notes for most of your presentations, let out a sigh of relief, because they are allowed. Just master them. Never let those little demons become a crutch or create a barrier between you and your audience. If you rely on them excessively—or worse, if you read from them—your audience will quickly become catatonic. That seldom (translation—*never!*) results in an engaging or a persuasive presentation.

19

Minimize Memorization

*I have never seen a human being who more perfectly
represented the modern conception of a robot.*

—Winston Churchill

Memorize your speech, by all means—but only if you aspire to sound like a robot. Why? If you speak by rote, you typically sound impersonal and detached. It seems as if you are reading to your audience—and you *are* reading to them, from the speech that you have engraved on a plaque in your memory. Do audiences leap for joy at the prospect of speakers *reading* to them? Unless your audience is composed of kindergartners, I doubt it.

The typical memorized speech lacks energy and any sense of spontaneity. As they listen to a memorized speech, listeners feel sedated, as though they have been drugged or they have spent entirely too much time watching C-Span. No one relishes that prospect. Most listeners are astute; they can spot a memorized speech from 100 yards: "Look over there; I see a rote talk headed our way! Run for cover!"

A speaker rarely connects with her audience while she is reciting a memorized speech. She is more concerned with what she will say next, and she is not interested in how her audience might be receiving her message. It is apparent to everyone but the oblivious speaker that her audience is bored silly. Most audiences, upon hearing a memorized speech, will mentally (or worse, physically) straggle off—quickly.

But this consequence of memorizing pales in comparison to the worst risk: going blank. I have visited that land; it is scary, and—believe me—you don't want to go there.

Perhaps my friend Clyde's harrowing tale will convince you. He had begun memorizing his speeches as a child because some well-meaning teacher had repeatedly praised him as a gifted memorizer; Clyde felt warm and fuzzy basking in that adulation. As an adult, he continued to memorize his speeches (it had always worked splendidly, after all), until one day his speaking world collapsed around him. I witnessed the implosion. It was pitiful.

❧

One ought, every day at least, to hear a little song, read a good poem, see a fine picture, and, if it were possible, speak a few reasonable words.

—Johann Wolfgang von Goethe

❧

He was speaking before several hundred people at a luncheon, and 3 minutes into his speech, he abruptly stopped, smack-dab in the middle of a sentence. He was mentally paralyzed, unable to utter the next word—or any word, for that matter (although he did seem to be whimpering a prayer). The silence in the audience was eerie. Clyde's eyes darted to the ceiling as his mind whirred, desperately searching for his bearings in his mental script. His bewildered audience fidgeted and gawked at this spectacle.

His shoulders slumped, and he dejectedly dropped the microphone to his side. You could almost hear the clock ticking; 5, 10, 20 seconds passed. After approximately 30 seconds (which must have seemed like 30 minutes to him), he resumed speaking, *precisely* where he had stopped, in the middle of the sentence. Immediately after his speech, according to informed sources, Clyde entered a Speaker Protection Program, and he is now enjoying his cloistered life as a monk somewhere in Quebec.

Imagine that you are standing before an audience, with hundreds of people staring at you, anxiously awaiting your next words. Now stop reading and imagine standing silently for 30 seconds while your mind is blank. You cannot remember your next words; you are not even sure that you can remember your name. Unless you have ice in your veins, that prospect should horrify you and cause you to swear off memorizing.

Do I hear a dissenting voice? "But actors memorize their lines, and they are amazing speakers—right?" Many are, but here is the big fat distinction: they are professionals who have devoted a lifetime to mastering the speaking craft. They can polish their delivery until it sounds conversational. Most of us do not have unlimited time that we can spend practicing our speeches. Only a handful of speakers in the world (seven, at last count) can make a memorized speech sound natural—and then only when they don't go blank. It is unlikely you are one of the lucky seven.

Five Parts of a Speech to Memorize

The following may sound like a contradiction of what I just said (vacillation is healthy at times), but there are a few limited exceptions to the No Memorization edict. Although you should never memorize your entire speech (ponder Clyde's excruciating experience if you are still undecided), you can and should memorize *portions* of your presentation. Although that advice may seem paradoxical (and may make you indecisive, if not bewildered), it is not, because certain sections of your speech are so critical to your ultimate success that, to ensure that your delivery and timing are flawless, you should memorize them. Here is the select list:

1. **The opening.** Memorize your opening (principle 11). Once you begin speaking, you have a tiny window of opportunity to engage the members of your audience and convince them to listen to you. If you hesitate, misspeak, or muse during that period, your audience will quickly conclude that you are unprepared and will move on to more pressing issues (such

as their favorite daydreams or their lunch plans). And if you botch your opening, your confidence will vanish for the remainder of the presentation.

There should be no hesitation, uncertainty, or waffling about what will tumble out when you first open your mouth. Do not speak impulsively. Memorize *exactly* what you will say in the opening, look at your audience, and deliver the words effortlessly.

2. **Quotations.** Memorize shorter quotations (I know, I know—it's more work, but it's definitely worth the added effort). Apt quotations add sparkle to every speech, enhance your credibility, and impress most audiences (principle 15). If you memorize your quotations, you will sound eloquent and well prepared, and every audience appreciates it when a speaker honors them by preparing.

Sometimes, your quotation may be too long to memorize. Then practice reading it repeatedly so that when you share it with your audience, you seldom need to refer to your notes.

❧

Courage is the power to let go of the familiar.

—Raymond Lindquist

❧

3. **Punch lines.** Memorize your punch lines. Humor typically succeeds when the punch line (the surprising twist, the startling revelation, the pithy observation) is reeled off with perfect timing. If you stammer, break eye contact, repeat yourself, or—horrors!—forget the punch line, the humor generally flops.

For example, let's pluck a punch line from the abundant treasure trove of lawyer-bashing humor: "Q: How do you save a drowning lawyer? A: Take your foot off his head." Now, if you botch the punch line ("A: Take your foot off his hand"), you will confuse your audience, the humor will fizzle, and the silence will be disconcerting, if not mortifying. Memorize those knee-slappers.

4. **Key points.** Memorize your key points and examples (if they are not too complex or lengthy), such as a shocking statistic, your underlying premise, or your call to action. Every speaker fondly hopes that his listeners will perch on the edge of their seats, listen with rapt attention, and squirrel away his every word in a cranny of their memories. Unfortunately, that usually will not happen, so you need to help your listeners understand and remember your central points and examples. You increase the likelihood of that happening if you memorize these points and deliver them with conviction, with your eyes firmly fixed on your audience.

5. **The closing.** Memorize your closing (principle 16). You should close your speech with authority, not reading, not bungling words, and not improvising. Your closing is your final opportunity to connect with your audience and leave a lasting, favorable impression. That will not happen if you are focusing on your notes, introducing new ideas, fumbling for thoughts, or just winging it. Memorize your closing and practice it until it flows naturally. Know it and nail it.

Be extremely selective about what you memorize, and never memorize the entire speech. The limitations inherent in memorizing your entire speech far surpass any perceived advantages. Audiences want to hear a presentation that entertains and engages them, not a robot mechanically reciting a script. And what more can I say about the risks of freezing and forgetting your memorized speech? It is a nightmarish experience, so avoid it. Clyde concurs.

20

Eliminate Distractions

Rowing harder doesn't help if the boat is headed in the wrong direction.
—Kenichi Ohmae

Let's be honest: speaking can be a daunting task. For some speakers, anxiety surges at the mere prospect of speaking ("I can't breathe!" "My heart is thumping right out of my chest!"). Because of your anxiety, you sometimes unconsciously engage in bizarre behavior while you are speaking: you might gnaw your lips, tug on your clothing, fidget, mutter, fiddle with your notes (or anything else you can grab), stare at the ceiling (praying for divine intervention, perhaps?), or hypnotically sway as if you were standing on the bow of a ship at sea.

Seven Distracting Sins to Avoid

You should exude confidence whenever you speak (principle 30), so eliminate mannerisms that undermine your message. You will spot many of them as you analyze recordings of your presentations (principle 21), but here are seven of the most common and distracting idiosyncrasies that you should mercilessly eradicate. Just call them the Seven Sins.

1. **Lectern clinging.** A lectern lover caresses, clings to, and hides behind that hulking block of wood. Without it shielding her from her audience, she feels exposed and vulnerable.

   If you plant yourself behind a mammoth lectern, your audience may see only your head cautiously peering over the crest, and perhaps a sporadic waggle of your hand, venturing out before quickly retreating. The lectern has become a physical and psychological barrier between you and your audience.

   The sole purpose of a lectern is to hold your notes and writing instruments, not to prop you up or hide you. Lectern dependency highlights your nervousness and prevents any meaningful movement or gesturing. If you are a lectern lover, it is time for you to sever your ties with your inanimate friend. Just step away. You will be fine, I promise.

   ❧

   All things are difficult before they are easy.
   —Thomas Fuller

   ❧

2. **Bobbing and weaving.** A bob-and-weave speaker moves perpetually while he is speaking for no apparent reason other than to dissipate his nervous energy. He awkwardly shuffles and slides around, stepping from side to side, back and forth, or even in a triangular pattern.

   Unfortunately, dancing does not render you invisible; your audience still sees you. And your nervous movement distracts your listeners from your message. Instead of shuffling about, stand erect. Plant yourself confidently in a wide stance, with your shoulders squared to your audience and your knees slightly bent (principle 24). Move only with a purpose—for example, to signal a transition from one point to another, to emphasize a key idea, or to convey an emotion. Shimmy and shake on the ballroom floor, not when you are speaking.

3. **Playing with jewelry, clothing, or writing instruments.** A high-style speaker is festooned with garish bracelets and necklaces, and rings adorn her every finger. She looks like a jewelry infomercial spokesperson. Her flashy ornaments are constantly jangling or banging against the lectern, and she cannot resist fiddling with them. When you are speaking, it is not the time to make a fashion statement, so jettison the jewelry.

Yet another speaker has a peculiar fascination with his clothing or his writing instruments when he speaks. He nervously twirls his laser pointer like a baton, smoothes and tugs at his clothes, adjusts his glasses, or clicks his pen until he just about drives his audience nutty. As well as being distracting, these quirks send a blaring message to the audience: "I am scared silly." Eliminate them.

❧

Bad habits are easier to abandon today than tomorrow.

—Yiddish saying

❧

4. **Wringing, twisting, or slapping your body.** We seldom smack or punish ourselves in our daily conversations (at least, I hope you don't), but some speakers abuse themselves in front of an audience. As they speak, they unconsciously wring and contort their fingers, hands, and arms; pop their knuckles; knead their faces; scratch assorted itches; or clean their ears—yes, it happens, and I have recordings to prove it.

One speaker repeatedly slapped her leg so viciously as she spoke that I feared for her safety. She had no idea that she was doing it, and she adamantly denied that it was occurring until she saw it on the video—and found walloping bruises on her leg. Your mannerisms when speaking should never become a distraction or, worse, a health hazard.

5. **Jamming your hands in your pockets.** Sometimes a speaker will burrow one hand, and sometimes both of them, deep into his jacket or pants pockets while speaking. To keep his hands occupied while they are in their temporary home, he might jangle what sounds like a gigantic piggy bank full of pennies. This approach resolves the perplexing quandary of what to do with those annoying appendages (your arms and hands) that you are obliged to bring with you every time you speak, but it severely restricts your ability to gesture effectively, and it distracts the audience. Your listeners start to focus on the jingling, not on your message. Placing your hands in your pockets also closes you in, making you appear more like a wooden puppet than a dynamic speaker.

   To keep your listeners focused on you, you should use animated (but never excessive or erratic) body language and gestures (principle 25). Once you get fully engaged in your talk, your gestures will come naturally, so don't imprison your hands in your pockets. Bring them out to play.

❧

Habit is habit, and not to be flung out of the window
by any man, but coaxed downstairs a step at a time.

—Mark Twain

❧

6. **Grooming your hair.** A speaker with a wild or disheveled hairstyle often finds her hair flopping in her face as she speaks. She flips, tucks, and even blows the locks away, but within seconds, they return. Another speaker might choose to groom himself as he speaks by running his fingers through his hair.

   Before you speak, arrange your hair in a way that will not interfere with your presentation or annoy your audience. Think hairclips, gel, or bows; or for a really drastic fashion statement, consider shaving your dome. Just stop playing with your hair.

7. **Using unnecessary filler words.** Meaningless verbal clutter permeates many speeches, even those by very accomplished speakers. Rather than simply pausing between sentences or thoughts, these speakers segue by using such crutch words as *uh, um, and, ah, all right, you know, so, like,* and *okay.* These empty utterances grate on listeners. Purge them from your speeches. Instead, pause, be silent, collect your thoughts, and then continue (principle 23). You do not want to become the Wizard of "Ahs."

The Seven Sins are the most common eccentricities, but there are more, trust me, so add to your list as you find them. If you discover distracting intruders, write notes in the text of your speech to remind yourself: "No hand wringing," "Stop grooming," "Never pet the lectern," "Plant, don't rock," and "No leg slapping." Be ever vigilant, because these vexing oddities can creep into your speeches insidiously. If you allow one of them to hang around, unchecked, for a few speeches, the next thing you know—bam!—you have yourself a full-blown habit. Before that happens, ruthlessly root it out.

21

Critique with a Camera

Experience enables you to recognize a mistake when you make it again.
—Franklin P. Jones

The good news about recording your presentations: Mr. Camera reveals everything. The bad news about recording your presentations: Mr. Camera reveals everything. How about that for creating a little speaker neurosis?

As you view a recording of your speech, you may wonder, "Who is that person jabbering away?" "Who is that person making that droning noise?" "Who is that marionette? Certainly not me!" Yes, that's you, and that is exactly what your audience sees and hears.

It may not seem like it as you agonize and squirm watching a DVD of your presentations, but the advantages of befriending Mr. Camera outweigh the disadvantages by a whopping margin. If your anxiety is running rampant as you watch, a margarita can come in handy. Recording helps neophyte and professional speakers alike polish all aspects of their presentations: timing, pacing, pausing, vocal variety, gesturing, body language, and eye contact—the whole enchilada. I always record presentations made by the business executives whom I coach. They often wince, wail, and gnash their teeth at the prospect, but the value of doing this is undeniable.

I don't do this to discourage them or because I am sadistic (Jell-O Boy feels their pain, believe me). I do it because it is very instructive. I can tell them repeatedly about their distracting idiosyncrasies: "Stop caressing the lectern; people are beginning to gossip." "Don't stare at your belly button while you speak." "Plant yourself; don't pace frantically around the stage." They listen to what I've said, they nod in agreement, and they may even verbally agree to banish the quirks . . . but the next time they speak, they proceed to unknowingly caress, stare, and pace anyway. The recordings are invaluable, however, and they often result in an epiphany for the speaker. There is no better way for speakers to understand how effectively—or how ineffectively—they are communicating than by seeing it for themselves.

❧

Men's natures are alike; it is their habits that carry them far apart.

—Confucius

❧

Allow me to confess: for many years, I had the unconscious habit of unwittingly stroking my necktie as I spoke. This ritualistic tie fetish puzzled and amused my audiences. Unaware of my bizarre habit, I mistakenly concluded, as the audience members stared at me: "Wow! I am one fine speaker. They are captivated!" Of course, what my audiences were really thinking was: "What a weirdo! What's up with the tie thing?"

I don't know why, when, or where I developed this peculiar vagary (therapists were equally baffled). But the first time I saw it on a DVD, I was so distressed that I was unable to focus on anything I said or did in the speech, because the truth was crushing: I was a kooky tie stroker. Recording my subsequent speeches helped me gradually break the habit.

A video camera is an invaluable ally in your perpetual battle to eliminate annoying mannerisms such as those described in principle 20, which undercut your presentations. Seeing the unassailable truth on video is often surprising (and occasionally shocking), but it is always educational.

With that knowledge, you will be able to begin to eliminate your distracting mannerisms before you speak. And here's the bonus: you can later destroy all the evidence of your really strange and embarrassing idiosyncrasies (or at least lock the DVDs in a Swiss bank vault).

Before you become overwhelmed with recording angst, keep in mind that the camera is a learning tool, not a device for shattering your fragile speaking psyche. Any bad habit that you might have has probably crept into your talks unconsciously. Once you identify it, you can begin to eradicate it.

And here is another added bonus: you are just as likely to be pleasantly surprised, if not delighted, at what you observe. While you were speaking, you might have felt as though your face were burning, your knees were knocking, and you were on the verge of cardiac arrest, yet the recording might well depict a confident, poised speaker. Watching a recording of your presentation can actually bolster your confidence. Like everyone else, you have speaking strengths, and you will see them when you study the DVD.

ஃ

Any man is liable to err, but only a fool persists in error.

—Cicero

ஃ

Six Tips for Capitalizing on Recording

You have secured a vault for the DVDs, you have steeled yourself, and you are willing to plunge in and record your speeches. How can you extract the greatest benefit from this exercise? Here are six exceptional ideas:

1. **Be objective.** As you review the recording, resist any temptation to berate yourself unmercifully: "No, no, no, you blockhead! The word is *gizmo*, not *gadget*!" Get a grip on yourself. If you are not careful, you can quickly become your own worst enemy.

Analyze objectively and ask yourself questions such as the following: "Do my eyes dart furtively around the room, avoiding everyone?" "Do I anxiously rock from side to side like a metronome?" "Am I moving naturally, or do I look as stiff as an iron poker?" "Do I sound warm and friendly, or pompous and bored?" "Do I screech?" "Am I chattering or droning?" "Do I project?" And, of course: "Am I massaging my tie, my blouse, or any other object?"

In critiquing your presentation, also give yourself credit for what you did right. Relish every success, large or small: purposeful movement, compelling pauses, a conversational tone, a beaming smile, enhanced eye contact, a confident demeanor—soak it all in.

2. **Focus on the speech and the delivery.** Don't fixate on factors that are not relevant to the effectiveness of your speech, such as your bulbous nose or those extra 10 pounds (okay, 20) that you have been lugging around. Irrelevant analysis is neither constructive nor beneficial. Instead, focus on such criteria as those identified in the previous tip and analyze why your speech worked or, perhaps, why it missed the mark. Avoid the personal, extreme makeover analysis.

≈

Experience is not what happens to you; it is what you do with what happens to you.

—Aldous Huxley

≈

3. **Capture various perspectives.** Entice a friend to help you record your speeches, with the promise of a sugar cookie with sprinkles (or a new BMW if you are really desperate for her help), and threaten to bean her with a wooden spoon if she mocks you.

Why not just switch on the recorder and let it roll? Here's why: every time you speak, you are communicating with your audience not only with your words but also with your facial expressions, your eye contact, and your body language, so you need to critique every aspect of your delivery. When you are speaking in front of an unattended camera, you cannot record all these views, especially as you move around.

Ask your camera buddy to zoom in on your face, eyes, hands, and feet, and to capture your gestures and other movements throughout the speech. Instruct her to focus on any disruptive mannerisms. She should even record your audience, too (to help you gauge their reaction to your speech) and see if they are dozing, doodling, or drumming their fingers while you speak.

4. **Compare presentations.** Compare and contrast your presentations to determine if any new eccentricities or distractions have surfaced. You will also be able to measure your progress, and if you have been following the blueprint outlined in this book, you should be pleasantly surprised at the dramatic improvements you have made. Your accomplishments may come gradually, in incremental steps, not instantaneously. Put in the effort, and you will reap the benefits.

ੈੈ

A man who never makes enny blunders seldum makes enny good hits.

—Josh Billings

⚜

5. **Allow time for adjustments.** Allow enough time between your recorded practice sessions and the big event to review the recording, to recover if the speech was a dud (smelling salts help), and to rectify the problems. Some adjustments may be simple (move periodically; stop flopping onto the lectern; stop scratching yourself; stop biting your lips) and some may be more involved (experiment with vocal variety; incorporate more expansive gestures; sustain your eye contact). But if you wait to review the DVD until an hour before you are scheduled to speak, it is probably too late to make any meaningful changes. And most of us do not produce our best work under a dire deadline.

6. **Be realistic.** Do not expect perfection, because no presentation is flawless—not those given by professionals and, odds are, not yours. Speaking confidently is a learned skill, so don't anticipate miracles overnight. Don't be obsessive (or compulsive, for that matter) about addressing every problem immediately ("Next speech, I'll make these 59 improvements!").

   If you attempt to fix a barrelful of challenges at one time, you will be overwhelmed and frustrated. Instead, analyze the recording, decide where to best focus your energies, and continue to tinker. Target three goals for your next talk, and once you have rectified them, tackle another three. Gradually you will chip away at your list, until—behold!—an exceptional speaker will emerge from the cocoon.

ᴥ

Learn in order to teach and to practice.

—Talmud

ᴥ

You will benefit enormously from recording and critiquing your presentations. If you are honest (but not brutal), objective, and receptive, you will learn more in several recording sessions than most speakers learn in several years, and you will avoid many mortifying speaking moments. That bonus alone is priceless. Excellent speakers understand and harness the incredible power of the video camera. You should too.

22

Project Vocal Power

Eloquence lies as much in the tone of the voice, in the eyes, and in the speaker's manner, as in his choice of words.

—François, duc de la Rochefoucauld

Raise your hand if you have ever heard any of the following speakers:

- The *plodder,* who speaks at a painfully ponderous, halting pace, pausing frequently and methodically weighing every word as if it were profound beyond belief
- The *jabberer,* who races lickety-split through her speech, never pausing and seldom breathing, talking so fast that her listeners fear for her welfare
- The *screecher,* who sounds so high-pitched and strident that her listeners fear for *their* welfare
- The *droner,* who tediously hums along, sounding lifeless and bored, and, as a result, boring his audience

I see quite a few hands. Listening to these speakers is a chore, even if it is a titillating topic.

Now raise your hand if you have ever heard a speaker who uses his voice to engage his audience, who sounds natural and relaxed, and who varies the pacing of his delivery. Or how about a speaker who employs vocal variety and energy in a manner that is congruent with her message? Not as many hands, I see, and for good reason: very few speakers do this. Most speakers barely scratch the surface of their vocal potential.

You can make dramatic strides toward enhancing your power as a speaker by learning to use your voice more effectively. Ironically, in a one-on-one conversation, you probably speak in a natural, relaxed manner without giving it any thought. The person to whom you are speaking can close his eyes and still know exactly how you feel: excited, passionate, angry, disgusted, frustrated, indifferent, or relaxed.

Unfortunately, an amazing transformation often occurs when you stand to speak: your normal manner of speaking becomes abnormal, and you sound diffident, monotonous, strident, or unnatural. Or perhaps you have become—drum roll, please—the authoritative-sounding speaker, someone who is brimming with seriousness and pomposity. It is not long before the audience says, "Enough of you."

&⫯

Enthusiasm begets enthusiasm.

—Henry Wadsworth Longfellow

&⫯

Eight Vocal Power Secrets

All right, you prefer to sound confident and natural. You might be asking, "How do I do that?" That's a good question, so here are eight excellent ideas:

1. **Warm up your voice.** If you were to bounce out of bed (or tumble out, for you sleepy-heads), grab a microphone, and immediately begin speaking, your voice would sound raspy, discordant, and probably a little scary. Why? Because your vocal cords are not warmed up.

Before you speak, always warm up your vocal cords; otherwise, you risk straining them. Hum a few bars of a song (avoid gangster rap), or deliver a portion of your speech to an imaginary audience (the one that gave you seven curtain calls, remember?). If you are tense before you speak (and some of you do look a little taut and ashen), this warm-up will relax you and help you prepare your voice to speak.

2. **Listen to your voice.** Enhancing your vocal power calls for cold, callous analysis, so stop whining, "I hate my voice" or "I sound like a dope." We are going to fix that. Remember our good friend, the one we met in principle 21, Mr. Camera (or his cousin, Mr. Recorder)? Let's usher him back onto the stage and put him to work.

   Record your presentations and analyze how you sound. Ask yourself the following critical questions: "Would listeners have known how I felt if they had only heard my presentation, without actually seeing me speak?" "Do I emphasize key words or thoughts in my delivery?" "Is my voice congruent with my message—angry, soothing, or self-assured?" "Do I sound like someone I would enjoy listening to—an energetic, engaged speaker?" Make vocal adjustments to address any shortcomings.

   ❧

   There are some people who leave impressions not so
   lasting as the imprint of an oar upon the water.

   —Kate Chopin

   ❧

3. **Don't mumble.** Occasionally a speaker gets lost in Speakerland and forgets that he is standing before an audience. As he weighs his thoughts or inspects his notes, he becomes introspective and begins to mumble. He seems to be carrying on a fascinating monologue with himself.

   If you talk to yourself regularly, counseling might help. In the meantime, be aware that when you are in the speaker spotlight, your listeners are focusing on you at all times. And they can hear you. Pause, collect your thoughts, look at your audience—and only then speak.

4. **Neither plod nor jabber.** At the beginning of this principle, I introduced you to the plodder, that speaker who trudges along, pausing awkwardly and frequently. His pauses make him appear uncertain or even dense. His delivery is halting, sometimes unfolding at the speed of cold molasses. It is maddening to the audience ("Jeez, hurry up for goodness sake!" his listeners silently implore).

A plodder also sounds like a stuffed shirt, intoxicated with his own self-importance as he bloviates away. If the plodder characterization sounds anything like you, you may be taking yourself much too seriously. The historians will contact you in due course, when it's time to memorialize your scholarly musings; until then, zip up the pace and get to the point.

I also introduced you to the antithesis of the plodder: the jabberer, who spews words so rapidly that no one can understand her. Listeners can neither process nor absorb the message; indeed, they can hardly catch their breath as the jabberer races along. Listeners are suspicious of this fast talker, assuming that she must be trying to slip something by them. Consciously force yourself to slow down and interpose pauses (principle 23). Experiment until you find a speaking rate that is neither too fast nor too slow.

5. **Expand your vocal range.** Slip into your imaginary physician's smock (okay, grab a stethoscope, too), and graph your voice the way an electrocardiograph monitors the activity of a heart—with high, low, and middle ranges. If your voice remains in a limited vocal range for a protracted period, like a droner, your listeners simply cannot focus on your message. Audience lethargy is imminent.

Because of the anxiety that speaking causes, you might also sound shrill or high-pitched. If you do this too often or stay up there too long, you officially join the Screecher Club.

A squeaky-sounding speaker does not instill confidence in any audience. Screeching is usually caused by nervousness and improper breathing. If you are struggling with the pitch of your voice, practice some of the suggested breathing exercises that are discussed in the recommended resources listed at the end of the book. Aim for a natural, conversational pitch.

Also, don't rant and rave at your audience in an effort to persuade them. That is seldom effective. Irritating, yes; persuasive, no. And don't continually speak in hushed tones, almost whispering your words, because your audience will decide that you are an indecisive wimp, unconvinced of your own position.

In summary, using a limited vocal range dilutes your message. To maintain your audience's attention and emphasize your key concepts, vary both the pitch and the volume at which you speak. Now, remove the smock. We have work to do.

6. **Experiment with different voices.** This is a great vocal exercise: practice incorporating the dialogue of different characters in your presentation. Tweedledum and Tweedledee, Mutt and Jeff—you get the point. For example, tell a story involving a surly taxi driver (but sanitize the language) or a jilted lover (*really* sanitize that language). Attempt to capture their emotions in your voice: surprise, joy, antipathy, bitterness, or frustration. Using different voices will force you outside of your limited and comfortable vocal patterns.

➳

Man never rises to great truths without enthusiasm.

—Luc de Clapiers, marquis de Vauvenargues

➳

7. **Adjust your voice to your environment.** Adapt your vocal volume to your environment, considering such factors as the size of the room (a tiny conference room versus a grand ballroom), what other activities are taking place in the room while you are speaking (meals being served, audience members milling around), and the acoustics in the room (high ceilings,

hard surfaces). For example, if you are in a quiet conference room, you would project your voice quite differently from how you would if you were speaking at a Town Hall meeting on the steps of City Hall with car horns blaring, protestors chanting, and an angry mob threatening to crack your kneecaps. Know beforehand what conditions prevail at your speaking venue so that you can be prepared (principle 26).

8. **Sound enthusiastic.** Do not expect your audience to get excited about your message if you are not. A lifeless speaker moves no one because he himself sounds unmoved. If you are a droner, one of those passionless speakers who merely shares facts ("Just the facts, Ma'am"), your listeners will be yearning for a glimmer of a real person, any sign that blood might be flowing in the veins of the bionic man they are witnessing. If you are periodically banging cymbals to wake up your audience, you need to add a little zing to your voice—pronto!

Sound enthusiastic! Your voice should convey the same passion you felt when you excitedly told anyone who would listen (including strangers on the street) that your college basketball team won the national championship, or the elation you felt when you told your family about your promotion to Chief Muckety-Muck. Your audience will find your enthusiasm contagious.

❧

Only passions, great passions, can elevate the soul to great things.

—Denis Diderot

❧

Study the best political speakers (all eight of them walking the planet), professional speakers, and historic speeches if you want to see how some of the masters harness the power of their voices. Explore the History Channel's Web site (www.history.com/video.do?name=speeches); it contains more than 100 of the greatest speeches of all time. You can also search the Web sites listed in principle 8 and review the recommended resources at the end of this book for additional examples.

Capitalize on your voice to inspire, persuade, and engage your audiences. Separate yourself from the gaggle of plodders, jabberers, screechers, and droners, and vow never to rejoin them. Why? You are far more likely to deliver a memorable and compelling presentation—something seen and heard as rarely as the Loch Ness Monster. You may not get those seven curtain calls right away, but start making your presentations sparkle with vocal energy, and you will have a much better chance of doing so.

23

Capitalize on Potent Pauses

The most precious things in speeches are pauses.

—Ralph Richardson

A journalist once asked Isaac Stern, one of the world's preeminent violinists, what distinguishes the great violinists from the merely proficient, when all of them play the correct notes in the proper order. His response was insightful: "The important thing is not the notes. It's the intervals between the notes."[1]

Pausing—those intervals between the words—is also an excellent strategy when you are speaking. In fact, here is a sobering truth: a timely pause is often more compelling than anything you might have said to fill up the silence. Why? *Less said is often more.* I'm sorry if that lets a little air out of your speaking ego, but it's true.

You should pause at many junctures in your speech, for various reasons, such as: to make transitions in mood or topic, to emphasize critical points, to alert the members of your audience that you are about to share something significant, to heighten the suspense, to enable them to reflect, and to let them laugh (hopefully with you, and not at you). Simply stop talking and reap the enormous benefits.

So, why don't more speakers capitalize on the powerful pause? Two reasons. First, there is a spectrum of fear associated with speaking. At one end of the spectrum, speaking can make you mildly anxious ("My heart is racing"); at the other end, you can become completely terrified ("End my misery—shoot me, please!"). When you are anxious, you may tend to rattle on because your overriding concern is to finish the speech as quickly as possible, minimize the damage to your self-esteem and reputation, and bolt away from the watchful eyes of your audience. Pausing would only prolong your agony.

ᐧᐁ

Silence is wisdom where speaking is folly.

—William Penn

ᐧᐁ

I have seen this in the courtroom. Allow me to illustrate. I once prepared a skittish witness (let's call him Bert) to testify at trial. I repeatedly advised him to answer my critical question directly: "Bert, just testify that 'it was 3:15 p.m.,' and then stop talking. All right?" Bert smiled and nodded in agreement with my simple instruction.

When the fateful moment arrived, I asked the question at trial; Bert responded and then, just as we had planned, paused. "Success," I thought. Nope, because almost immediately, with everyone staring at him, Bert began to nervously fidget. Under the unbearable weight of what was apparently, to him, a lengthy silence (it was approximately two seconds), he quickly unraveled and began blathering on like a nitwit: "It was 3:15 p.m. . . . . I know, because I was screeching out of the Gulp & Guzzle Tavern parking lot after knocking back eight or nine beers with my fishin' buddies . . . ." Pausing had become an alien concept to the suddenly chatty Bert. I settled that case—quickly.

The second reason for not pausing: you failed to budget any time to pause when you were preparing your speech. Your mind may have been blazing with ideas, and you could not identify the crucial ones, so you didn't discriminate. You just crammed every idea into the speech. You attempted to shoehorn a 25-minute speech into a 10-minute slot; there was no time for pausing ("Not a second to lose!"), because you were on a crusade to cover as much ground as possible.

Vice president Al Gore did this during his acceptance speech at the 2000 Democratic National Convention in Los Angeles. Throughout the speech, he trampled on the laughter and applause of his adoring audience because he was intent on completing his speech during prime-time television. As a result, he was often forced to repeat himself, and he blunted the impact of his message.

ε•

Sometimes you have to be silent to be heard.

—Stanislaw J. Lec

·s

Nine Ways to Pause with Impact

If pausing makes sense to you (and I hope it does), consider this plan. Don't just haphazardly pause for the sake of pausing ("Bingo, got another pause squeezed in!"), because that will make your delivery jerky and defeat your purpose in pausing. Instead, pause at specific junctures in the speech. Here are nine exceptional ways to benefit from the power of the pause:

1. **Allow time for pauses.** Speech time limits are sacrosanct (principle 33), which is a rule that many speakers flout. If you fail to allow time for pausing, either you will trample on the time limits or you will speak too rapidly, trying to cram everything in. Neither approach is prudent. As you practice and time your presentation, budget time for pausing.
2. **Practice pausing.** Pausing may seem unnatural, especially when all you *really* want to do is wrap up your speech quickly and scram. So as you rehearse your speech, practice pausing to replicate as nearly as possible every aspect of your delivery. Because you are likely to speak faster if you are anxious, insert the word [PAUSE] in your outline or notes to remind yourself as

you are speaking. Written delivery cues are invaluable reminders when your anxiety is soaring into the stratosphere as you speak.

3. **Pause before you begin.** If you are eager to tear into your speech, and you begin chattering before the welcoming applause has subsided, rein yourself in, Impatient One. Let your audience size you up and get comfortable with you. You want to project confidence from the moment you are introduced (principle 30), and pausing helps you do just that.

    Step up to the lectern, smile, and pause before you utter your first word. Wait until you have your listeners' undivided attention (usually two to three seconds). Your pause alerts them: "I am confident, and you do not intimidate me." (Even if they do intimidate you, you will never have to tell them.)

ﻬ

Silence is not always a sign of wisdom, but babbling is ever a mark of folly.

—Benjamin Franklin

ﻬ

4. **Pause when you are sharing complex details.** Listeners lose their direction easily, and it is your job as their tour guide to hold their attention and to keep them focused. Evaluate both your listeners (principle 6) and your speech, and determine whether they will understand your topic, or whether it is likely to fly right over their puzzled heads. The language and terminology that you use every day (academic, legal, technical, or scientific mumbo jumbo, for example) may baffle many listeners ("The gizmo interfaces with the whatchamacallit, which, of course, controls the thingamajig . . . *yada yada*").

    Although you understand all the subtle nuances of your topic, your listeners may not. Before you begin to share complicated or technical data, pause. If the complexity of the topic warrants it, consider pausing *and also* alerting them that what you are about to say might be confusing. With this preface, your listeners will concentrate carefully on what follows—something that they might not have done if you had simply launched into your complexities without pausing and alerting them. Also, pause *after* you have shared the information, to enable them to digest it. Not everyone may grasp your technical data, but pausing certainly improves the odds.

5. **Pause before and after quotations.** You have already seen the benefits of sprinkling quotations throughout your presentations (principle 15). To highlight each of these pearls of wisdom, pause both before and after you deliver it. Enable your listeners to reflect upon the quotation's import. If you zip right through the quote without pausing, you diminish its impact; in fact, your listeners may not even realize that you shared a quotation.

❧

Trust the man who hesitates in his speech.

—George Santayana

❧

6. **Pause after you ask a question.** You will engage every audience if you ask questions, but—and this is important— only if you pause immediately after asking them. If you pose a question and then speed ahead without pausing, you signal to the members of your audience that you really did not expect them to think about it or answer it, so they will do neither. Do that repeatedly, and you communicate to them that you do not care about their perspective. Soon they will be ignoring all your questions (and maybe ignoring you). If you want your listeners to contemplate your questions, pause.

7. **Pause when they laugh.** If you take a stab at humor, as you should, and—praise the day!—your audience laughs, be still. Do not talk. Just smile, pause, and enjoy the moment, because, trust me, sometimes the silence following your punch line is eerie. I know that eerie silence all too well.

Never stifle the laughter of your listeners. If you keep talking while they are laughing, they will not hear you. Even worse, your talking will cause the laughter to die down much more quickly than it otherwise would have. So just pause, relish the laughter, and think: "They like me; they *really, really* like me."

8. **Pause to create suspense.** Pause before you disclose a critical fact, to build suspense: "I could not believe it when, sobbing, he confessed: [PAUSE] 'Yes, I jammed my thumb into the bottom of each of the chocolates, searching for caramels. I am so ashamed!'" A pause before a revelation alerts your audience to pay close attention. And once again, if you really want to magnify the impact, pause *after* you disclose the critical information as well.

❧

The deepest rivers flow with the least sound.

—Quintus Curtius Rufus

❧

9. **Pause when you conclude.** Don't be one of those speakers who is so anxious to skedaddle as she approaches her conclusion that she begins packing up her materials and walking away as she mumbles her final words. This will send the message that you are eager to conclude, and you will end with a resounding thud. Your closing is critical (principle 16), so to heighten the dramatic impact of your message and to convey your confidence, do the following: just before you utter your final words, and again afterward, pause.

❧

Well-timed silence hath more eloquence than speech.

—Martin Farquhar Tupper

❧

Weave pauses into your speech judiciously. If you pause too often, your speech will become tiresome and choppy. And if you never pause during your breakneck delivery, you will diminish the full force of your message. But well-placed pauses will highlight critical points and send an unmistakable message to your audience: "I am self-assured." It works for Isaac Stern, and it will work for you, so pause and capitalize on those critical intervals between the words.

24

Stand Tall

[D]o not let [fear] into your house. . . . Stand up straight.
—John Cheever

Contrast the following two speakers. After being introduced, Sluggo Sammy lethargically shuffles to the front of the room like a big oaf. His shoulders slump, his spine curves, and his energy is apparently depleted. He props himself against the lectern, virtually draping himself over it. His eyes are riveted on his notes rather than on his audience ("What audience?" he wonders). Sammy stifles a gaping yawn, and his gestures are feeble. He seems so limp that you fear that at any moment he will crumple to the floor.

Enter speaker two, Perky Peggy. She strides confidently to the lectern, quickly arranges her notes, and then steps away from the lectern. She smiles, pauses, and establishes immediate eye contact with her listeners. Her shoulders are back, and her feet are firmly planted. She leans toward her listeners to engage them.

As a member of the audience, you have not heard one word from either speaker, but answer these questions: What are your immediate impressions? Who appears to be more confident, more professional? Are you thinking, "Whoa! Sluggo Sammy will surely have a doozie of a presentation. I can't wait!" I doubt it.

Unless you are Sluggo Sammy's mother, you dread his talk. His body language is screaming: "I am a wet noodle!" Maybe that is an inaccurate and unfair assessment, but the audience is likely to form that conclusion immediately. Sluggo Sammy has handicapped himself from the outset. In stark contrast, Perky Peggy's demeanor, posture, and stance instantly command her listeners' attention and arouse their interest.

☙

This world belongs to the energetical.

—Alexis de Tocqueville

☙

Every audience will choose an energetic speaker *every* time, one who approaches the opportunity of speaking with gusto over one who seems to approach it as pure drudgery. Your audience is evaluating you from the moment its members first see you. Your body language and demeanor speak volumes, signaling whether you are excited to be speaking or whether you seem to be approaching the task indifferently, with all the enthusiasm of a man headed to the gallows. Listeners are remarkably perceptive, so your nonverbal communication is critical to the success of your presentation. In fact, it may have a greater impact on your listeners than what you actually say.

If you trudge to the lectern apathetically, slouch, and violate all the rules of posture that your mother drilled into your head since childhood ("Stand up, or you'll become a hunchback!" "Chin up, Mopey Face!"), you are signaling to your audience that there are dozens of places you would rather be at that moment. You are constantly communicating with your body language, so be careful what message you send.

Eight Guidelines for Posture and Movement

All right, so you want to join the perky club—a wise choice. How should you position yourself and move around in front of your audience to convey confidence? Here are eight outstanding suggestions:

1. **Remove physical barriers.** Any object that stands between you and your audience becomes a physical and psychological barrier. The usual suspects: the mammoth lectern, of course, but also the microphone stand, a desk or table, a pad of paper, a writing instrument (not much cover there), and even your intertwined fingers and folded arms. As a speaker, you want to seem accessible, confident, and trustworthy, so stand tall, remove the barriers, and let the audience see all of you.

2. **Never plant yourself in one spot.** Sometimes a speaker remains riveted to one spot for the entire presentation ("I ain't movin', no way, no how!"). Like a prospector in the Gold Rush, he has staked his claim to a plot of stage, and he will guard it just as fiercely. Oh, he may glance to the left or right, and if he is feeling especially spunky, he may even pivot at the hips. But his feet might as well be buried in cement.

    Can you say, "*R-I-G-I-D*"? Loosen up! It will not matter if you are revealing the secret formula for concocting Coca-Cola or sharing your exploits climbing Mount Everest in your swimsuit; it will be extremely difficult for you to maintain your audience's attention if you have become, essentially, an inanimate object. Move around (an excellent reason to avoid a microphone attached to a lectern, which is discussed in principle 35) but heed the next three guidelines.

3. **Never pace.** Sometimes a speaker will nervously pace back and forth like a caged zoo animal anxiously awaiting a feeding. Perhaps she has deluded herself into thinking that constant movement renders her invisible. Are you anything like her?

Sorry, your audience still sees you. Your perpetual pacing contributes nothing to your speech and eliminates any doubts that your audience might have had that you are nervous. Avoid the zoo-animal syndrome.

4. **Never dance.** Then there is the speaker who suffers from that peculiar malady, Happy Feet. His feet are perpetually moving as he speaks. Sometimes they are sliding from side to side or back and forth; other times they step in a rhythmic, repetitive pattern. Occasionally, the speaker just bounces and taps his feet. All this occurs for the sole purpose of dissipating nervous energy. Take command of your feet, and restrict your dancing to the dance floor.

5. **Move with a purpose.** As you practice your presentation, consciously decide when you should move—for example, when you make a transition from one story or point to the next, when you segue from your analysis of the problem into your proposed solution, when you want to signal a change in the mood of your presentation, when you need to illustrate distance or location, or when you are portraying a conversation between several individuals.

You can also move when you are covering less significant information, but then, when you want your listeners to really concentrate on the words you are about to share with them, stop, pause (principle 23), plant yourself, and deliver your point. The contrast between your movement and your sudden stop helps to ensure that your audience will focus on you at a critical point in your speech.

Purposeful movement helps you project a confident image and enhances the prospect that the audience will remain focused as you speak.

❧

Self-assurance reassures others.

—Garry Wills

❧

6. **Stand with conviction.** You want to exude confidence whenever you speak, so make sure that your body cooperates. Position yourself in the following manner: Assume a spot in the center of the stage. Align your feet with the outside of your shoulders; pressing your feet together will appear unnatural (even worse, you may teeter and possibly tumble over—never a great confidence booster). Pull your shoulders back, and keep them squared up with your audience. Let your arms drape at your sides. Shift your weight slightly forward onto the balls of your feet. Bend your knees slightly; if you lock them, you restrict your blood flow (and increase your chances of fainting, yet another way to undermine your fragile speaking psyche).

7. **Face your audience.** Speakers who use visual aids often fall into the habit of orienting themselves toward the visual aid rather than toward the audience (see more on this topic in principles 29 and 37). When you speak, look primarily at your listeners to engage them in your presentation. Step toward them to signal that you want their attention and to communicate the message that they do not intimidate you. Avoid turning your back on them, because you will lose eye contact and miss all the vital signals that they are sending: nods of agreement and note taking, or puzzled looks and spitballs flying across the room. Face the crowd.

8. **Study a recording of your movements.** It's time to break out Mr. Camera again (it is a genuine love/hate relationship with him, isn't it?). Begin recording from the moment you approach the lectern and don't stop until you return to your seat. Then study the DVD. Scrutinize your body language and ask: "Do I stride to the front of the room with confidence?" "Do I nervously fidget, rock, or shift my weight?" "Are my shoulders back and squared to the audience?" "Do I move fluidly, or do I appear as stiff as a board?" "Do I lean toward the audience, or am I constantly retreating, almost plastering myself against the wall at the front of the room?"

Next, turn the sound off and fast-forward the DVD. This is always an enlightening and sometimes an entertaining exercise that will reveal whether you are hypnotically swaying from side to side or back and forth, and whether any of your movements seem annoyingly repetitive. Don't blame Mr. Camera, because he is just the messenger. Your audience is seeing exactly what he records, so ensure that your nonverbal body language is commanding.

❧

Nothing is stable. Nothing absolute. All is fluid and changeable. There is an endless "becoming."

—Benjamin N. Cardozo

❧

Stiff, lethargic, or erratic body language undermines your authority as a speaker. Be aware of the message you are sending to your audience. Trust me: your listeners will give Perky Peggy their undivided attention, and they will cringe and groan when Sluggo Sammy shuffles to the front of the room to speak. Listening to a slouching, spiritless speaker looms as a chore. Engage your audience with animated, purposeful, and confident body language.

25

Gesture with Conviction

Suit the action to the word,
the word to the action.

—William Shakespeare

It is the mother of all speaking bugaboos, *the* burning issue for many speakers. It torments neophyte speakers and even vexes some speaking pros. Some agonize over it and suffer sleepless nights; some turn to drink; others pray for divine inspiration to unravel the mystery. The perplexing question is: "How in the world do I gesture?" Many speakers would pay a king's ransom for a magic potion, *Gestures in a Bottle*.

The irony is that in your daily conversations, you gesture freely and naturally, without the slightest hesitation. Your hands and arms flow with your words as you speak. You are animated, relaxed, and engaged in your exchange. You make chopping motions with your hand to emphasize your point, jab your finger into your palm to drive home your message, and even pound your fist for impact. And you do this without ever thinking about it.

But some mysterious metamorphosis occurs in those fateful few steps from your warm seat in the audience to the loneliness of the lectern. Anxiety grips you, and suddenly—poof!—you are immobilized. Your gesturing becomes positively anemic, or you become as rigid as a plank of wood—and neither will impress your audience.

So how do some speakers attempt to address the gesturing conundrum? In peculiar ways—most of them unnatural, and some of them remarkably bad. One speaker clutches the lectern with a white-knuckled, viselike grip. Another speaker locks his hands at his belly. Still another speaker plasters her elbows against her ribs (in a position aptly described as Velcro Elbows). There is also the speaker who fiercely clasps his hands behind him (protecting his buttocks) in a formal military stance. Another folds her hands below her waist in a modest fig-leaf position that conjures up images of Adam and Eve. Yet another crosses her arms tightly in an authoritative, defiant stance. And finally we have the speaker who simply crams his hands deep, deep, *deep* into his pockets; those hands never see daylight for the duration of the speech.

Problem solved, right? No, problem compounded. Each of these "solutions" in the all-star lineup of gesturing don'ts will severely handicap you as a speaker and will undermine the confident image you want to project. Why? You appear perfectly wimpy, robotically stiff, and ridiculously tense. In the worst case, rigor mortis seems imminent.

So what is the solution, you ask? You may snort in disdain at the pure simplicity of the answer, but more than 25 years in the speaking arena, coaching literally thousands of executives around the country, have convinced me of its validity: *forget about yourself and focus on the audience.* That's it.

❧

Men trust their ears less than their eyes.

—Herodotus

❧

Speakers who are tied in knots about their gesturing are typically focusing on how they appear *to* the audience rather than on how their message is received *by* the audience. Consider every presentation as something that you want to say to people who want to hear it. Take the focus off you and place it on your audience (principle 29). The critical question should never be, "How do I gesture?" Rather, it should be, "How do I *connect* with my audience?" Answer that, and you will resolve the gesturing puzzle.

Eight Gesturing Tips

Those of you who suffer from gesturing phobia might be thinking (or obsessing): "Fine, but can you give me specific gesturing guidance?" Certainly. Help is on the way in the subsequent paragraphs, and here's the real bonus: the gesturing solution does not involve therapy, tranquilizers, or hypnosis. To help you transform your handicap into a genuine asset, here are eight gesturing nuggets of wisdom:

1. **Believe in your message.** First, never approach any presentation with the attitude that it is "just another speech." Why? Because it never is. If you think it is, don't speak. If you can't say what you have to say with enthusiasm and conviction, perhaps you simply should not be saying it at all. If you don't believe that your message is important, neither will your audience. I am sure there is a more perceptive group of people in the world than an audience, but I have not met such a group. If you approach your speech as though you were merely delivering a rote recital, you are guaranteed to leave your listeners yawning.

   Instead, develop the mindset that your listeners need and want to hear what you have to say. And they actually do. They are there to hear you speak for any number of reasons: to be informed, to be persuaded, or perhaps to be inspired. They don't want to waste their time listening to a detached, blasé bore. Become engrossed in and excited about your message, and your gesturing self-consciousness will melt away.

2. **Make the gesture fit the emotion.** Your gestures should match your emotions and accentuate your message: more restrained if your message is informational; more animated if you are selling or persuading. For instance, suppose that you had been passed over for a promotion—for the ninth time—and you were justifiably livid. If, as you pleaded your case to the honchos on the promotion review panel, you gestured with a puny wave of your hand, you would be belying your anger. Instead, you should punctuate your points by pounding your fist, thumping your finger on the flip chart, or twirling away in disgust. (Just don't go berserk if you want to be around to be passed over the tenth time.)

3. **Never cling to the lectern.** Some of you (and you know who you are) cower behind that hulking lectern (many of which are about the size of Noah's ark) and cling to it fiercely (perhaps fearing that you might be swept away in the Great Flood if you loosen your grip). As a result, your movements are limited to head bobbing and shoulder shrugging—gestures that are hardly likely to enhance your message.

   Okay, Lectern Lovers, try this: take a step back so that you will have to stretch your arms forward to grasp your wooden friend. The stretch may feel awkward (as it should), but it will remind you that lectern hugging is forbidden.

   Now, if you are feeling audacious, step away from Mr. Noah periodically as you speak so that your audience can see you. The sky will not fall, I promise, and the audience will be instantly impressed with your adventuresome approach. You may even feel remarkably liberated. Don't worry: if you start to wobble on your newfound speaking legs, you can dart back in a pinch to the safety of Mr. Noah.

⁊

Gestures and facial expressions do indeed communicate, as anyone can prove by turning off the sound on a television set and asking the watchers to characterize the speakers from the pictures alone.

—Peter Farb

4. **Drop your arms to your sides.** Your arms are useful for emphasizing key points as you speak. Unfortunately, if you are busy nearly massaging your hands raw, if you cross your arms in front of your chest, or if you press your elbows against your ribs, you cannot use your arms in any meaningful way. Instead of handicapping yourself, simply drop your arms to your sides. As you become engaged in sharing your message with your audience, your arms are then in a position to gesture naturally.

5. **Incorporate planned gestures.** If you are in dire straits, really struggling with your gestures, incorporate a few planned gestures into your presentation. For instance, you might try holding your hand up, displaying three fingers, and counting off while you tell the audience the three reasons why you should never be compelled to speak: "First, the written word is intrinsically beautiful; second, speaking is wickedly cruel; and third, sweating profusely from anxiety is neither glamorous nor endearing."

    As you begin to discuss each point in detail, gesture again: "Let's discuss point one, the beauty of the written word. . . ." But be careful: you do not want to look like a marionette gesturing, so practice this technique until it seems natural, not jerky or mechanical. Your comfort level will rise with practice.

6. **Add variety to your gestures.** Repetitive gestures quickly become monotonous. They seem choreographed and predictable. Their impact, and the audience's attention, quickly plummets. And since many audiences have a limited attention span, you must use every tool in your speaking arsenal to keep them engaged. Spice up your presentation with a little gesturing variety: sweeping your arms, raising your hand, or counting off your points on your fingers.

7. **Make the gestures fit the space.** Diminutive gestures may be effective if you are speaking in a smaller venue, such as a classroom or a boardroom, but they will be lost in a larger setting, such as a cavernous hotel ballroom. In that type of mammoth arena, your gestures must be expansive and sweeping.

Find out about the facility where you will be speaking (principle 26), and practice using the type of gestures that you will need to use in a venue of that size.

8. **Study your gesturing.** Analyze recordings of your presentations (principle 21), both from your practice sessions and from your speeches before audiences. This is an excellent way to spot and eradicate any feeble, distracting, or ineffective gestures.

Be warned, however: sit down and breathe deeply before you begin watching your DVD, because this gesturing analysis can be downright scary. You may gasp in dismay at your erratic or lifeless gestures. The good news is, the sooner you identify any ineffective or distracting gestures, the easier it is to banish them, preferably before they blossom into full-blown habits.

ଈ

*Every act of conscious learning requires the willingness
to suffer an injury to one's self-esteem.*

—Thomas Szasz

ଈ

For more detailed information on gesturing and nonverbal communication, see the recommended resources at the end of this book, which offer advice and exercises to help you conquer your gesturing phobia.

Your goal is to gesture with authority and conviction. Purposeful and commanding gestures will enhance your presentation and convey your emotions in a way that words alone cannot. They will make you stand out like a real person in a speaking world riddled with robotic speakers. No one likes watching a speaker who displays all the gesturing flexibility of an iron statue. Until the magic *Gestures in a Bottle* potion hits the market, concentrate on the audience and how you can effectively connect with your listeners. Do that, and the gestures will soon flow naturally.

PART V

FOCUS ON THE DETAILS

At last, it is nearly showtime. It has been an arduous journey, with many zigs and an occasional frustrating zag along the way. But you made it. You have revised and polished the text of your speech, repeatedly practiced and refined your delivery, and recorded and critiqued your presentation. You are ready to speak and amaze the throngs.

&

> *A word is dead*
> *When it is said,*
> *Some say.*
> *I say it just*
> *Begins to live*
> *That day.*

—Emily Dickinson

&

So, with all the grunt work accomplished, all you need to do is show up at the designated time and place, speak, and a stellar performance is virtually guaranteed—right?

Sorry, there is more work to be done. (I know—will it ever end?) Specifically, you have to attend to all the critical details that, if not addressed, could potentially diminish your effectiveness at best and undermine your speech at worst. Part V outlines the steps you should take to make sure that you have anticipated and planned for everything when you speak—unless living dangerously invigorates you.

26

Plan Carefully

A man's accomplishments in life are the cumulative effect of his attention to detail.

—John Foster Dulles

Do details *really* matter? After all, isn't the message all that really counts? Well, as Clint Eastwood would say: "[Y]ou've got to ask yourself one question: 'Do I feel lucky? Well, do ya'. . . ?"

If luck is not always on your side, then remember this: there are *no* insignificant details. Ignore them, and, at a minimum, you will heighten your anxiety. But if you overlook the wrong detail, your presentation may implode before your very eyes. I have had the misfortune of participating in a few of those debacles, and I can assure you this: a speaking disaster is one gut-wrenching experience that you want to avoid.

In a *perfect* world, your only job as a speaker would be, appropriately enough, to speak. You would arrive at the designated speaking location and find an ideal environment. The room would be arranged exactly as you had requested, the temperature would be cool and comfortable, soothing classical music would be wafting through the room, and the AV equipment would work flawlessly. Best of all, eager assistants would be at your beck and call, promptly addressing your slightest whim and desire. You would be treated like royalty, because, after all, you are (drum roll, please) the Speaker. That, my friends, is a speaker's utopia.

Now, back in the *real* speaking world, things *very rarely* work that smoothly. "Never" might be an overstatement, but not by much. It is very risky to simply show up to speak expecting that all the details will have been handled (because this rarely happens) or that you will have ample time to address them (because you seldom do). You are just as likely to arrive at the venue and encounter bedlam: saunalike conditions, recalcitrant AV equipment, no lectern, nothing that you previously requested, and—worst of all—no eager assistants, no meeting host, and nary a human being in sight.

If you leave the details to others, then minutes before your presentation, you may find yourself scrambling around wildly, sweating like a pack mule, dragging cumbersome chairs, shoving unwieldy tables, cursing the unresponsive LCD projector, and juggling a cornucopia of unimaginable problems. In this frenzied state, you will invariably overlook something. And rest assured: your oversight will eventually surface at the most inopportune moment—such as smack-dab in the middle of your presentation.

So, do ya' feel lucky?

An individual who is observed to be inconstant to his plans, or perhaps carry on his affairs without any plan at all, is marked at once, by all prudent people, as a speedy victim of his own unsteadiness and folly.

—Alexander Hamilton

The best advice for every speaker, in any speaking situation, is this: leave nothing to chance. Assume that if you do not personally handle the details, or personally see that they are handled, they will not be handled. That cynical view may not comport with your sincere belief that people will always do what they promise to do when they promise to do it, but that kind of Pollyannaish faith is sorely misplaced when you are the speaker.

And here is the worst part: when your presentation flops, your audience will fault *you*, not the people behind the curtain and not those who failed to deliver. Instead, your listeners will blame you for everything: the screeching microphone, the botched introduction, the illegible PowerPoint, and the miserable conditions in the room. The whole shebang. You can protest the unfairness until you are blue in the face, but don't be surprised when the disappointed masses turn surly on you. Only your mother cares about excuses; your audience expects results.

Ten Things You Need to Know for Every Speech

So, besides grousing and stomping your feet in protest, what can you do to ensure that neglected details do not undermine your speech? If you are prudent, you will use the extensive checklist set forth in principle 28 when preparing for every speech, particularly the critical ones (like when your job hangs in the balance). But the following 10 items deserve special attention, because if they are treated cavalierly, they have a proven record of sabotaging speeches with lightning speed:

1. **Know who is in charge.** Determine who is responsible for handling all the issues (and there will be many) that arise between the date when you agree to speak and the date when you actually speak. Make that person your new best friend. That expert can answer questions, provide support, and help you avert calamities. Fawn shamelessly if necessary and resort to bribes (marshmallow Rice Krispie treats, warm chocolate chip cookies, cash) in a pinch.

2. **Know whether plans have changed.** Particularly when you make speaking arrangements months in advance, circumstances can and often do change. What might change? The size of the audience, the length of time you are expected to speak, the topics of other speakers, or the location or time of your presentation. Sometimes the plans have changed (critical plans, such as, for instance, the theme of the meeting and the

topic of your talk) and—surprise!—no one has bothered to tell you. Nothing will dampen your enthusiasm for speaking faster than staring at a room packed with audience members gazing at you with befuddled looks. Stay abreast of all developments.

3. **Know the head count.** The size of the audience will dictate how you should prepare for many aspects of your presentation, such as which visual aids will be suitable, the number of handouts you should prepare, your need for a microphone, and how the room will be arranged. Addressing an intimate gathering of 30 people poses an entirely different set of challenges from speaking to a boisterous crowd of 1,000.

❧

Plans must be simple and flexible. . . . They should be made by the people who are going to execute them.

—George S. Patton

❧

4. **Know the terrain.** Know the layout of the room where you will be speaking. Know, for example, whether you will have theater seating in rows, a classroom setup with tables, or just rows of chairs. Why do you need to know this? You want the people in your audience to be as close to you as possible so that you can interact with them, field their questions, and read their reactions. (On the other hand, if you anticipate that your message will cause a violent response (a Town Hall meeting on gun control or health-care reform spring to mind), you may prefer to speak by videoconference—from another country.)

Certain room conditions cannot be remedied, such as inherent acoustical limitations or columns that might interfere with sight lines. Although you may not be able to correct these problems, if you are aware of them before your presentation, you can mentally prepare to deal with them when you speak.

5. **Know the lectern options.** Preferred option: a tabletop lectern which will allow you to move around freely. Second option: a small, freestanding lectern suitable for holding only a few

notes and your favorite pen. Worst option: a hulking mound of wood about the size of New Hampshire.

A massive lectern will dwarf you as the speaker and severely limit your visibility, your gesturing, and your body language. If that is your only option, insist that you have a hands-free, wireless microphone, which will allow you to move around the room. And if all else fails, bring a shiny, sharpened ax to whittle down the lectern.

6. **Know your microphone needs.** How best to describe microphones? All unique, most unreliable, and every single, sneaky one anxious to betray you as you speak. Principle 35 provides a list of microphone rules. If your presentation requires you to use a microphone, don't skim that chapter. Rip it out, laminate it, and even put it under your pillow if that will help you absorb the rules.

❧

We're all, it seems, saving ourselves for the senior prom. But many of us forget that somewhere along the line we must learn to dance.

—Alan Harrington

❧

7. **Know the visual-aid rules.** It is a statistical dead heat as to which can gut a presentation faster: microphones or visual aids. Visual aids present a sweeping array of challenges; the rules for using them are discussed in detail in principles 36, 37, and 38. Here are the salient points: ensure well before the masses arrive that the visual aids are in the room and working, and set aside ample time for testing them. Balking visual aids torpedo hundreds of presentations every day, and in all likelihood, at this very moment, they are sinking a few speakers. Don't trust them.

8. **Know when you are speaking.** You need to know the time of day when you will be speaking. Content-heavy presentations work best in the morning, when attention levels are at their highest. At the end of the day or following a meal, attention

plunges dramatically, so if you are speaking then, eliminate 30 to 50 percent of your content (I know, I know—it's all fabulous material, but some of it has to go, sorry).

Speaking during a meal can be especially challenging. You will be required to compete for your audience's attention with scrumptious desserts or the clanging of dishes, glasses, and silverware as the waiters clear the tables. You need to mentally prepare for these distractions.

I was once scheduled to speak at a luncheon, presumably after the meal had ended. Unfortunately, the members of this audience had apparently not eaten a solid meal in over a week, judging by the zeal with which they were attacking the food. With shirtsleeves rolled up, they were devouring everything in sight. In the middle of this feast, while the audience members were gorging themselves, my introducer leaned over to me, his jowls firmly packed with food. As he wiped the gravy off his chin, he mumbled, "We're running behind, and . . . [Chew] we promised you 30 minutes for your talk. [Chew] So, why don't I go ahead and introduce you now? [Swallow] You can begin speaking while we're eating."

As I observed the ravenous crowd, I knew that not only would my message be ignored, but the audience members would resent my insensitive intrusion on what appeared to be a truly religious eating experience. Without any hesitation, I replied, "No, why don't you allow them to finish? I will adjust the time of my speech to meet your schedule."

Did that require instantaneous adjustments to my speech that were a wee bit unnerving? Certainly. But as a result, this particular audience was more receptive, because I was not competing with a meal for their attention. Perhaps a portion of my message stuck. I will never know for sure, however, since the audience members were clamoring for a second dessert when I left.

9. **Know who else is speaking.** If others are speaking with you on the program, ask these questions: "What are their topics?"

"How long will they speak?" and "When are they scheduled to speak?" Why? Because you may encounter a boorish speaker who unilaterally decides to address your topic rather than his. Or perhaps another speaker will determine that his allotted time is inadequate for someone of his stature—after all, the audience cannot possibly hear too much from him—so he will flout the time limits, gobbling up large chunks of your time.

Unless you relish dancing on the head of a pin with hundreds of people watching, or unless you are remarkably gifted at improvising, know these risks beforehand and plan accordingly.

ঌ

To know things well, we must know them in detail.
—François, duc de La Rochefoucauld

ঌ

10. **Know who will introduce you.** Never—that is, N-E-V-E-R—let anyone "wing it" on your introduction. Not your grade school best buddy, not your limelight-seeking boss, not even your favorite rabbi. Surrendering control over your introduction is a recipe for disaster. Invariably, someone will bungle it if given the chance. This issue warrants an entire principle (principle 27), because it is critical. For now, just remember one word: *never.*

Nagging details can make or break any presentation. Gamble at the roulette wheel, at the racetrack, or in the office pool, but never while you're preparing to speak. A confession: I have felt lucky a few times, and I ignored the details. I was confident that my wealth of speaking experience would save me from any calamity. I was wrong. Don't gamble in the speaking arena.

27

Prepare Your Introduction

What makes a plan capable of producing results is the commitment of
key people to work on specific tasks.

—Peter F. Drucker

You have carefully crafted, honed, and practiced your presentation, and in mere moments, you will stand up to speak and mesmerize the audience. But then you realize—oops!—you forgot to prepare the script that your host will use to introduce you.

Not a problem you think. You can just scribble a few ideas on a scrap of paper and pass it to your introducer (a big mistake), or you can simply tell her: "Say whatever you want. You know me" (a mammoth mistake). Why is each of these solutions a mistake? Because the introduction sets the tone for the speech. An exceptional introduction will generate interest and excitement, but a bad one can sully the entire speech. Don't stumble before you even begin.

Do I hear dissenting voices? I know what you are thinking: "It is *just* an introduction, for goodness sake! No big deal." Wrong. It is a huge deal, because introductions are regularly botched. They suffer greater than a 50 percent failure rate, and here is how: an inept introducer may mispronounce your name: "Mr. Demsie? Mr. Denskey? Mr. Dempster? Whatever—the speaker." He may mutilate the introduction in his vain struggle to pronounce words containing more than three syllables. She may randomly select tidbits from the introduction that you carefully crafted: "Let me see what's important here. . . ." He may deliver the introduction like a perfect zombie, which is unlikely to entice your audience to hang around. Or she may improvise: "One really funny thing that *nobody* knows about ole Buck . . . "—words that will surely send chills down Buck's spine.

And what's the result of those introduction debacles? Your listeners may be laughing for the wrong reasons; they may be disoriented, scratching their heads and wondering who you are and why they should listen to you; or they may be focusing on the bungled introduction rather than on your critical first words. You have been handicapped before you open your mouth to speak. You will need to waste valuable time cleaning up the mess, establishing your qualifications, and refocusing your audience.

Here is a simple rule: never take a chance on something that is so important to the success of your presentation. Your introduction should answer the following three questions for each audience member: "What is the topic?" "Why does this topic matter to me?" and, "What qualifies this speaker to address this topic?" Your audience should know the answers to these questions before you begin speaking because you have ensured that your introducer has told them.

ᨦ

No plan originated by another will be as sympathetically handled as one's own plan.

—Conrad H. Lanza

ᨦ

Eight Critical Introduction Rules

Use your introduction to entice your audience to listen. These are the rules for doing that:

1. **Prepare your introduction.** Carefully craft the introduction yourself. Never allow your introducer to improvise: "Our speaker today is Ms. Chatterbox. I don't know what she has to say, but I bet she will be interesting—at least, I hope so. Give her a rousing round of applause!" Few audiences will be giddy with anticipation about hearing poor Ms. Chatterbox. Your introducer should say exactly what you want him to say— nothing more, nothing less.

2. **Tailor your introduction to the presentation.** Every presentation has a purpose (and if yours doesn't, then you must have skipped principle 9). Tailor your introduction with that purpose in mind. Focus on your qualifications or experiences that are relevant to your presentation. For instance, an audience of homeowners who are worried about spiraling tax assessments in their subdivision will care deeply about the speaker's expertise gained while she worked in the county tax assessor's office; they will care very little about her prizewinning recipe for succulent salmon.

   If you are making an entertaining after-dinner presentation, your introduction should set the tone for your speech and alert your listeners that they will have fun: "Our speaker graduated in the bottom 10 percent of his college class, but he no longer has to stand on interstate exits holding a sign that reads 'Will Clean Gutters for Food!' He is encouraged by these advances in his career."

ঌ

Brevity is the sister of talent.

—Anton Chekhov

✽

3. **Make it brief.** Resist the urge to use your introduction to chronicle all your stellar achievements over the past 30 years. Here is the litmus test: if your introduction is longer than your speech, pare it down—by about 90 percent. Make it relevant, informative, enticing, and, above all, brief. Generally, it should not exceed one page in a large font size, and always keep in mind that shorter is better.

4. **Defuse hostility.** If you know beforehand that the audience is hostile, use the introduction to defuse the hostility. For example, if you are speaking to the Plastic Bag Society of America about the glories of paper sacks, your introduction might read: "Our speaker today realizes that many of us are utterly contemptuous of paper sacks and are frankly suspicious of their advocates. But Jim Bob grew up in a family of plastic bag aficionados, so he understands the challenges confronting us. He believes that we can peacefully coexist."

   This more conciliatory approach may not convert the plastic bag purists to your way of thinking, but it may slightly blunt their hostility. And they may be less likely to seethe and sling hard objects at you.

5. **Type your introduction.** Always prepare your introduction in a large font size (18- to 22-point) and triple-space the text to make it easy for the person introducing you to read it. Do this for three reasons: your handwriting is probably not as fabulous as you imagine, the lighting in caves is brighter than some lectern lamps, and you do not want the blind-as-a-mole introducer squinting and craning his neck to decipher the microscopic words crammed on the page. Help the introducer do his job.

6. **Exhort the introducer to practice.** It seems like so very little to ask of the person introducing you to practice your introduction beforehand and then to deliver it in a somewhat conversational manner, exactly as it was prepared. That is a perfectly reasonable expectation, right? Apparently not, because it seldom happens. Introducers stumble herky-jerky

through introductions, mispronouncing words, skipping vital details, or delivering them like perfect cyborgs. So, how do you avoid that?

Give your introducer a copy of the introduction days prior to your presentation. Stress the importance of her responsibility to set the right tone for your speech. Ask her (plead and threaten mayhem if necessary) to review and practice the introduction until she can recite it comfortably and not sound like a crashing bore. Finally, emphasize that veering from the script is not an option (see rule 7). Assert yourself.

Are these steps overkill? You may think so, right up until some bonehead butchers your introduction or launches into a monologue that you have never heard, and hoped you would never hear, when being introduced.

7. **Restrain the introducer.** You want an introduction, not a comedy routine. The unrestrained introducer often aspires to be witty, but there is a huge problem: he's not. Worse, his inane comments are typically directed at you. For example, he may share embarrassing personal information that you earnestly desired to forget: "We used to call Charles 'Chowdown Chuck' in the good ole fraternity, because that boy could cram down five jumbo chili dogs in mere seconds."

I was once introduced by a bozo who, sneering, tossed aside the introduction I had meticulously prepared for him and instead delivered this snappy witticism: "I would like to introduce David Dempsey, because, well, that's his name. Please give him a round of applause." Strangulation, anyone?

These introductions undermine your professional image and leave your audience clueless. Muzzle the comedic introducers.

ॐ

It is by the goodness of God that we have in our country three unspeakably precious things: freedom of speech, freedom of conscience, and the prudence never to practice either of them.

—Mark Twain

♣

8. **Bring extra copies.** Even if you have delivered your introduction to your introducer several days before you are scheduled to speak (which you should), bring several extra copies with you when you speak. Why? Because other than car keys, nothing on the face of the earth is lost more frequently.

Your introduction should pique your audience's interest in your presentation and signal that an expert is about to speak. There is too much at stake for you to cross your fingers and hope for the best. It is okay to trust your banker, trust your partner, and trust your mother—provided they are not introducing you. But never trust an unprepared or unrestrained introducer. You will regret it if you do.

28

Check Your Checklist

Your plan should foresee and provide for a
next step in case of success or failure.

—B. H. Liddell Hart

With apologies to Charles Dickens, when speaking, I have seen the best of times, and I have seen the worst of times. Allow me to share the worst.

I had agreed to speak to more than 100 prominent business executives ("The Hotshots Roundtable" or something like that) at 7:00 a.m. in the private dining room of an Atlanta restaurant. Weeks before my speaking engagement, I had painstakingly addressed all the details, and several days before the event, I had reconfirmed everything. The host was affable and accommodating. He repeatedly assured me that I was in the hands of a professional, with many years of event-planning experience. His exact words: "Relax. This is not my first rodeo." Thus soothed, I trusted that he would do what he said he would do. Big mistake.

At 6:00 a.m. on the day of the presentation, our agreed meeting time, my host was nowhere to be found. That, however, was the least of my worries, because the room was a disaster. It had been the scene of a gluttonous bachelor party the evening before, which appeared to have ended only a few moments earlier. The putrid stench of cigars, beer, and anchovy pizza permeated the air, and plastic cups, confetti, and garments of every type littered the room. The revelers had apparently showered each other and the room with beer, because I had to peel my shoes from the sticky floor. Chairs and tables were toppled, soggy banners with inspiring messages ("Your Life Is Over, Loser Boy!") hung limply from the walls, and the strobe light above the dance floor was still spinning and flashing.

With my heart pounding and my throat constricting in panic, I tracked down the restaurant manager, who was sleepy, unshaven, and slumped over the counter, gulping coffee. He had attended the party, and he assured me that it was "one fine wingding!" I explained that we had less than one hour to convert the den of iniquity into some semblance of a meeting room. Unfazed, he smiled and glibly stated, "No problem, man! The cleaning crew should be arriving around 6:30 or *thereabouts.*" That nonchalant comment was hardly a confidence builder.

I had two choices: bolt out of the front door and go into hiding for several years or roll up my sleeves and get to work. I plunged in with wild-eyed frenzy. I fashioned a lectern out of plastic milk crates and propped it on the head table. I covered the empty beer kegs with greasy tablecloths and tossed the pizza remnants into a closet. I raced around the room like a whirling dervish, dragging tables, heaving chairs, and gathering trash. Practicing law suddenly seemed appealing again.

❧

In Fair Weather prepare for foul.

—Thomas Fuller

❧

My presentation was mediocre at best, delivered under barely tolerable conditions, and that was my fault. Why? As the speaker, I was responsible for everything related to my presentation.

You are responsible for everything when you are the speaker as well. If your listeners are uncomfortable, if the visual aids are difficult to see, if the handouts look unprofessional, or even if a strobe light is flashing— your listeners ultimately blame you. That may be unfair, and you can squawk and howl all you want, but it's a fact. Audiences expect results, not excuses, and this is particularly true of business audiences who are invest-ing their valuable time in listening to your presentation.

Exceptional speakers obsessively address every detail that affects their presentations. They do everything possible to ensure that each pre-sentation is a roaring success. Sometimes things will not work out the way you had planned, and you may need to hold the program together with a little baling wire and duct tape, but that is exactly what you must do. Canceling is never an option—ever. And you must do your best to keep any problems behind the curtain:

> As a presenter, you are the actor, the director, and usually the crew. The audience must always have the feeling—from you—that it's effortless.[1]

The Perfect Presentation Checklist

I am going to make the wild assumption that you would prefer to avoid a speaking debacle like mine, so I have provided an exhaustive list of issues that you should consider before every presentation. Admittedly, not every item on this checklist will apply to every presentation, but the checklist will help guarantee that you at least consider every detail. You may scoff at some of these suggestions as excessive, merely the musings of a worrywart. I would have felt the same way, too, prior to my dining-room disaster.

Let me recommend that, as you work through the checklist, you get commitments from people in writing. Written commitments will elimi-nate confusion and clarify who is responsible for which task. Enlist others to help and delegate tasks, but never forget that you are in charge of, and ultimately responsible for, everything, including the following:

1. **Prepresentation details.** By addressing the following items as early as possible, well before the date and time you speak, you can adapt your speech to the real circumstances you will face, and you can prepare appropriate visual aids or handouts:
   - Who is responsible for fulfilling all of your AV requirements?
   - Who is responsible for copying and distributing your written materials?

- Who is responsible for handling your speaking requirements, such as setting up the room (principle 26) and testing the microphone (principle 35)?
- When and how will attendees be notified of the meeting (printed invitations sent in the mail, e-mail distribution, Web site posting)?
- What time will you speak?
- How much time will you have for your speech (principle 33), including Q&A (principle 34)?
- How long is the entire program?
- How many people are expected to attend?
- Who are the other speakers on the program, what are their topics, and how long are their presentations (principle 33)?
- Will any other business be addressed during the meeting?
- Will a meal be served before, during, or after your presentation?

2. **Program assistant details.** Make sure you have contact information (office, home, and cell phone numbers and an e-mail address) for everyone involved in the program, including the following:
   - The host
   - Alternative contacts to the host, such as an assistant
   - The person who will introduce you
   - An on-site technician to assist with AV requirements and problems on the day you speak
   - A building engineer or a building manager to assist you with technical problems with the room (access, lighting, temperature)
   - A contact with building security

3. **Building details.** Answer the following questions, to become familiar with all the details of the facility where you will speak:
   - Is the building easy to find?
   - Will directions to the meeting room be sent to the attendees or posted on a Web site?

- Are there traffic challenges around the building (rush-hour congestion, limited access) that might delay the arrival of your attendees?
- Is public transportation available and accessible?
- Is there adequate parking?
- Are there parking fees?
- Is valet parking available?
- What are the details of ingress and egress (stairs, elevators, alternate routes, emergency exits)?
- Is there wheelchair accessibility?
- Will you or the attendees need building security clearance?
- Are the building personnel and security guards familiar with the meeting details?
- Will you have access to the meeting room outside normal business hours, to set up and practice?
- Are there copying and faxing facilities on-site?
- Is there a building cafeteria, a vending machine, or a snack shop?

4. **Meeting room details.** Study the room where you will speak, and eliminate potential problems. If they cannot be fixed because of inherent structural limitations (poor lighting, a column obstructing views), prepare mentally to work around those limitations. Ask these questions:
   - What is the size of the room?
   - Does the room have adequate seating capacity for the anticipated number of audience members?
   - Has the room been arranged with tables and chairs according to your specifications?
   - Will extra chairs be removed?
   - Are rows sectioned off to encourage attendees to sit toward the front of the room?
   - Is there ample aisle space?
   - Will each audience member have an unobstructed view?
   - Does the room have a stage or raised platform?
   - Can you move easily off the stage and into the audience?

- Is the requested lectern properly placed?
- Are there tables for your notes, books, writing instruments, and handouts?
- Is there a sign-in table, with a registration list and a program agenda?
- Will whiteboards, chalkboards, or flip charts be available?
- Can you control the lighting for the room?
- Will there be adequate heating and air conditioning to ensure that the room will be comfortable for the attendees?
- Are there separate thermostat controls for the room?
- Will there be sunlight glare at any time during the day, and, if so, will you be able to lower the blinds or shades?
- Are there any unavoidable distractions (lights, traffic noise, scenic views)?
- Have avoidable distractions been addressed (intercom system muted, signage posted on doors for the meeting in progress)?
- Is there a place for coats and bags?
- Will audience members have water pitchers and drinking glasses, writing instruments, and pads for taking notes?

5. **Equipment details.** You need to assure yourself that any equipment that you plan on using will be working properly (part VII). Make sure that you have tested and retested the equipment (right before you retest it again) and that you have all the accessories and emergency supplies readily available. Here are some questions to ask:
   - Do you have the type of microphone you requested (fixed, hands-free, hand-held)?
   - What restrictions, if any, does the microphone set up present?
   - Have you conducted a sound check for the microphone (principle 35)?
   - Have you tested all visual-aid equipment (principles 37 and 38)?
   - Is the equipment situated properly?
   - Is there built-in AV equipment in the room?

- Are electrical outlets reasonably accessible?
- Do you have a backup laptop computer?
- Is your laptop computer compatible with the AV system in the building?
- Do you have an extra computer mouse, a laser pointer, and a presentation remote?
- Is your computer battery charged?
- Are there additional cables for the computer, projector, and DVD player?
- Do you have extra extension cords and three-pronged electrical adapters?
- Do you have extra lightbulbs for all the equipment that needs them?
- Have you tested the remote controls for all the equipment?
- Do you have new batteries for all the equipment?
- Is there a surge protector for your equipment?
- Can the audience see the flip chart, screen, television monitor, and meeting room boards from every vantage point in the room (principle 37)?
- Are all DVDs and CDs properly cued?
- Do you have a fallback plan if the equipment fails?
- Is there a separate USB flash drive or CD with the entire program and handouts saved on it?

6. **Supply details.** Bring all the tools and supplies that you will need before and during the program. Use this checklist so that you do not overlook any of the following:
   - A printed agenda
   - Additional photocopy-ready handouts
   - Name tags and place cards on the tables for the attendees
   - Extra business cards
   - Extra copies of your introduction (principle 27)
   - Duct tape for taping down carpets and cords (and, in a pinch, for holding the program together)
   - Fresh markers for the flip chart, whiteboards, and name tags

- Adequate paper for your flip chart
- Thumbtacks and masking tape for hanging sheets of paper
- Erasers and cleaner for the chalkboards and whiteboards
- A laser pointer
- Pens and highlighters
- Post-it notes in various sizes
- Paper clips and binder clips
- Stapler and staples
- A clock or large watch to monitor the time (principle 33)
- Bottled water for you
- Throat lozenges for you
- Food for you (energy bars, raisins, nuts) to eat during the breaks

❧

The final test of a plan is its execution.

—U. S. Army Field Manual

❧

I know exactly what you are thinking. Yes, this is a lot to consider, and yes, some of these items will not apply to every meeting. And sometimes, despite your utmost efforts, even exceptional plans will go awry. But your goal is to avoid unexpected surprises that will heighten your anxiety and diminish the impact of, or completely undermine, your speech.

So, obsess over the details. Anticipate everything and overlook nothing. The details make a monumental difference. And if your host ever utters the words, "Relax. This is not my first rodeo," sound the alarm.

PART VI

DAZZLE WITH DELIVERY

As a child (before the advent of electronic games and MTV), I played for hours with a nifty device about the size of a notebook. It was called an Etch A Sketch. I used two plastic knobs to move a stylus horizontally or vertically to sketch any picture I wanted with the black aluminum powder on the screen. But the real beauty of this toy was this: if I disliked what I had drawn, I simply picked up the box and shook it; that cleared the screen, and it was ready for me to start over.

ஃ

Three things matter in a speech: who says it, how he says it, and what he says—and, of the three, the last matters the least.

—John Morley

ஃ

You do not enjoy a similar luxury when you are speaking. Every time you speak, you have only *one* chance to make a lasting impression.

If you fail to deliver your message with confidence and conviction, all your hard work will be for naught. You have no ability to quickly wipe the slate clean.

Part VI discusses the techniques that will help you avoid that fate and truly dazzle the crowd with your delivery.

29

Focus on Your Audience

Some writers take to drink, others take to audiences.

—Gore Vidal

Do you focus on your audience when you speak—*really* focus—or does every audience look alike to you, just another sea of blank faces? Be honest (it's okay, you don't have to share your answer with anyone).

All right, it's test time. Perform an honest self-assessment now, by asking yourself the following questions: "When I speak,"

- "Do my listeners sometimes seem detached or disinterested?"
- "Do I respond to nonverbal body language from my listeners, or do I unwaveringly stick to my script?"
- "Do I analyze how my listeners are reacting, or do I concentrate primarily on what I have said and on what I will say next?"
- "Do I attempt to involve my listeners in the presentation through questions or audience participation, or is it always just a monologue?"
- "Do I *really* listen to and process their questions, or am I more concerned about sounding authoritative?"
- "Am I primarily concerned about looking and sounding good?"

Study your listeners, and they will let you know how you are doing. If your speech is clicking, they will send unequivocal signals that acclaim, "Exceptional presentation!" What type of signals? Nods of agreement, rapt attention to your words and to your visual aids, sitting upright and leaning forward, feverish note taking, and smiling faces. When that happens, the sky is bluer, the birds are chirping, and—ta da! blare the horns—you have entered the speaker's Promised Land. Pat yourself on the back and cherish the memory. You may need to recall that moment on another day, when it feels as though you are plodding along in wet sand as you speak.

❧

I do not object to people looking at their watches when I am speaking. But I strongly object when they start shaking them to make certain they are still going.

—Lord Birkett

❧

Let's look at one of those wet-sand days, when your presentation is flopping and you are just not connecting with your listeners. Their signals are unmistakably telling you that you are on the fast train to nowhere: rampant fidgeting; furtive (or blatant) watch glancing; wincing; furrowed brows; distressed, puzzled, or downright antagonistic stares; clenched jaws; or defiantly folded arms. If you speak frequently, tackle challenging topics, or face such tough audiences as lawyers, doctors, or grade school children, you will encounter these signals. As painful as the signals might be, don't ignore them.

Never forget your primary purpose in speaking: to connect. It does not matter whether you are trying to sell, persuade, inform, inspire, or entertain; if you don't connect, you might as well not have spoken.

Understand that every audience member is tuned to a single frequency: WII-FM ("What's in it for me?"). The people in your audience want to know how listening to you will benefit them, so you had better answer that question—and stay tuned to their frequency. Throughout your presentation, broadcast a static-free message to your listeners that you understand their perspective and that they are important. Joel Weldon, a very successful professional speaker, describes his interaction with his listeners this way:

> By the time I'm introduced, all the preparation is done and there is no thought given to the material, the ideas, stories, examples, or the humor. My entire conscious focus is on the audience. I'm watching the audience, thinking what they are thinking, attempting to experience what they are experiencing. I'm looking for people who are buying in, signs of resistance, or things that might have passed over them that need to be restated in a simpler, clearer way.[1]

Eight Ways to Read and React to Your Audience

So, what do you do when you feel like you are dying on the platform, when it seems as if your speaking world is crumbling all around you? How do you react? Do you: (1) Ignore the signs, drop your chin, and barrel ahead? (2) Conclude that the audience is the problem? (3) Just talk louder and faster? (4) Disregard the audience and conduct a titillating monologue with your notes or with your PowerPoint slides? Or (5) wrap it up quickly, dart away, and hope to preserve a smidgen of dignity? None of those choices bodes well for your long-term speaking prospects.

The correct answer: get attuned to the members of your audience and the messages they are sending you, and react to those messages. Here are eight excellent ways to accomplish that:

1. **Eliminate disruptions.** If something or someone is interfering with your message, pause and address the problem. Crossing your fingers and wishing the problem away, talking louder, or simply ignoring the issue never helps. Ask the industrious waiters who are banging dishes to stop, or the buffoons in the third row who are yakking to put a lid on it. Politely suggest that you might bop them with a wooden spoon if they refuse (a variation of the "Speak softly, and carry a big stick" slogan).

Your listeners will appreciate it, and you will increase the probability that your message will be received. Taking control of distracting situations also demonstrates that you are confident and that you are concerned about your listeners' ability to hear your important message.

❧

There is always a single ear in the audience,
to which we address ourselves.

—Henry David Thoreau

❧

2. **Solicit questions.** The following recommendation may sound like pure heresy to the legions of speakers who memorize *every* speech (who, incidentally, are encouraged to reread—and memorize, if necessary—principle 19). Periodically deviate from your prepared text to solicit audience input. For example, pause and say: "I realize that I blazed through that material, and it might have been somewhat confusing. What questions do you have?"

   Audiences today want and expect an interactive presentation, and they are typically eager to participate and share ideas. Straying from the script is an exceptional way to accomplish that and to minimize confusion. Principle 34 delves into the intricacies of Q&A participation.

   But here is the stipulation: solicit questions only if you are willing to listen to them. Don't start thinking about what you will say next while the questioner is speaking. If you begin responding before you have a clear understanding of the question, you will gain little insight, probably alienate a few listeners, and merely compound your problems. Pause, listen, process, and only then respond.

3. **Refer to a specific audience member or event.** Periodically refer to someone in the audience by name (assuming that you won't embarrass him): "I was speaking to Mr. Big Wheel this morning about your competitor's products." And also refer to

recent events that occurred in the organization, such as a banner year in sales, an industry honor, or an upcoming retirement. Gather information about your audience from various sources (principles 6 and 7).

If you demonstrate that you have gone out of your way to customize your message for that particular audience—in other words, that this is not just another "canned speech"—you heighten your listeners' interest and enhance your credibility. Just be careful not to reveal confidential information ("Mr. Big Wheel really regrets that as a result of the economic downturn, he will be slashing everyone's compensation by 50 percent") if you hope to speak to that group again.

4. **Pause to allow for laughter and emotions.** If your listeners are laughing, stop talking and let them laugh (principle 23). Savor this moment, because at other times the silence after your witty lines can be deafening.

   If some listeners are emotionally upset, honor that moment as well. Pause and acknowledge their feelings: "I know this is upsetting to some of you, and that is understandable." Pausing and allowing for an emotional response shows that you respect your listeners, and it also gives you a chance to collect your thoughts.

5. **Take a short break.** If it appears that the energy in the room is waning (gaping yawns, glazed looks, snoring), take a short break. Encourage everyone to stand, stretch, and check her neighbor's pulse for signs of life—you get the point.

   Don't get your feelings hurt, because you may not be the source of the problem. People may be drowsy because it has been a long day, because the room is too warm, or because that triple cheese lasagna and Mighty Meaty pizza they ate at lunch is taking its toll. The speaking time you lose by taking a break will be offset by the heightened attention of your listeners for the remainder of your presentation. And next time, specify salads, melba toast, and caffeinated drinks for lunch.

6. **Break the pattern.** If your listeners seem numb (eyes are rolling back; heads are drooping; doodling is rampant), be honest: you may be the problem (I know that's hard to imagine). Maybe your delivery has grown tedious, maybe you have overwhelmed your audience with information, maybe the topic is complex or boring, or maybe your energy has waned. Whatever the reason, it is time to change course quickly and spice it up.

    What can you do? Pause, vary your pacing, change your volume or tone, move around, step toward the audience, expand your gestures, incorporate slides or videos in the program, refer to the handout, engage in some audience participation exercises, or ask questions. Do anything (within the bounds of good taste) to snap people back to attention and to refocus them.

❧

I have just got a new theory of eternity.

—Albert Einstein (after listening to a long-winded speech)

❧

7. **Shorten the presentation.** Sometimes your listeners have already sat through several presentations by the time you speak, and they are satiated with information. They have had enough, and they are sliding into full-scale shutdown. If you are facing that situation, you could be sharing the winning numbers in the Mega Millions lottery for the drawing that will occur the next day, but they don't care and won't listen. It's time to employ a quick exit strategy. Try this.

    Slash a portion of your prepared presentation and address only the key points. Let your audience know that you are doing this: "I was scheduled to speak for one hour, but I realize that you have already been inundated with information. So if you will just give me your attention for 15 minutes, I will highlight four points that are particularly important to *you* [audience focus always] and then stop. If you have questions, I will be available to speak with you individually after the program, or you may e-mail your questions." Your audience members will appreciate your sensitivity, and they will typically return the favor by focusing on what you have to say.

❧

There can be no fairer ambition than to excel in talk;
to be affable, gay, ready, clear, and welcome.

—Robert Louis Stevenson

❧

8. **Accept the inevitable.** You have tried everything to connect, but the audience vibes are still distinctly negative: locked jaws, rigid body language, heads shaking in disagreement, or—worst of all—the evil eye. What then?

   First, recognize that no matter how eloquent you are, you will not always sway everyone, so stop trying. Acknowledge those who disagree with you, and thank them for their willingness to listen to your viewpoint (which, of course, as you know, is the correct one).

   Second, solicit the naysayers' input. You may not convert them to your way of thinking, but it affords them an opportunity to vent, it livens up the program, and it sends the message to everyone that you are confident in your position. But avoid this option if you feel it will result in chaos.

   Finally, resign yourself to the reality that you sometimes just encounter a bad audience. Some audiences are unreceptive, grumpy, and convinced that you could not possibly have anything valuable to share with them. Smile, do the best you can under the circumstances, and go home. No presentation is final or fatal. But—and this is important— don't use the "it was a bad audience" rationalization unless you know that you have done *everything* possible to guarantee an exceptional presentation.

Concentrate on connecting with your audience. Always remember the frequency that every listener is tuned to: WII-FM. You may not like the signals that the audience is sending you, and you will need to be nimble whenever you decide to deviate from your prepared comments. But if you stay focused on your audience, you greatly enhance the chances that your message will be understood and favorably received. And after all, isn't that the primary reason for speaking?

30

Act Confident

Whether you believe you can do a thing or not, you are right.

—Henry Ford

I could not wait to finally hear Professor Muck-a-Muck speak. He was the preeminent authority in his field, an esteemed Ivy League professor who had written several treatises on his expertise. He had even appeared on the *Oprah Winfrey Show*, so I knew that he stood at the pinnacle of his profession. I arrived early, determined to secure a front-row seat. As I stepped into the auditorium, he was already on stage, and what I saw shocked me.

Professor Muck-a-Muck exuded fear. He was wringing his hands, scribbling notes, and frantically flipping pages in the mounds of books scattered around the head table. He appeared to be researching his talk at the last minute. Sweat dripped off his forehead, which he repeatedly mopped. Old Muck-a-Muck was fighting a colossal battle with his glasses, which persistently slid down his shiny, damp nose, only to be shoved back into place. Occasionally, he would glance apprehensively and furtively at the people who were trickling into the auditorium, but this seemed only to exacerbate his anxiety and quicken his pace. He looked like a condemned man. I feared that he might injure himself before he began speaking. His pretalk behavior was both comical and pathetic.

This was hardly the image I had expected. Before he uttered his first word, I had formed a negative opinion of him. I began to question his qualifications, based solely on his appearance and conduct, which was unfair, and probably inaccurate, but I could not help myself. And I was not alone. From the bewildered looks around the room, it was apparent that others shared my surprise.

Every time you speak, remember this: you are communicating with your audience members from the moment that they first see you. They immediately begin to evaluate you and form conclusions based on your appearance and conduct. I know that contradicts the admonition we heard repeatedly as children: "Never judge a book by its cover." Sorry, we may have learned it, but most of us don't apply it, and neither will your audience.

Your audience expects you to be a self-assured expert when you speak, so you had better look, sound, and act confident, poised, and focused. You immediately place yourself at a huge disadvantage if you resemble a milquetoast, a disheveled pack rat, or—worst of all—a Professor Muck-a-Muck. All of the following mannerisms undercut your confident image:

- Pacing or swaying for no apparent purpose
- Fidgeting
- Clinging tightly, almost desperately, to the lectern
- Clasping, shuffling, or rattling your notes
- Scribbling on, editing, or reviewing your text
- Emitting strange sighs, grunts, or yawns
- Darting your eyes
- Staring at the floor, at the ceiling, or out the window
- Licking, biting, or sucking your lips
- Contorting your hands
- Touching, rubbing, or scratching your face (or other body parts)
- Fiddling with your hair
- Twirling your rings or other jewelry
- Adjusting your clothing or glasses
- And (my favorite) stroking your tie

Audience members quickly zero in on all of these distracting quirks. Soon, they forget your message and simply enjoy the spectacle that you have become.

Eight Ways to Project Confidence

Here are eight steps that are guaranteed to enhance your confidence *and* to send the unmistakable message to your listeners that you are self-assured:

1. **Dress up and strip down.** Audiences expect speakers to look polished and professional. You risk undermining your credibility if you wear flashy, trendy, or sloppy clothing when you speak. What are the rules for appropriate dress?
   - Be one of the best-dressed people in the room.
   - Dress conservatively and professionally. If you want your listeners to take you seriously, save your snazzy purple shirt, cartoon-character necktie, leather miniskirt, fishnet nylons, argyle socks, or white buck shoes for a really big date night.
   - Shine your shoes (or pray that patent leather becomes fashionable). Audience members notice.
   - Empty your pockets. You look slovenly if your jacket or pants pockets are jammed with a week's worth of receipts, your jumbo key chain, or a bursting wallet the size of a ham sandwich.
   - Remove your technology. Do not march to the front of the room with your cell phone, pager, calculator, iPod, BlackBerry, or any other technology draped on you.
   - Minimize jewelry. Layers of necklaces, rows of bracelets, and fingers covered with gaudy rings distract your audience and become an alluring diversion for you to play with as you speak.
2. **Mingle and greet.** Arrive early, mingle with the audience members, and introduce yourself before you speak. Let them know that you are genuinely excited and honored to be

speaking to them. Why? It relaxes you, it gives you a few friendly faces in the audience (you can never have too many of those), and it heightens their interest in your talk. But avoid any alcohol during your meet-and-greet session; it will not relax you, and that is the first step on the treacherous slope to a speaking calamity.

❧

Knowing is not enough, we must apply.
Willing is not enough, we must do.

—Johann Wolfgang von Goethe

❧

3. **Do not review or edit your notes.** When you are about to speak, you should already know what you are going to say. If you are unprepared when the curtain is about to rise (Is it possible that you skipped principles 1 through 29?), forget about reviewing or editing your notes. It is now too little, too late. Despite all your success working under self-inflicted, dire deadlines in college, desperate cramming will seldom improve any speech; it will probably only exacerbate your anxiety. It also alerts your audience that you are unprepared. Give it your best shot, deal with the repercussions, and prepare properly for the next speech.

4. **Pause before you begin.** Some speakers begin jabbering the minute their name is announced—before the applause has subsided, sometimes even before they reach the microphone—as if the speech were a race to jam in the most words in the time allotted. This behavior sends one unmistakable message: "Man, oh man, I am one Nervous Nellie!"

   Instead, approach the lectern with confidence, arrange your notes quickly, and pause before beginning (principle 23). Let your introducer return to her seat, and wait for everyone to quiet down. Insist on total silence and your audience's undivided attention before you begin. Opening in this manner signals: "I am confident and poised. You, Dear Audience, do not intimidate me."

5. **Do not apologize.** If you are unprepared to speak, do not apologize. You don't need to; it will probably be obvious that you are unprepared, and your apology will not improve the speech. Resist the urge to appeal to your audience's sympathy at this stage, because such an appeal only undercuts your credibility and highlights the problem. Do the best you can under the circumstances and learn from the experience. (And cross your heart and vow to always prepare in the future.)

ঽ৶

We shall never know all the good that a simple smile can do.

—Mother Teresa

◂§

6. **Monitor your facial message.** Your facial expressions should send the message that you are genuinely delighted to be speaking. I have to constantly remind myself to smile when I speak, because I get engrossed in my talk, and I look frighteningly intense. To remind yourself to enjoy the process, make notes on your text (a smiley face or the word "SMILE" will work).

    Even worse than a serious sourpuss is Mr. Pomposity. You know, the pontificator who stares down his nose at you through his bifocal reading glasses, who frowns while he condescendingly lectures, and who harrumphs repeatedly. Spare us. Nothing alienates an audience faster than some blowhard who patronizes the audience. Act that way, and your speech is kaput. Period.

7. **Connect with eye contact.** Your audience can see you. Do you see them? If so, actually look at them. Establish and sustain eye contact with as many audience members as possible. Once again, this signals that you are confident. To learn exactly how to capitalize on using your eyes to connect, see the seven eye-contact secrets in principle 32.

8. **Defuse hostility whenever possible.** If your audience is hostile toward you, acknowledge the animosity and attempt to neutralize it. You might say, "I recognize that many of you disagree with me on this issue. Thank you for your willingness to listen. I hope I can persuade you, but perhaps we will simply have to agree to disagree." There are two advantages in doing this: you are showing respect for your listeners and their opposing (and, of course, woefully misinformed) viewpoint, and you are communicating to them that you are not afraid of contrary opinions.

Your listeners are watching and judging you all the time. Are you sending the right message: that you are confident, friendly, and prepared? Or are you signaling that you are puffed up, petrified, or disorganized? Don't undermine your credibility. The nonverbal signals are often more powerful than anything you say (just ask Professor Muck-a-Muck). Let your actions and words convey one message: "I own the stage!"

31

Persuade with Passion

The eloquent man is he who is no beautiful speaker, but who is inwardly and desperately drunk with a certain belief.

—Ralph Waldo Emerson

A persuasive speaker is passionate about his message. Within seconds after he begins, his listeners lean forward in their seats, drawn in by his compelling delivery. He speaks with contagious energy, animated body language, sustained eye contact, and captivating vocal power. His style is always dynamic. But more important, he moves his listeners because he himself is moved. He is passionate about his ideas and determined to reach his listeners.

What about you? If you are not on fire with your message, don't expect your listeners to do cartwheels with excitement.

"Does passion really matter?" you might ask. Absolutely, and here is why: it makes a huge difference in how you connect with your audience. Especially if your primary purpose is to persuade, in an intensely competitive marketplace, any edge is significant. If you can ignite your audience with your passion and conviction, you are far more likely to be persuasive.

The benefits of honing your skills as a persuasive speaker are tremendous. You are viewed as an expert, your status as a leader soars, and you motivate your listeners to act on, or at least carefully consider, your viewpoint. And let's be honest: a persuasive speaker sells more of his products, ideas, and services, and (if I might be crassly commercial for a moment) that often translates into cold, hard cash. That should be a particularly compelling incentive if you ever hope to have that shiny red Ferrari parked in your driveway.

❧

Persuasion is achieved when the orator's speech is so spoken as to make us think him credible; when the speech stirs our emotions; when the speaker provides logical arguments.

—Aristotle

❧

So, how do you become an exceptional persuasive speaker? It's time for you to pull out the playbook of the masters again (remember, it's all right to emulate the best). Start by studying the consummate persuaders: motivational speakers. Anyone who has ever attended a motivational rally has probably been swept up in the groundswell of enthusiasm. Before long, audience members have shelled out hundreds of dollars for books, tapes, DVDs, posters, and assorted paraphernalia guaranteed to revolutionize their lives. The most highly successful motivational speakers do more than just share words; they infuse their messages with passion.

Consider the following insights from a few professional speakers at the pinnacle of their profession, Anthony Robbins, Dr. Wayne W. Dyer, and Mark Victor Hansen:

> I would say that the most important key to speaking is not to be perfect or to know exactly what you're going to say or how you're going to say it. But rather, that you have incredible passion about what you're speaking about. Your emotional intensity is what people will remember.[1]

> I speak to an audience in the same way I would speak to somebody in the living room of my home. From my heart, with integrity, and with enthusiasm. . . . [I]f you are truly enthusiastic about what you are thinking about, and not acting out a role, not playing "rent-a-speaker," not being an actor, not delivering a script . . . [if] you are enthusiastically, excitedly delivering your talk, it will come across.[2]

Great speakers have a calling within them to communicate; they communicate exceedingly well. They are absolutely passionate and intense. They have the eye of the tiger, the magnificent obsession. I can tell within thirty seconds of meeting someone whether they're on purpose toward some goal, because they start spilling over with effervescent enthusiasm about it.[3]

Passion is what distinguishes these exceptionally persuasive speakers from the majority of speakers—those who may know their topic, who may even have strong convictions, but whose delivery is lifeless. I often question whether some speakers have blood pumping in their veins as they methodically grind along.

A dry, pedantic recitation of facts may be informative, but who is going to listen? Speak like that, and you will be neither persuasive nor interesting, and it is likely that your listeners will not hear most of what you say. They will simply check out. And you won't have to worry about scheduling subsequent speaking engagements; audiences will avoid you like the plague.

৵

Speech that leads not to action, still more
that hinders it, is a nuisance on the earth.

—Thomas Carlyle

৵

Three Styles of Persuasion

So you want to genuinely connect with your audience and be a truly persuasive speaker? You need an effective method for channeling your passion. There are three proven styles of persuasion: empirical or logical, psychological, and personal. Each style is described here. Work with me: this is as close as I come to psychological gibberish in the book, so I will make it quick.

1. **Empirical or logical persuasion.** With empirical or logical persuasion, you sway your listeners to accept a particular point of view through inductive reasoning (empirical persuasion) or deductive reasoning (logical persuasion). A few examples may help.

With inductive reasoning, you first present all the facts and reasoning, and then ask your listeners to take a particular course of action. For example, let's say that Tiny Tim has been summoned to the principal's office because of his involvement in a playground scuffle. In pleading for clemency, Tiny Tim might argue: "I was sitting there [fact], absorbed in the titillating tales of Cicero in my book *Latin for Nerds* [fact], when that half-wit Buster shoved me down [fact], snatched my lunch [fact], and stomped on my banana [fact]. Everyone knows Buster is a bully [fact]. I was only defending myself when I beaned him with my backpack [logic]. So, I say, hurl Buster into detention and toss away the key [call to action]."

❧

A speech has two parts. Necessarily,
you state your case, and you prove it.

—Aristotle

❧

With deductive reasoning, on the other hand, Tiny Tim would begin with the result he wants: (1) The playground should be safe from hooligans, and all hooligans who disrupt the playground should be sentenced to decades of detention without leniency. (2) Anyone who stomps on the banana of a nerdy student who is reading the tales of Cicero is a hooligan. (3) I am a nerdy student. (4) Buster stomped on my banana while I was absorbed in reading *Latin for Nerds*. (5) Therefore, Buster is a hooligan, and he should be sentenced to decades of detention.

Both inductive and deductive reasoning are effective, and Buster will enjoy many years of cleaning erasers and scraping gum off desks after school.

2. **Psychological persuasion.** With psychological persuasion, you appeal to the self-interest of your listeners (remember the WII-FM—"What's in it for me?"—radio frequency that we discussed earlier?). For your appeal to be effective, you need to know why the action you are proposing will benefit them. Always answer

the following question first: "If my listeners act as I request, will it satisfy one or more of their basic needs or interests—*biological* (hunger, thirst, sleep), *security* (money, protection, a sense of order), *affiliation* (family, love, friendship, association with a particular organization), or *recognition* (success, pride, doing the right thing)?"

At the risk of stating the obvious, understand that psychological persuasion works only if you have researched your audience (principles 6 and 7) and you can answer its WII-FM question. Know the members of your audience— their likes, dislikes, goals, history, experiences, hopes, the whole enchilada—and you will enjoy a huge advantage when you attempt to persuade them.

⚓

Speech is power: speech is to persuade, to convert, to compel.

—Ralph Waldo Emerson

⚓

3. **Personal persuasion.** A personal appeal is based on a speaker's reputation, credibility, or influence. For example, a president with a high approval rating can persuade the public to act in a particular way, sometimes even if many of the citizens do not agree that it is in their best interest.

Following the terrorist attacks on the World Trade Center and the Pentagon on September 11, 2001, President George W. Bush enjoyed widespread personal appeal and had the support of the majority of Americans (his job performance approval rating exceeded 80 percent). Over the next several months, President Bush was able to spend some of that political capital persuading most of the public that our national interests justified a costly and dangerous military action in Iraq. He was persuading through his personal appeal.

In contrast, although former president Bill Clinton is very charismatic, the public was skeptical of his call for military action in the Middle East during his presidency, because it came during his impeachment process, when his reputation and credibility had been sullied.

Personal appeal can be very powerful when you are attempting to persuade, so look for ways to burnish your reputation and credibility. (Stomping on a nerd's banana will not help.)

❧

Nothing great in the world has been accomplished without passion.

—Georg Hegel

❧

You can use any or all of these styles of persuasion when delivering your message. When coupled with your passionate delivery, they greatly enhance your chances of persuading your listeners. Study all the secrets of speaking with passion that are given in the recommended resources at the end of the book. And don't forget to review recordings of memorable persuasive presentations, both current and historical (principle 8).

If you want to persuade your listeners, speak with genuine passion and conviction. Don't expect your audience to be persuaded, excited, or even interested if you drably deliver a string of platitudes; you might as well save your listeners trouble by letting them nap at home rather than in your audience. Instead, communicate with a "magnificent obsession" to share your message. Do that, and you will move the hearts and minds of your listeners—and truly persuade them.

32

Look 'Em in the Eye

Eyes can speak and eyes can understand.
—George Chapman

Listeners today are not content to tag along passively wherever the speaker leads them. They want to be part of the speaking experience. No matter how many people there are in the room, each listener wants to feel as if the speaker were talking directly to her. One of the best ways to produce this feeling requires a bit of courage: look directly into the eyes of your listeners and speak with confidence and conviction. Do that, and you not only enhance your chances of connecting with your listeners, but you also send a tacit message: "You can trust me."

Many speakers seem oblivious to their audiences and rarely look at them in meaningful ways throughout their entire presentations. Let's meet five typical eye-contact transgressors:

- The *gazer*, who stares pensively out the window (fascinated by any activity in the parking lot) or at the back of the room (apparently spellbound by the wonder of a beige wall)

- The *sweeper*, who rhythmically and hypnotically sweeps her eyes back and forth across her audience, never sustaining eye contact for an instant
- The *transfixer*, who becomes mesmerized by his notes or his visual aids, studying them as if they were the Holy Grail
- The *worshipper*, who focuses primarily on the floor (maybe hoping that the earth will swallow her and deliver her from her plight) or on the ceiling (maybe hoping for divine intervention)
- The *navel ogler*, perhaps the most entertaining of the lot, who delivers his presentation with a bowed head, staring directly at his belly button

If you belong to any of these clubs, it is time to resign your membership.

If you accept the premise that eye contact is essential (and you should), why do so many speakers look anywhere and everywhere *except* at the audience? Let's examine the typical excuses.

First, there is the speaker who focuses primarily on her notes or PowerPoint slides because she is unprepared and has no idea what to say next. She has no time to worry about her audience, because she is desperately searching for her next words. If you are unprepared, don't expect to engage your audience with your message.

Then there is the speaker who gets the jitters from speaking. He fears that he might crumple into a blubbering mass if he were actually to *look* at someone. Sorry, but as painful as it might be for you skittish ones to glance at your audience periodically, avoiding eye contact actually exacerbates your anxiety and alerts your audience that you are tense.

Finally, there is the speaker who is just indifferent or pompous; she considers her audience to be a huge annoyance, just lucky to be graced by her presence. That attitude alienates any audience within seconds, so instead of avoiding eye contact, this speaker should avoid showing up, thereby sparing everyone from a wretched experience.

One thing is certain: if you are not using your eye contact to create a positive connection with your audience, you are squandering a golden opportunity and diminishing your effectiveness. Avoiding eye contact makes informing, persuading, inspiring, or entertaining any audience far more challenging for you.

Seven Eye-Contact Secrets

If you appeared on the list of eye-contact transgressors (and let's be honest, we have all made at least cameo appearances), and your excuses seem feeble (as they should), consider these seven excellent ways to enhance your delivery and convey self-assurance and sincerity with your eye contact:

1. **Get ready.** Without belaboring the point (all right, only slightly belaboring the point), be prepared. If you are well prepared, you can focus on your audience rather than concentrating on your notes, the memorized script in your head, or that apparently intriguing spot on the back wall. Enough said.

2. **Make friends.** Speaking can be intimidating (now, there is a revelation, right?). You are alone in front of the audience, staring at a sea of faces and grappling with that old hobgoblin: fear. So, what should you do? Before you speak, work the crowd like an eager politician. Enthusiastically introduce yourself to the audience members as they enter the room, and thank them for attending. Show a genuine interest in them, and they will reciprocate with undivided attention. When your audience is brimming with smiling, attentive faces, it is much easier to establish eye contact.

3. **Connect before you speak.** If you begin speaking before you have visually connected with your audience ("What audience?"), trumpets will blare and a heavenly voice will proclaim: "Scaredy-cat!" Instead of dashing into your speech, do the following: after you have been introduced, assume a commanding stance, pause, breathe, smile, and—this is important—look at your audience. Your listeners will not bite.

With your eyes, send the unmistakable message: "I am confident, and you will enjoy this." Then, and only then, begin speaking. That will quiet those trumpets.

4. **Read and react.** If you are preoccupied with your notes, the ceiling tiles, your shoes, or your belly button, you will miss those harbingers of trouble that are evident throughout the room: droopy eyelids, furtive glances, skeptical expressions, and rampant note passing.

But if you are attuned to your audience, you can pick up on these signals and react (take a break, ask a question, vary your delivery). If you miss the signals because you never look at your audience, your speaking ship may be headed for the bottom of the deep blue sea, and you will not realize it until it is much too late. Stay focused on the vital passengers on your speaking voyage, the members of your audience (principle 29).

❧

The eyes have one language everywhere.

—George Herbert

❧

5. **Sustain eye contact.** If your eyes dart about or drift aimlessly around the room, landing everywhere except on your audience, the members of the audience will conclude that you are shifty, unwilling to look at them when you speak. Shiftiness is not a desirable attribute for a speaker. And unless you are a hypnotist, intent on lulling your audience into a trance, don't rhythmically sweep your eye contact back and forth across the room.

Try to establish and sustain eye contact, for a few seconds at least, with as many people as possible. In smaller settings, you should establish eye contact with each listener several times. But be careful not to stare intently, because that might intimidate the listener. Even worse, some listeners may become defiant if you stare, and they will reciprocate by staring menacingly back. Menacing glares can cause your knees to buckle, so avoid stare-downs with your audience.

6. **Divide a large audience into sections.** If you are speaking to a large audience, establishing eye contact can be challenging (so many faces, so little time). Try this: divide the room into quarters, then speak to each section of the room for a short period, attempting to make eye contact with as many people in that section as possible. Then shift to another section. Most audience members in the general vicinity of your gaze will believe that you are looking only at them, and you never have to tell them otherwise.

7. **Deliver key points to individuals.** Identify the significant points in your speech (poignant quotes, startling revelations, challenges, or calls to action). When you approach each of these points, pause, plant yourself, and then deliver the words slowly and with emphasis while looking directly at one individual in the audience.

   This will make your delivery more forceful, and you will seem more sincere. Repeat this practice with each key point, focusing on a different audience member each time. (If you look at the same individual repeatedly, others will feel slighted, and gossip will run amok.)

ै\.

To speak much is one thing; to speak well another.

—Sophocles

\.§

If you really want to connect with the members of your audience, maintain eye contact with them. Don't gaze, sweep, transfix, worship, or—worst of all—ogle your navel (or anyone else's navel, for that matter). Let your eyes send a message of utter self-assurance and trustworthiness.

33

Adhere to the Time Allotted

One never repents of having spoken too little,
but often of having spoken too much.

—Philippe de Commynes

Have you encountered the inconsiderate windbag speaker who believes that his audience cannot hear enough from him? He rambles on and on *and on*, flouting the prescribed time limit for his presentation as if it were merely a suggestion. He is wrong, of course. He may never want to stop talking, but his listeners feel otherwise. At times, they want to stand up and shout, "Enough!" Hell hath no fury like an audience scorned.

Listeners are not renowned for their patience. We want everything fast. How fast? It is telling that we can now get married at a drive-through window, and Twitter compels us to condense our thoughts into tidy little tweets consisting of no more than 140 characters. Don't encroach on your audience's precious time. The inviolable rule regarding time is: speak for the scheduled amount of time (or less) and sit down.

I once attended a presentation titled "Ten Secrets to Ridiculous Riches." It was about seven secrets too many. The financial wizard was scheduled to speak for 20 minutes, but when he reached that landmark, he was still yammering about Secret Number 3 ("To become rich, spend less and earn more . . ." or something equally astute). Unfazed by the time, he continued to trudge along until he mercifully concluded after 45 minutes.

Had the blabbermouth bothered to glance at his audience after 20 minutes, he would have seen his listeners impatiently flipping ahead in the handout, glaring at the clock (and at him), and squirming restlessly. Clearly, we were irked by this intrusion on our time. After he blew by the 20-minute barrier with no glimmer of light at the end of the speaking tunnel, attention and patience began to plummet. At 30 minutes, his listeners were openly grousing; at 40 minutes, we were preparing to storm the stage and toss him off.

&c

The less said, the better.

—Jane Austen

&c

Brevity is beautiful when you are speaking. Always strive to deliver your message in a memorable way, in the fewest words possible. Typically audiences are delighted whenever a speaker concludes early. They are likely to hail you as an outstanding speaker if you cut it short; end early on Friday afternoon, and they may deify you.

Seven Rules about Speaking Time

Adhere to the following guidelines to ensure that you are not flying right through the speaking stop sign and agitating your listeners:

1. **Time it.** When you are practicing your speech (you are practicing it, right?), time it *after* you have made your final revisions. If you time it during the drafting phase, as you are adding and deleting material, you will get a distorted idea of its length. Your goal is to make your delivery fit into the time allotted. If it does not, continue tinkering.

Be flexible, because various factors may affect your time. You may be anxious (yes, even you) when you speak, which may cause you to jabber or to forget a few thoughts. You may get caught up in the spirit of the moment and insert new comments. Or—thank goodness!—your audience may laugh at a few of your witticisms. All of this affects your time, so don't be absurdly inflexible ("Okay, I will complete my opening at 2 minutes and 15 seconds, wrap up point 3 at 9 minutes and 30 seconds, and finish with 10 seconds to spare"). Unless you are an accountant, that type of unrealistic, mathematical precision shackles you, so build a little leeway into your time frames.

❧

Have more than thou showest, speak less than thou knowest.

—William Shakespeare

❧

2. **Prepare to jettison.** Time not only the entire speech, but also each section. Why? Because you could be forced to scrap portions of your speech (a point, a story, an example) to meet time constraints for any variety of reasons, such as if the program runs late (not uncommon); if your audience's attention has become very limited (again, not uncommon); or if a prior gasbag has monopolized your time (a capital offense).

In any of those events, you should cut your speech short. Even if you did not cause the timing problems, you will be regarded as the culprit if you encroach on your audience's sacred times: lunch, scheduled breaks, and quitting time all spring to mind.

Alert your listeners that you are shortening your speech to respect their time and offer to be available afterward to address any questions. You will then bask in the warm glow of your audience's admiration.

❧

Far more numerous was the herd of such,
Who think too little, and who talk too much.

—John Dryden

❧

3. **Control the meeting flow.** Begin your presentation on time, and if there are breaks during your presentation, reconvene on time. Why? You can assume that the attendees, like children, will test your authority. If they determine that you are a pushover, and that the times you announced are merely suggestions, they will cavalierly disregard them, knowing that they can arrive late and not miss anything important. These stragglers invariably arrive with a noisy flourish and cause a commotion as they squeeze into their middle seats (they *always* have middle seats), stomping on everyone's toes along the way and loudly apologizing ("Oops! Sorry, sorry.").

   If audience members arrive late, ignore them. Continue speaking unless they become so disruptive that you must pause and allow them to get settled. Reward those who arrived on time by not repeating what you have already said.

4. **Monitor your time as you speak.** Monitor your time, because it evaporates quickly, and it is very easy to lose track of time in the midst of your presentation. Place a large watch on the lectern, locate a wall clock that is visible from the stage, or designate an audience member to periodically but discreetly signal how much time you have remaining. Avoid glancing at the watch you are wearing while you are speaking, because that sends the unspoken message that you are either bored or anxious to bolt.

❧

The secret of being a bore . . . is to tell everything.

—Voltaire

❧

5. **Keep 'em posted.** Let your listeners know that you are sensitive to the time constraints. This builds audience rapport, which is always a worthy goal. The bonus for you is that they are much more likely to pay attention.

Such comments as "In the 15 minutes I have with you today . . . ," "In the final few minutes, I would like to discuss . . . ," or "Let me be brief . . ." signal that you respect your listeners' time. But here is the caveat: after you make any of those announcements, you had better abide by them. Never raise expectations with promises that you don't intend to keep, because your audience will be miffed and will feel betrayed. And, as you know, "Hell hath no fury . . . ."

ﾀﾑ

I should be glad, if I could flatter myself that I came as near to the central idea of the occasion, in two hours, as you did in two minutes.

—Edward Everett to Abraham Lincoln

✒

6. **Do not exceed your audience's attention span.** Under most circumstances, the attention of your audience members tends to dwindle after 10 minutes, and it nearly vanishes after 20 minutes. If the speaker is a crashing bore, she may be lucky to hold their attention for 1 minute.

   It may seem hard to imagine, but the time races by when you are speaking, so you should distill your message to its essence. I know, all your points are critical, but you may have to sacrifice a few brainy insights if they cause your talk to run long.

   I was once intent on impressing a coveted prospect with the depth of my expertise, so I puffed: "I have 10 compelling reasons why you should hire me as a presentation skills consultant." Without missing a beat, the prospect leaned forward, smiled wryly, and said: "I'm sure you do, but I am extremely busy, so why don't you just give me your best 2?" Lesson learned.

   This is great advice for speakers, too. Make one lasting impression with a few crisp, direct points rather than creating a haze with a barrage of words. Give them your best points— quickly—and then go home.

7. **Allow time for questions.** Before you speak, clarify with your host whether you will be provided additional time to address audience questions, or whether you are expected to answer them within your allotted speaking time (principle 34). Field questions whenever feasible, because this is an excellent way to engage your audience, but have a clear understanding of the time limits. Don't encourage questions without budgeting time for them, because if you run out of time during a Q&A session, your audience will feel cheated, and you will seem evasive.

❧

Think before you speak; stop talking before they say "enough."

—Sa'di

❧

Abide by the time limitations in every presentation, unless your audience or your host invites you to continue and you are not encroaching on subsequent speakers' time. Don't get swept away in the heat of the moment and delude yourself that your audience is anxious to hear more. Audiences generally prefer less (a harsh but accurate assessment). Make your points, and then, while your audience is intoxicated with your words and nodding in agreement, sit down.

34

Take Command of "Q&A"

Before I refuse to take your questions, I have an opening statement.

—Ronald Reagan

Here is a bitter truism that those who are rigidly tethered to the script of their speech do not want to hear: most speakers do more to inspire, persuade, sell, and inform their listeners by responding to audience questions confidently than by *anything* they say during their prepared speech. I can hear the "say-it-ain't-so" wails of anguish from the disciples who never deviate from their prepared speech. Sorry, it is time to leave that safe cocoon.

These unpredictable question-and-answer sessions give you an excellent opportunity to clarify and reinforce points, elaborate on issues, solidify your expertise, address any misunderstandings, and perhaps persuade those who seem unpersuadable. Yes, you up the anxiety ante when you venture away from the safety of your carefully planned presentation and invite audience input, but the rewards outstrip the risks by a tremendous margin.

A question-and-answer session typically crackles with energy, often generating more interest than the prepared presentation did. What accounts for its appeal? One reason is that the audience members get to participate, which increases their interest and learning. Also, during a question-and-answer session, the speaker traipses into uncharted territory. Perhaps it is the same phenomenon that compels us to gawk at a car wreck (be honest, you know you have done that): it is dangerous and unusual. When the questions start flying, everyone, even the drowsiest listener, snaps to attention and perches on the edge of his seat, especially if the exchange promises to be heated (such as when the speaker is advocating plunking a halfway house in the audience's bucolic neighborhood).

Now, for the bad news (I know, what a killjoy!): a question-and-answer session is a tremendous opportunity—listen, because this is important—*if*, and *only if*, you are prepared (do you detect a theme developing in this book?). If you are unprepared, the session can quickly become a treacherous minefield, the kind that has doomed even exceptional speakers. If you are unprepared, cower and pray when the questioning barrage begins.

&a

I was gratified to be able to answer promptly,
and I did. I said I didn't know.

—Mark Twain

&s

There are manifest rewards for handling audience questions deftly. Yet sometimes a speaker gives them absolutely no forethought; he just wings it: "I was just strolling through the Q&A neighborhood, and thought, 'What the heck! Why not take a few questions?'" That is a sure recipe for disaster. With no planning, this foolhardy speaker is often perplexed by even the most predictable questions. Staggered, he lamely mumbles an unresponsive reply, or he reaches into his handy grab bag of canned answers. If you do that, you can put one gigantic check mark in the squandered-opportunity column. And while you're at it, let a little air out of your "expert" balloon to boot.

Seventeen Q&A Rules

So, you are willing to add a little zest to your talk by answering questions. Now what? Unless the prospect of public humiliation exhilarates you, don't enter the Q&A arena without a plan. Here it is. Study these rules before you invite the first question:

1. **Know the terrain.** Don't simply cross your fingers and fervently hope that the members of your audience will not ask the questions that you are dreading. They will. In the same way that a predatory animal can sense fear, an audience has an uncanny ability to zero in with amazing accuracy on just those particular questions. So you had better be prepared, lest you find yourself under the heat of the spotlight, babbling incoherently.

   What can you do? Start by knowing as much as possible about your audience before you speak so that you can anticipate the questions and plan your responses (principles 6 and 7). Ask yourself the following questions:
   - "Are the questions likely to be pointed and probing or friendly and fluffy?"
   - "Do my listeners understand the issues?"
   - "What do the audience members *need* to know?"
   - "What do the audience members *want* to know?"
   - "What is the opposing position?"
   - "What are the strengths of the opposing position?"
   - "Am I advocating something that threatens my listeners (tax increases, health-care decisions, lifestyle choices)?"
   - "Am I dealing with emotional or inflammatory topics (stem cell research, same-sex marriage, Coke versus Pepsi)?"
   - "What are the weaknesses in my position?" (There are always some.)
   - "Should I concede anything in my response?"
   - "Do any listeners have a hidden agenda?"
   - "What questions do I hope the audience members will *not* ask?

- "How will I respond to inane, provocative, or irrelevant questions?"
- "What will I do if an audience member becomes confrontational?"

Know the terrain, your risks, and your vulnerabilities before you solicit questions.

2. **Devise a plan.** Before you speak, decide whether you will field questions during or after your prepared speech. In your introduction or in your opening comments, clarify for your audience which approach you will take. Each has inherent advantages and disadvantages.

Accepting questions during the speech typically heightens the interest for everyone; it enables you to gauge your audience's response and level of understanding immediately, and it gives you an opportunity to correct misunderstandings quickly (what seems clear to you may be murky to your audience). This approach can be risky, however, if one of the questions is only marginally related to your topic (it happens) or if it baffles you (this also happens). In addition, the questions might divert your audience's attention from your message. Finally, if you accept questions during the speech, your allotted time can quickly evaporate, so plan accordingly.

On the other hand, if you hold all questions until you have completed your speech, you will be able to cover all your points without interruption. Unfortunately, without immediate input from the members of your audience, you limit your ability to evaluate their reaction to your message. Moreover, your listeners may forget their questions or be reluctant to raise questions regarding a subject that you covered much earlier.

Either approach will work, but you need to pick your path before you begin to speak.

3. **Understand the question.** Here is a simple rule: if you don't understand a question, don't guess and don't answer. No one will think that you are a dunce if you ask the questioner to explain or clarify the question. That is definitely preferable to

taking a wild stab at it and answering unresponsively or incorrectly. If you are clueless, but you plunge into a response anyway, you may create confusion; irritate the questioner, who will conclude that you are being evasive or flippant; and irk the other audience members, who may conclude that you are patronizing one of their kindred spirits in the audience. Any of these results will open Pandora's box for you, so clarify before responding.

4. **Schmooze.** If you want to encourage questions, create a friendly, nonthreatening atmosphere. Solicit participation with an open-ended invitation for questions: "I know I covered that topic quickly. What questions do you have?" Also acknowledge and thank audience members for their participation: "Thank you for that question." This respectful attitude toward those who ask questions—yes, even when all you really want to do is sock the bozo, whose goal it is to agitate you, in the nose— helps to build audience rapport.

But, avoid saying, "That is an excellent question," because you risk offending others who have already asked a question ("Hey, what about me? My question was better than his!"). Audiences can be hypersensitive, so don't single anyone out for special praise.

❧

Think before you speak, pronounce not imperfectly, nor bring out your words too hastily but orderly and distinctly.

—George Washington

❧

5. **Repeat the question.** If your audience is large, repeat the question before responding to ensure that everyone has heard it. The listeners will appreciate your audience focus (principle 29), and you will gain additional time to consider your response. (If you are momentarily stumped, even a few seconds can help while your brain whirs away in a desperate search for a reasonably intelligent thought.)

6. **Reframe the question.** Occasionally, some ninny in your audience will plop a disjointed, convoluted, or complex question in your lap. Address such queries cautiously, because they can undermine you quickly.

   Paraphrase the question if it is confusing: "Let me see if I can restate your question so that I am sure I understand it." If it is a compound question, break it into bite-size segments: "I think you have asked several questions, so let me attempt to respond to each one separately." Finally, if the question is irrelevant, smile, say so, and move on: "Thank you for the question, but that is really beyond the scope of my talk today." Your goal is to respond in a direct, logical fashion and to remain focused. If the question causes your intuitive alarms to blare "Danger! Danger!" proceed warily.

7. **Be responsive.** You will seldom persuade your listeners with ambiguity or evasiveness (a principle no politicians have learned). Stop futzing around and answer as honestly and as directly as possible. Don't stall, hoping that a pithy insight will pop into your noggin. If you ignore the question, or if you launch into your "speaking points" to rehash your position, your evident elusiveness will undermine your credibility. Of course, if you are honest and responsive, there is a price to pay as well: you will have eliminated your prospects of running for political office.

❧

Speak properly, and in as few Words as you can, but always plainly;
for the End of Speech is . . . to be understood.

—William Penn

❧

8. **If you do not know, admit it.** Some speakers feel that saying "I don't know" will cause them to turn to stone. But it is not merely okay to admit ignorance; it is preferable at times. Unless the question is clearly one that you *should* know the answer to ("Is it not true that Giovanni 'The Hatchet Man' Gotti handed you a greasy duffel bag filled with $50,000 in

crisp $100 bills?"), it's perfectly acceptable to respond by saying, "I am sorry, but I don't know the answer. I will try to find out and get back to you."

Understand, however, that there is no substitute for thorough preparation, and if you are intentionally unresponsive ("A greasy duffel bag jammed with cash? Let me think . . . I'm not sure") or cagey ("That depends on what your definition of *is* is"), your audience will quickly become exasperated, and you will undermine your credibility.

❧

Teach thy tongue to say, "I do not know."

—Moses Maimonides

❧

9. **Exude confidence with your body language.** Your goal is to exude confidence when you speak (principle 30), so don't forget that when you begin to take questions. Here is a laundry list of what not to do: don't stand ramrod stiff, clutch the lectern with ferocity, recoil, flop over the lectern, prop your chin in your hand, scowl, wince, or draw your face taut. Such body language and facial expressions diminish the message of self-confidence that you want to convey, and frighten small children and animals.

Look interested and relaxed. Being prepared (there is that gosh darn Mr. Preparation again!) will do wonders for your confidence and your stage presence.

10. **Remain composed.** Stay positive and composed despite questions and comments that are antagonistic ("Your position is just double-dumb!"), personal ("I would not expect an insensitive half-wit like you to understand!"), or irrelevant ("Can vegetarians eat animal crackers?"). Do not let hostile questioners provoke an angry response from you. That response is often precisely what they want to accomplish. Rather, be firm but polite. Smile, grit your teeth, and agree to disagree. Shouting invectives may be cathartic, but it is neither helpful nor persuasive.

✸

Our anger and annoyance are more detrimental to us than the things themselves which anger or annoy us.

—Marcus Aurelius

✸

11. **Target the majority.** You will rarely convince everyone to accept your position, so don't waste valuable time and energy addressing questions from the malcontent minority and attempting to persuade them. Focus instead on the concerns of the majority of your audience. Some members of your audience would not accept your position if it were an edict chiseled in granite and delivered from heaven. Move on confidently, smugly knowing in your heart that they are wrong and you are right.

12. **Be brief.** Get to the point. Don't ramble, filibuster, or browbeat when responding. This only annoys your listeners, creates confusion, and generates more questions. Your listeners will better understand and remember concise, focused answers. Being brief also enables you to address more questions in the time allotted. Answer succinctly and let your listeners get on with their lives.

13. **Follow up.** After you have responded to a question, occasionally ask a follow-up question, such as "Does that make sense?" or "Does that answer your question?" This demonstrates that you are genuinely interested in seeing that the questioner understands your point. But avoid follow-up if it prevents you from addressing questions from other audience members, if the questioner is argumentative, or if you are anxious to move on to the next question (just be darn thankful that you were able to mumble something marginally lucid in your answer).

14. **Maintain control of the room.** Sometimes, multiple conversations or even heated arguments—complete with name-calling, finger-pointing, and fist waving—will erupt during a question-and-answer session. Disruptions can escalate into chaos if you ignore them.

Pause and politely ask those who are causing the disruption to hold their comments so that everyone can hear both you and the person asking the question. Allow the agitators to be heard only if you have time on the program and are so inclined. It is your responsibility as a speaker to maintain control of the room. If all else fails, suggest that they settle their disagreement by arm wrestling in the hallway; resort to your crowd-control mace and tasers only in dire circumstances.

ᴥ

If you can't answer a man's argument, all is not lost;
you can still call him vile names.

—Elbert Hubbard

✎

15. **Monitor the time.** Always adhere to the time allotted for your presentation (principle 33). So when you are preparing your speech, budget time for questions. If your time on the program has expired, stop. Don't continue to field questions, especially if others are speaking after you. Instead, inform your audience that you will be available to answer all their questions one-on-one after the program or through e-mail.

16. **Practice Q&A.** Round up all your inquisitive, annoying, and stubborn friends (don't tell them that this combination of characteristics is why they were selected) and role-play. Practice responding to their questions with concise, well-organized responses. This will hone your ability to think on your feet and to formulate crisp, responsive answers. Have your inquisitors ask every conceivable type of question, because that is exactly what you can expect from your audience: compound, convoluted, and confrontational questions posed by bewildered, inarticulate, and hostile questioners.

Some of the questioners in your audience will have amazingly fertile imaginations, others will have hidden agendas, and still others will just be dunderheads. Inevitably there will be at least one who relishes the sound of her own voice and will welcome any opportunity to pontificate. The practice sessions will help you prepare for all of them.

17. **Study recordings.** Compose yourself first; then dive in and analyze recordings of both your practice sessions and your live presentations involving Q&A (principle 21).This study may be painful, but it will be profitable, I promise.

Be analytical and ask yourself these questions: "Was I responsive, or were my answers gibberish?" "Was I focused, or did I blather?" "Did I sound confident, or did I sound confused?" "Did I focus on the questioner, or did I allow my eyes to dart around?" "Did my body language and facial expressions convey poise, or did I look like a crazed, trapped animal?" Mr. Camera reveals exactly what your audience will see, so study the recordings, internalize the lessons, and address any deficiencies.

Deftly fielding questions is a skill that you develop only with preparation and practice. Study the additional resources regarding question-and-answer sessions that are given in the recommended resources at the back of the book.

Venturing from your script can be unnerving, but you can calm your jitters and minimize the risks with careful planning. Handle questions adroitly, and you will distinguish yourself and enhance your stature and credibility with every audience. But never enter the question-and-answer briar patch unprepared; many speakers have done that, and they have not been heard from since.

PART VII

TALK WITH TOOLS

The process of using a microphone looks effortless from the comfort of your seat: you walk up, grab it, and just start yammering. Simple, right? Hardly. That seemingly harmless microphone can sabotage you lickety-split if you are unfamiliar with all of its quirks.

❧

Things seen are mightier than things heard.

—Alfred, Lord Tennyson

❧

Speakers also regularly incorporate visual aids into their presentations, and for good reason: a visual aid can transform a pedestrian presentation into an extraordinary one. When you use a visual aid in your presentation, your audience is more attentive, learns more, and retains the message longer. But that happens only *if*—and this is a colossal *if*—the visual aid is created and used skillfully. When it is poorly designed or handled clumsily—and it frequently is—a visual aid frazzles the speaker, vexes the audience, and undercuts the presentation. If this happens when you are speaking, you will rue your decision not to have become a cloistered scientist.

Part VII addresses a variety of presentation tools, the advantages and disadvantages of each, the nuts and bolts of fickle Mr. Microphone, and the secrets of using a visual aid flawlessly.

35

Master the Microphone

The wisest thing to do with a fool is to encourage him
to hire a hall and discourse to his fellow citizens.
Nothing chills nonsense like exposure to the air.

—Woodrow Wilson

I know exactly what you are thinking: "What could be difficult about using a microphone? Don't you just flip a switch and start rattling away?" Yes—if you enjoy living dangerously. Microphones harass grizzled veteran speakers, and they can befuddle neophytes. In the worst of times, speaking greenhorns can completely unravel. So that you will recognize your microphone risks, let's start with a quick lineup of the Eight Egregious Microphone Sins. Please step forward as your name is called.

> *Sin 1* occurs when a speaker holds the microphone too close to her mouth, nearly inhaling it. This causes her to sound shrill, amplifies her anxious breathing, and produces sounds that terrify small children.
>
> *Sin 2* surfaces when a speaker forgets that his sniffling, snorting, and paper-shuffling sounds are fully amplified for his audience.

Sin 3 happens when a speaker plants her chin on her chest, focuses on her feet, and speaks directly into the microphone, which she is holding right next to her belly button. She might as well be speaking into a bucket.

Sin 4 occurs when a speaker treats his microphone as he would a deadly cobra, clutching it with a steely grip and holding it a stiff-arm away from his mouth. His microphone is useless, and there is an added drawback: he resembles the Tin Man from *The Wizard of Oz.*

Sin 5 crops up when a lanky speaker, rather than pausing and adjusting the microphone stand higher, decides to simply droop down several feet to the microphone's level, which makes him look like a giant slouch.

Sin 6 takes place when a speaker gestures wildly during her talk with the hand that is holding the microphone; only haphazardly, whenever the microphone happens to cruise by in the general vicinity of her mouth, does she project a random word or two.

Sin 7 comes into play when the speaker discovers to his misfortune, as he tumbles either to the floor or into the orchestra pit, that— yes, yes indeed—there is a cord attached to the microphone.

And finally, *Sin* 8 (drum roll, please), the worst of all the transgressions for a speaker, but, without question, the most entertaining for her audience, is when she forgets that her microphone is on before she steps up to speak, and she broadcasts her juicy observations and scurrilous accusations throughout the room. Her mother cringes in shame, and the speaker wonders where she will find her next job, *gosh darn it!*

So, do you still think that all it takes is a flip of the switch?

Three Microphone Options

You might as well resign yourself to the reality that you will need to use a microphone sometime in your speaking career, so you need to know your options. There are three main types of microphones, each with its own inherent advantages and disadvantages (it is never easy, is it?). Let's study each of them.

1. **The fixed microphone.** As its name implies, a fixed microphone is attached to the lectern. You can typically make minor adjustments in the height of the microphone, but not much else. After adjusting the height, you simply turn it on, test it, adjust the volume, and talk. Other than staying close to the microphone as you speak, there is no other fussing required. You are free to gesture with both hands (provided you have not locked your hands in the lectern death grip), and there is no risk of tripping over that pesky microphone cable.

   But you pay a hefty price for this apparent simplicity. The biggest drawback is that you are stuck behind the lectern for the entire presentation, a position that saps your power. You are unable to use several important communication tools such as body language and expansive gestures. The lectern also creates a buffer between you and the audience. It is even worse if you find yourself standing behind a hulking monster of a lectern that required all the lumber from several giant redwood trees to build. This behemoth lectern obscures your audience's view of everything except your bobbing head. That is a huge disadvantage in every situation, so avoid the fixed microphone whenever possible.

   Finally, if you are tall, don't forget Sin 5: adjust the microphone's height upward, because a slouch seldom projects power or confidence.

   ❧

   A lot of managers aren't bad at public speaking.
   But "not bad" ain't good enough.

   —Tom Peters

   ❧

2. **The handheld microphone.** You can detach a handheld microphone from the lectern or microphone stand and move

about with relative freedom. Once you become proficient with a handheld mike, you can also use it in various ways to enhance your voice. Many professional speakers prefer it for that reason.

But much like its relative, the fixed microphone, a handheld microphone has inherent limitations. First, since you are holding the mike, you can gesture with only one hand at a time (unless you commit Sin 6, and if you do, you should confess it and resolve to stop). Second, many of these microphones have cables, which limit how far you can wander. Third, you must constantly monitor the microphone cable's location. Otherwise you risk stepping on it, thus yanking the microphone from your hand, or you tripping over it, thus looking like a buffoon. Both predicaments will require nimble improvisation on your part. Finally, it takes practice to master where and how to hold the microphone to amplify your voice correctly, positioning it neither too close (which produces sounds similar to those made by alley cats) nor too far away (which produces no sounds).

3. **The lavaliere microphone.** A lavaliere microphone is a tiny mike that clips to your shirt collar, jacket lapel, or necktie. It has many advantages. You can wander about and gesture freely and naturally with both hands. It is typically cordless, eliminating concern that you might step on or trip over a cable. And you can speak naturally, without constantly monitoring whether you are holding the microphone in the proper position to amplify your voice.

Lavaliere microphones have three drawbacks, however. First, some are not cordless, which limits your movement and interjects that tripping bugaboo. Second, you need to make sure that your microphone is not attached to some piece of clothing that moves, swishes, or crinkles, because that will produce disturbing noises. And third, you can easily forget that you are wearing this unobtrusive device; if you do not vigilantly monitor when it is on, your uncensored Sin 8 comments may haunt you.

Seven Microphone Guidelines

Now that you know your options, let's consider seven pearls of microphone wisdom:

1. **Practice with a microphone.** Familiarity breeds confidence (or was that contempt, but I digress), so get accustomed to holding the microphone as you practice your presentation. If you don't have a spare mike lying around your office or home (doesn't everyone?), hold a pencil, a rolled-up magazine, or a Tootsie Roll Pop to replicate the feeling while you practice.

   Holding a mike in place while speaking is not as easy as it might look, so practice this repeatedly. Record yourself to see whether you are using the microphone correctly (principle 21). If you spot any problems (the microphone careening about wildly, erratic projection, your striking resemblance to a robot), address them and continue practicing until you have mastered the mike.

   It may seem unnatural to stand for long periods with your elbow bent, pressed against your ribs, holding an object next to your mouth, but you will become more comfortable with practice.

⏺

Speech was given to the ordinary sort of men whereby to communicate their mind; but to the wise men, whereby to conceal it.

—Robert South

⏺

2. **Befriend an expert.** If the venue where you will be speaking has an on-site AV specialist, track this person down and enlist his help in testing the sound system well before the program begins, ironing out the glitches, and exorcising the microphone demons. Try to ensure that he will be readily available to help you if the microphone begins to balk when you are speaking.

Give him your unconditional love, cash, or both, because it will be one of the best investments you make in your presentation.

3. **Always test the microphone.** Raise your hand if you have been in the audience when some numbskull has trudged to the microphone after his introduction and then repeatedly thumped it with his chubby fingers while reciting the only microphone mantra apparently known to the human race: "Testing, testing, 1-2-3, is this on? Can you hear me?" Unfortunately, we can, and we now realize that we are in the hands of a hack speaker.

   Test the microphone well before your audience arrives. Enlist someone to move around the room as you speak, while you are also moving around; listen for dead spots where the microphone sound mysteriously disappears (call that the Bermuda Triangle for Microphones). Tinker with the microphone settings: Does it emit shrill feedback? Do you need to adjust the volume? Do you know where to hold it for ideal projection?

   Microphones are notoriously unpredictable, and even identical models can sound noticeably different. Leave nothing to chance: test it. And stop thumping it.

4. **Position the microphone.** To amplify your voice properly, keep the microphone close to your mouth as you speak. Otherwise, you will hear such unsettling catcalls as "Speak up!" "What'd ya say?" "Can't hear you!" As a general rule, position the microphone about three to four inches from your mouth and about one inch below your lower lip, and get used to holding it there for your entire presentation. The elbow of the arm holding the microphone should be held next to your ribs (not flying around). That will steady the microphone (and disguise your trembling hand).

   Be careful not to hold the microphone too close to your mouth, because you might smack your teeth or spit on it. When it is too close, it also creates discordant, shrill sounds that will make your audience cringe. On the other hand, if, as you get caught up in the spirit of the moment, you forget that you are using a mike and you don't hold it close enough, your voice will fade in and out. That is recommended only if you are weaseling out of sharing bad news and secretly hoping that your audience will not hear you. Experiment until you find the ideal positioning.

5. **Be leery of the cable.** While you are speaking, that seemingly harmless microphone cable lurks, just waiting for its first opportunity to entangle your feet and wreak havoc. It can quickly transform a confident speaker into a klutz. Use your free hand to control the cable and push it aside. Unless you relish pratfalls, never lose track of that insidious little demon.

6. **Control your gestures.** If you are speaking with a handheld microphone, you can gesture only with your free hand. Since you can hold the microphone in either hand, add a little variety by switching hands periodically.

    If you are an animated gesticulator, you may find it difficult to control your gesturing as you become engrossed in your message. If some of your grand gestures send your microphone several feet away from your mouth, your audience may miss the wisdom that you are so energetically imparting. If you speak regularly to groups large enough to require a microphone, consider investing in a lavaliere mike. If it enhances your delivery or helps you avoid even one nightmarish experience, it is a worthwhile investment.

7. **Act "microphone savvy."** Some speakers approach the microphone with absolute trepidation, as though it were about to snap at them. Become comfortable using the microphone. Before your audience arrives, practice removing the mike from its cradle, holding it, moving around with it, and placing it back in its cradle. Practice this until it feels and looks perfectly natural.

From the moment you step before a crowd and seize the microphone, every one of your actions should convey a simple message: "I am confident, because I have done this many times." If you can convey that message, your audience will never know that this is your first adventure with fickle Mr. Microphone.

All your diligent work can be washed away in an instant if you botch handling the microphone. If your listeners cannot hear you, if they are constantly distracted by booming, popping, or screeching feedback (frankly, if you commit any of the Eight Egregious Microphone Sins), you may be racing pell-mell toward microphone meltdown—not a place you want to visit. Practicing with the microphone may not make you perfect, but it will have a tremendous positive impact, so get to work.

36

Capitalize on Visual Aids

*Remember: It is ten times harder to command
the ear than to catch the eye.*

—Duncan Maxwell Anderson

Powerful visual images etch lasting impressions in our minds. Consider the following examples:

- John Kennedy Jr., as a child, saluting his father's casket as it passed
- Neil Armstrong stepping onto the lunar surface, taking "one giant leap for mankind"
- East and West Germans drinking champagne together atop the Berlin Wall
- Two commercial jets crashing into the World Trade Center, and the buildings collapsing
- A commercial airliner landing on the Hudson River—with no fatalities

Whether you witnessed these events as they unfolded or saw them captured on film, they created indelible impressions.

A visual aid can also have an enormous impact in most speeches, one that often surpasses the effect of anything you (yes, even you) might say. It can make complex concepts understandable and mundane topics engaging. Visual aids pack the following wallop:

- **Holding your audience's attention.** Let's be honest: whatever your objective when you are speaking, you are unlikely to be effective if your audience is physically present but mentally miles away, or even dozing as you speak. A visual aid increases the chances that your listeners will remain engaged and focused on your message.
- **Reinforcing your message.** The disillusioning truth is that the typical listener will quickly forget much of what you say, sometimes within moments after you say it. But if you toss in a compelling visual aid and employ it skillfully during your presentation, the equation changes. Studies consistently demonstrate that listeners understand and recall points that are reinforced with a visual aid better and longer. How much better and longer? In one study, audience retention increased between 38 and 200 percent when a visual aid complemented the message.[1]
- **Staying on target.** In the unlikely event that you are not as prepared as you should be (something that never happens, correct?), the visual aid can substitute for notes, helping *you* remain focused on your message.

But (you just knew there was a *but* coming, right?), don't start haphazardly incorporating visual aids into your presentation without first carefully considering how they might sabotage it. Here are three of the treacherous ways in which they might do that.

First, if your visual aid becomes monotonous (one tedious slide after another), its impact shrinks. Your listeners will quickly start concentrating on any convenient distraction, such as doodling, twiddling their thumbs, or counting ceiling tiles. Soon, both you and the visual aid become an annoyance, and your message is doomed.

Second, if you jam too much information into too little space, display too many complex details, or distract with too many whiz-bang features, you introduce confusion rather than clarity. You should always design your visual aid with your audience members in mind (principles 6 and 7). If you overwhelm them with content, or if you dazzle them with impressive special effects at the expense of relevant content, your message is doomed.

Finally, if you bungle around when using a visual aid (and bungling around is rampant in the visual-aid world), you will lose any advantage using the visual aid might have created. Worse, you may actually undermine your message. You can read more about this in principles 37 and 38, but you must be comfortable handling the visual aid and quickly resolving the glitches that will inevitably surface during your speech. These glitches can bedevil you if you are unprepared (they are notoriously recalcitrant). Witnessing a visual aid balking and a speaker imploding is painfully awkward for everyone. You do not want to go there, which I unfortunately know from first-hand experience. And if you do go there (did I mention this already?), your message will be doomed.

ɝ

Eyes are more accurate witnesses than ears.

—Heraclitus

ɝ

Nine Visual-Aid Options

Speakers enjoy a startling array of visual-aid options, from the simplicity of a snapshot to the complexity of a stunning multimedia extravaganza. This is both a blessing and a curse. All visual aids have both advantages and limitations—advantages that can be enthralling, but limitations that can be crippling.

You should select your visual aid carefully, and meticulously plan how you will weave it into your presentation. Your goal is to create suspense, heighten interest, and solidify your message. Examine the following list to select the right visual aid for your presentation. Then master the rules for using a visual aid set forth in principles 37 and 38.

1. **Handouts.** By having your listeners fill in handouts as you speak, you will reinforce your message and improve listener recollection. Another bonus is that your listeners will typically refer to the handouts after the presentation to supplement your message. Finally, you can provide additional information in the handout that you simply did not have enough time to cover in your prepared remarks.

    But this is important: handouts should *always* be well organized and look professional. If they are disorganized, cluttered, or sloppy, or if they appear to have been created on a 1930s-era mimeograph machine, they reflect poorly on you.

    You want to provide rich content in your handouts, but don't go overboard. If they are too detailed (about as lengthy as *War and Peace*, for instance), they become a distraction. Your listeners may end up reading them and ignoring you. Being ignored as you speak can be disconcerting; worse, it bruises even the heartiest ego.

2. **Objects.** Almost anything that you can easily handle and display fits into the object category: a scale model of a building, a baseball bat, a book of artwork, or a water gun (unloaded, please). An object typically commands the immediate attention of your audience, particularly when you skillfully incorporate it into your presentation.

    A precaution: your object should be neither so small that it is nearly invisible to most of the audience (cuff links or a paper clip) nor so hulking that it is unwieldy (a refrigerator or a 50-gallon barrel of olive oil). Neither choice will enrich your presentation. And as a rule, avoid any visual aid that has the potential to cause a hernia as you clumsily attempt to shove it around.

3. **Photographs.** A photograph can captivate your audience, but only if the image is clear and large enough to be seen by

everyone, including those introverts clustered at the back of the room. If the photograph fits in your wallet, it will be appropriate only for a very small audience—say, two people.

A blurry or tiny photograph only frustrates your listeners, and they will quickly lose interest. Consider enlarging your photographs and mounting them on stiff foam boards to make them easier to display. And never pass a stack of photographs around as you are speaking, because they—not you—will become the center of attention.

❧

Seeing is believing all the world over.

—Miguel de Cervantes

❧

4. **Diagrams.** Whether you prepare it ahead of time or, assuming you have some rudimentary drawing skills, draw it while you are speaking, a diagram can help clarify your message. You can use it to reinforce your points, for example, by showing the hierarchy of an organization, an architectural plan, or vehicle paths during an automobile accident.

But sometimes a diagram looks like a labyrinth of disjointed lines that are more likely to confuse than to enlighten. A few determined audience members may attempt to decipher the maze (while concentrating so hard on the puzzle that they miss what you are saying), but many will just give up. Strive for clarity and simplicity.

5. **Graphs.** A graph can be useful when you need to explain a topic that is loaded with mystifying statistics, mind-numbing data, or technical jargon, especially when your audience is not conversant with the topic. There are three popular options:

You can use a *line graph* to depict trends or developments over time, such as your company's dramatic spike in sales immediately after you launched the exciting "Piddle-Paddle" line of cutting-edge swimwear. A *bar graph* can help you illustrate trends and percentages, such as when you want to compare the disparity in the income levels of I. Rolin Dough, the swaggering, blue-blooded, Ivy League graduate, and Ralph Sipowitz, a high school dropout. And a *pie graph* can delineate percentages—for example, when you want to clarify the portion of the pastry market cornered by that juggernaut Doughnut Decadence.

Like a diagram, a graph must be visible, simple, and easily understood. If it is too complex, it is worse than worthless—and that is bad.

6. **A flip chart.** The preceding three visual-aid options— photographs, diagrams, and graphs—can be incorporated into the final four options: the flip chart, overhead transparencies, slides, and electronic presentations.

A flip chart is the workhorse in many presentations, for several good reasons: it is the essence of simplicity, you can use it in a variety of ways, and you do not risk a gut-wrenching electronic snafu. When you write on a flip chart during your presentation, you reinforce your message, and you can immediately record audience input. Also, you can tear off sheets from the chart and post them around the room for repeated reference.

But like all visual aids, the flip chart has a few limitations. It is suitable only for a small audience—say, of 20 to 30 people. A larger audience will not be able to read the text. And if your scrawl is horrendous ("Is that cryptography?"), either you will need to entice someone to write the information beforehand so that you can flip to the appropriate page during the presentation, or you will need to enlist a volunteer with stellar handwriting to help you while you speak. Swallow your penmanship pride and make sure that your flip chart text is legible.

❧

Eloquence is the power to translate a truth into language perfectly intelligible to the person to whom you speak.

—Ralph Waldo Emerson

❧

7. **Overhead transparencies.** Although the overhead projector is somewhat outdated technologically (the Pilgrims used this device at the Plymouth town hall meetings), it is still regularly used by many speakers because it offers distinct advantages: it is simple to use, you can face your listeners, you can present information easily to any size group, you can instantaneously record listener input, and you can prepare colorful transparencies before the presentation.

   As with all electronic visual aids, you may need to lower the lights in the room, and this can be a dicey proposition, especially if your topic is slightly tiresome or if you tend to drone on (never a good idea with or without a visual aid). You will need to raise the lights periodically to guarantee that your audience does not become drowsy. More on this topic in principles 37 and 38.

8. **Slides.** Slides are an excellent way to reinforce your message and captivate your audience for a long period of time. Unfortunately, even the simple task of loading the slides into a carousel can be unnerving. I have seen them loaded upside down; backward, producing mirror images; and in the wrong order. Also, although it is relatively easy to operate, a slide projector can and does jam, usually at the most inappropriate moment. The typical result is a tug-of-war battle with the projector. The battle is usually entertaining (especially if you are not one of the combatants), but always unprofessional, so try to avoid it.

9. **Electronic presentations.** After surveying today's visual-aid market, you may conclude: "So many alluring, snazzy visual-aid toys, and so little time!" You now have at your disposal a huge array of video, computer, and multimedia visual aids that have the potential to rivet your audience; these are discussed in principle 38. But before you race helter-skelter down this high-tech path, be sure that you know what you're getting yourself into. It can be a perilous journey for any speaker.

We have only scratched the surface, but if you intend to rely on a visual aid in your presentation—and you should—study the recommended resources that are listed at the back of this book.

A visual aid can pack enormous punch when it is carefully designed and skillfully used, but many speakers fail one or both of those requirements. A visual aid should never become a crutch, never substitute for thorough preparation, never be used excessively, and never overwhelm the audience—rules that are ignored far too often. But if you harness its power by knowing and applying the rules described in principles 37 and 38, a visual aid can help make your message engaging and unforgettable, which are excellent results with every presentation.

37

Know the Visual-Aid Rules

Believe nothing of what you hear, and only half of what you see.

—Anonymous

You have studied principle 36 and carefully selected the ideal visual aid, and now you are hankering to go. All you need to do is schlep it to the front of the room, prop it up, and presto! It works like magic, right? Only in fantasyland.

Either you had better know how to use your visual aid proficiently, or you can plan on some embarrassing moments. It takes detailed planning, tenacity, and plenty of practice to ensure that your visual aid complements rather than undermines your talk. Why? Because it is never a question of *whether* something will go awry with your visual aid; it is only a question of *when*. Take every precaution to avoid that experience, because visual-aid calamities can rattle speakers, as the following episode illustrates.

One of my university public speaking students was demonstrating the steps involved in repotting a plant. She carefully laid out her trowel, a clay pot, a pile of dirt, and the plant. Unfortunately, she had not practiced with her visual aid before her speech, and she had overlooked a critical detail: her clay pot has a big, pesky hole in the bottom.

As she spoke, holding up the pot so that it was visible to the entire class, she troweled dirt into it, and, just as quickly, the dirt poured onto the table. The logical way to address this untoward development was simply to pause and plug the hole. But there was no logic involved, because she was flustered, and her brain was frozen. She elected to handle her perplexing problem in a peculiar manner: by scooping faster— much, *much* faster. She was hell-bent on trying to shovel the dirt into the pot more quickly than it was pouring out, but she was losing the race and growing ever more frenzied. Her rate of delivery quickened, and she ripped through her 10-minute presentation in less than 3 minutes, winded and ankle deep in dirt. The class was tremendously amused; it's too bad she had not intended to deliver an entertaining speech. She is now a huge fan of silk plants.

Twenty Rules for Using Visual Aids

Scrupulously adhere to the following rules when you plan on using a visual aid. Some of them may seem excessive, but you should always plan for the unexpected. I am confident that Murphy's Law was conceived with visual aids in mind, and the likelihood of complications increases the more you rely on complex high-tech gadgetry. This principle addresses the rules applicable to all visual aids; principle 38 covers the unique challenges that multimedia visual aids pose.

1. **Study the speaking venue.** The omnipresent "P" word— prepare—surfaces again. Before selecting your visual aid, analyze the room layout to identify any limitations that might adversely affect your using it during the presentation. Ask yourself the following questions:
   - "How large is the room?"
   - "Are the electrical outlets, screens, and lights easily accessible?"

- "Will the room's sound system, lighting, or acoustics present any challenges?"
- "Are there any barriers in the room (columns, walls, chandeliers) that will obstruct my audience's view?"
- "Will I be speaking on an elevated stage separated from my audience?"

You cannot select or create the appropriate visual aid without specific information about the venue where you will be speaking, so to avoid nasty surprises, answer these questions sooner rather than later.

2. **Make your visual aid visible.** I know what you are thinking: "Make it visible? What a brilliant concept!" But speakers regularly violate this rule. One speaker will use visual aids that he has jammed with a maze of cryptic words, cluttered points, and minuscule graphs. Another speaker strains mightily to read the itsy-bitsy lettering on her visual aid, even though she is standing right next to it. A third speaker displays objects so small that they could rattle around in a thimble and wonders why his audience is not engrossed.

Make sure your visual aid is visible from every vantage point in the room. The members of your audience will not spend much time concentrating on a minuscule or perplexing visual aid. They will quickly give up and divert their attention to more pressing matters (newspapers, BlackBerrys, daydreams), none of which involve you or your message. Don't assume that your visual aid will be visible; know it. If you cannot assure yourself of its visibility, either replace it or eliminate it from your presentation.

3. **Use only professional-looking visual aids.** A sloppy, disorganized, or amateurish visual aid damages your professional image and handicaps your presentation. And unless your purpose is pure entertainment and silliness (you are presenting to an audience of second graders, for example), avoid hand puppets, cartoons, home videos, or any Halloween costumes. That kind of buffoonery is more likely to annoy than to amuse your audience.

You have only one chance to make a lasting, favorable impression, so don't squander it. Your visual aid should convey the following message: "I am a professional and a well-prepared expert." If you cannot muster the time, resources, or expertise needed to create (or have someone else create, following your specific directions) professional visual aids, do not use them. No exceptions.

4. **Use vibrant colors.** Judiciously add a smattering of color to your visual aid. From their exposure to television, movies, and the Internet, audiences today are accustomed to bright colors and striking images, so black-and-white visual aids can seem drab to them.

   Use colors to highlight key points, to focus your audience's attention, and to show contrasts on graphs or charts. But don't go wild with dozens of colors; too many colors become distracting. Choose two or three per visual aid. And, avoid the gaudy, fluorescent shades that are visible from a quarter mile away; you don't want to daze the audience members.

5. **Design horizontally.** In most cases, you should design your visual aid so that as you reveal a point, your audience reads it from left to right. Why? Because audiences are accustomed to reading material that way, not diagonally or vertically. Don't disorient them; they can do that by themselves.

6. **Select clean block lettering and fonts.** Suppress any latent desire to express your individuality or your artistry when you design your visual aid. Fancy calligraphy is generally illegible, and multiple fonts will confuse your viewers.

   Use basic, crisp block lettering such as Arial, Verdana, Times New Roman, or Garamond. That style may seem boring, but in the visual-aid world, being easy to read is far more important than being ornate. Use no more than two font styles per visual aid.

   The size of the lettering depends on the size of your audience. As a general guide, consider using a 36-point font for titles, a 30-point font for subtitles, and no smaller than a 24-point font for text. The litmus test is always the same: is it visible? A visual aid that may be appropriate in a cozy conference room will be impractical in a large ballroom—simple common sense that is consistently flouted.

7. **Highlight the key concepts.** Highlight the crucial points in your visual aid, but not every point. I know: "It's all crucial." Perhaps it is to you, but it probably is not to your listeners. You will stupefy them with a tsunami of information. Your greater risk is that the essential points will wash right by in that tidal wave, and the groggy listeners will not notice them ("What was that? Was it important?").

   Another drawback of laying out every topic in detail is that your audience may opt to read the visual aid rather than listen to you. Soon your voice will become only an annoying background droning noise.

   You should use the visual aid to guide your audience to the essence of your message, and then point it out ("Look, right there: that is crucial!"). Ask yourself these questions when you create your visual aid: "What is the most effective way to make my point with the fewest words and images?" "What are the three or four crucial points that my audience *must* remember?" If the information is not crucial, pare it out. Make simplicity and clarity your watchwords.

ও

When the eyes say one thing, and the tongue another,
a practiced man relies on the language of the first.

—Ralph Waldo Emerson

ও

8. **Use signposts.** Don't make your listeners work to follow along, because most of them will not do so. If your material looks like one big, unbroken blob of words and sentences, then it reeks of hard work and boredom—both of which will cause your listeners to zone out. It is your job to guide your listeners through your talk. Do not invite them to stray from the path with a muddled, complicated visual aid. Rather, make your visual aid memorable and concise. How?

To focus attention and to facilitate understanding, use numbering, lettering, or bulleting in your visual aid. Limit the number of bullets per slide or per page to four or five to minimize the clutter. And limit the number of lines per visual (four to six at most, and fewer is preferable) if you want your listeners to comprehend your information. Present your information in phrases rather than in complete sentences.

Finally, organize and group the information on the visual aid in the most logical, understandable way: pros versus cons, advantages versus disadvantages, brawny versus brainy.

9. **Create suspense.** Think of yourself as a master storyteller or a magician (yes, you may have a wand and a top hat if you must). Use your visual aid to delight and surprise your audience. To add suspense, heighten the impact, and maintain your listeners' fickle attention, carefully orchestrate when and how you will reveal the information. Why?

If you display all the points of your message immediately, rest assured that the members of your audience will read ahead; they are headstrong that way. Soon, they will lose interest in your presentation, because they already know exactly what you intend to say. Alternatively, if you fail to hide the points that you previously discussed, your listeners may lag behind while you have moved ahead to your next point. Either occurrence guarantees that they will not be focused on what you are saying when you are saying it.

Reveal your points only as you make them. For example, if you have a bulleted list entitled "Seven Fashion Blunders," highlight blunder number 1 ("White Shoes and Black Socks: A Deadly Duo") only while you are addressing it, and only as long as you want your audience to focus on that point. Conclude your discussion of that fashion faux pas and then highlight blunder number 2 ("Gold Chains and Hairy Chests: A Tacky Twosome"). Revealing information in this way helps you maintain the audience's attention on the point you are addressing.

10. **Proofread the materials.** *Surely* everyone proofreads any
    material that will be displayed to an audience, right? *Surely not.*
    Few oversights will undermine your professional image and
    credibility more quickly than typographical or grammatical
    mistakes. You can apologize profusely, curse the gremlins in
    your computer, look petty and blame everyone else, or even
    engage in self-deprecating humor as a face-saving last resort,
    but you are unlikely to recover from this embarrassing setback.

    Before you unveil your visual aid to the world, have
    several qualified individuals who have not been involved in
    creating the visual aid proof it. And then have several more do
    it for good measure. It takes far longer to undo the damage
    created by sloppy work than to get it right the first time.

11. **Limit the number of visual aids.** Speakers sometimes look
    like circus ringmasters as they ricochet from one visual aid to
    the next—PowerPoint slides, handouts, flip charts, videos,
    whiteboards, and models. Adding such layers of complexity to
    your presentation will exacerbate your anxiety and diminish
    the overall impact of all the visual aids. Select one or two
    clear, concise visual aids to use during your presentation. If
    you still have the urge to multitask, join the circus or take up
    juggling as a hobby.

    ❧

    It is quality rather than quantity that matters.

    —Lucius Annaeus Seneca

    ❧

12. **Practice with your visual aid.** When your visual aid works
    flawlessly, it can amaze your audience, reinforce your
    message, and make you look like a real genius. And after a
    few flawless presentations, you can easily delude yourself into
    believing that visual aids are your reliable, loyal friends and
    that you can always trust them. Sorry, but they will betray you
    eventually, and no amount of sniveling, cursing, or head
    banging will save you from your plight. Master the visual aid

before you make your presentation—unless living on the edge of disaster exhilarates you.

Repeatedly practice your entire presentation, using your visual aid exactly as you intend to use it when you speak. Iron out all the logistics: the timing, where you will stand, and how you will display the visual aid. Practice flipping the pages, playing the videos, writing on the transparencies, and changing the slides. It should seem effortless when you are speaking. If possible, practice using the visual aid in the room where you will make your presentation. That experience will enhance your confidence when you speak, because you will have eliminated surprises and challenges.

13. **Protect your visual aid.** Be careful with the visual aid you have so painstakingly created. Store it in a dry, secure place before your talk; do not stack it in your garage or broom closet, or sling it into the car trunk next to your gym bag full of sweaty clothes. Photographs, posters, and charts are easily damaged: edges become tattered, pristine charts become soiled, and greasy smudges mysteriously appear. A sloppy visual aid undermines your professional image.

One speaker stored his charts in a tube for several weeks before he spoke, then whipped them out during his presentation. He spent the remainder of his talk tethered to his display stand, using one hand to hold down the obstinate charts that repeatedly rolled up into the tube shape. Avoid such predicaments.

14. **Bring your tools.** Review the checklist in principle 28 to determine all the accessories you will need when you are using your visual aid, such as nonpermanent markers, duct and masking tape, binder clips, Post-it notes, extension cords, backup files for the program materials, and spare lightbulbs for your equipment. And invest in a nifty laser pointer to help you direct the attention of your audience to the details on the visual aid (and to entertain yourself before the program).

And don't forget: immediately after you have finished using your accessories, set them down. Do not distract your audience by twirling, bouncing, spinning, gnawing on them, or jamming them in your ear (anxiety causes eccentric behavior—beware).

15. **Coordinate logistics.** Unless you enjoy sweating like a pack mule from lugging a cumbersome visual aid around right before you speak, or agonizing over whether it will work, plan ahead. You should have your visual aid set up, tested, and ready well before your audience arrives. Your listeners will be forming opinions about you before you begin to speak; if you are red-faced, flustered, and scrambling around as they begin to filter into the room, they will conclude that you are rattled and disorganized. That behavior will not generate confidence in you or your talk.

16. **Focus on your listeners.** Sometimes a speaker (not you, of course) becomes so engrossed with her visual aid that she forgets about her listeners. She turns her back to them and begins reading her visual aid, engaging in what is, apparently to her, a fascinating monologue with it. She stares at it like it is the Holy Grail, the most fascinating document ever. She is so spellbound by her visual aid that she probably would not know if her listeners left the room during the speech.

    Always focus on your audience (principle 29), not on the visual aid. Your listeners will get cranky if you ignore them. And don't use the visual aid to avoid looking at your listeners because you are nervous. They can still see you, and they are far more important than the visual aid. You do not need to persuade, inform, or motivate the visual aid—it's indifferent.

17. **Substitute the visual aid for notes.** As long as you have prepared (and it is a capital crime if you have not), you can quickly refer to the points on the visual aid to prompt yourself so that your presentation flows as planned. Substituting the visual aid for notes also gives you the flexibility to move

away from the lectern, which results in a more natural, conversational presentation.

But—and this is a really big *but*—the visual aid should *never* become a crutch or an excuse for not practicing. If you are unprepared and you read to your listeners from your visual aid, you will hold their attention for one minute, maybe two if they like you. They can read, so they don't want you to read to them. It dredges up unsavory memories of their boring ancient history teacher from high school.

18. **Stand to the left.** Face your audience, stand on the left side of the visual aid (your audience's left), and point or gesture toward it with your left hand, because this is how the audience reads text.

    Do not position yourself or point to the visual aid in any way that causes you to turn your back on your audience (never a good idea, and probably a really bad idea with a hostile group) or to gesture across your body (such as standing on the right side of the visual aid and pointing with your left arm). You will look like a contortionist.

19. **Allow your listeners time to study your visual aid.** Observe the audience members before you remove the visual aid or move to your next point. Are they still studying it or taking notes? Is the material depicted on the visual aid so complex that it requires extra time?

    Remember, a topic that you are very familiar with because of your detailed preparation may be new and confusing to the members of your audience. Let them study and absorb the information on the visual aid. Be sure they have digested the current point before you move to the next one. Pace yourself and adjust your rate of delivery as necessary. That increases the likelihood that your message will stick.

20. **Add variety.** If you darken the room for long periods while using a visual aid, your audience's attention will drift away. Worse, your audience may become drowsy, and snoring distracts everyone.

Keep the members of your audience alert and engaged by adding variety to your delivery: periodically switch on the lights, ask questions, solicit their ideas, vary the pacing, or take a break. You will never connect with audience members if they are not listening.

When you have finished referring to a visual aid, remove it from view. Turn off the projector, darken the screen, or flip the chart to a blank page. Otherwise, many listeners will stay focused on the visual aid in a zombielike trance rather than focusing on listening to you, especially if the visual aid is vibrant (or your presentation is wearisome). Listeners are easily distracted and amused, especially when they are bored.

Stay alert, because visual aids can ruin your presentation in a flash, and they seem to enjoy doing that. Never trust them. But if you plan and practice carefully, a great visual aid can convert an ordinary presentation into an extraordinary one. And always remember: plug the hole in your clay pot.

38

Create Multimedia Magic

Technology . . . is a queer thing. It brings you gifts with one hand,
and it stabs you in the back with the other.

—C. P. Snow

"Learn to master the power of PowerPoint," the tempting flyer promised. The program guaranteed that attendees would discover how to harness PowerPoint's potential to their advantage, how to mesmerize listeners, and how to blend words and images in a stunning visual package. How could any speaker resist? I couldn't, and I didn't, but I wish I had.

The speakers on the program intended to dazzle the audience with their multimedia presentations. Instead, they fizzled. Their embarrassing gaffes ran the gamut from simple glitches to inexcusable oversights. Their computers were incompatible with the facility's equipment, resulting in awkward and lengthy delays. Their glitzy software programs froze repeatedly. The lettering, graphics, and images were cluttered, confusing, and virtually impossible to decipher. And the speakers were ill prepared; they fumbled along until they ultimately resorted to simply reading what was projected on the screen.

In the ample spare time that I had while the speakers floundered, I wondered if they could have planned a worse demonstration. Most of the attendees quickly lost patience; instead of listening, they chose to read newspapers, send text messages, make cell phone calls, or vote with their feet and leave. Rather than convincing the audience members to embrace PowerPoint in their programs, the speakers inspired a renewed appreciation for the simplicity and reliability of the flip chart.

Unfortunately, the speakers' bungling did a disservice to the potential of multimedia. Multimedia can seize your audience's attention, add sparkle to your presentation, and enhance your credibility, expertise, and professional image. High-tech presentations are increasingly becoming the standard in the industry. The graphics can be stunning. The latest multimedia presentation software available from a variety of sources such as Microsoft, Adobe, Corel, and IBM Lotus all heighten the enormous impact of visual aids by offering the following significant advantages:

- You can incorporate graphs, slides, photographs, animation, video clips, and sound to help your audience visualize your message.
- You can scan material from books or magazines and incorporate it into your presentation (but be wary of the dreaded Copyright Police).
- You can download thousands of documents from the Internet to include in your presentation.
- You can quickly add, delete, or modify material, which is difficult with many visual aids.
- You can produce handouts from the slides in your presentation to reinforce the message.
- You can choreograph your program so that specific material will appear at a predetermined time during the presentation, or you can control the timing with a wireless presentation remote.

Now, for the bad news: although multimedia presentations can amaze, they can just as easily flop. The more complex the technology, the greater the likelihood that it will eventually fail. And here is the cruel reality:

by some twist of fate, these calamities typically occur in a room packed with clients, prospects, competitors, and, of course, your boss. And they occur at the most inopportune moments in your presentation: as you attempt to close the sale, offer recommendations, or share an epiphany.

When they occur—and they will—logic and reason vanish into thin air, and a Herculean struggle between man and machine begins. At these moments, the evil twins—Mr. Hardware and Mr. Software—will do exactly what they want to do, and no amount of cajoling, nudging, swearing, or desperate banging will persuade them to do otherwise. They mulishly refuse to work. The machinery prevails all too often in these epic battles.

Even when they do work as planned, multimedia presentations are not always a blessing. Often they are neither memorable nor helpful if they are not carefully designed. Mastering the tools and software necessary to create powerful multimedia presentations poses special challenges, including all of the following:

- Listeners who are overwhelmed by a staggering presentation often succumb to sensory overload and miss much of your intended message.
- A multimedia presentation that will not confuse and frustrate your listeners requires meticulous planning and attention to detail.
- You must design your multimedia presentation so that you control when and how much information is revealed.
- You must master the basics of setting up and operating the equipment for each multimedia presentation, adding to your overall preparation time.
- As the complexity of the technology increases, so does the likelihood of a snafu or even a total equipment failure.

Twelve Steps to Multimedia Power

You are not prepared for the complexity of a multimedia presentation until you have mastered the basics of creating and using a visual aid, so if you skipped principle 37 (and why would you?), retreat and study that principle.

The guidelines below supplement those in principle 37 and specifically address the problems associated with multimedia visual aids. Always follow these steps before unveiling a high-tech show:

1. **Know the basics.** If you are a technological tenderfoot but you are making a multimedia presentation, you had better take a crash tutorial titled "Surviving Multimedia Meltdown 101." Master the technology *before* you attempt to use it while standing in front of an audience. Be prepared to handle simple technical difficulties. It is probably not the best time for on-the-job training when your audience is impatiently staring, squirming, and scowling.

   Keep a handy list of your hardware and software specifications (the brand and model of your laptop, the type and version of your software) so that you can quickly refer to that information if you have a problem. Those details will escape you in the heat of the moment, when your mind is paralyzed and you are jabbering to the technician on the telephone about "the gizmo that flips the whatchamacallit thingie next to the doodad." That enlightening description of the problem will not prove helpful. If you skip this precaution, have the telephone number for the Dial-A-Prayer hotline readily available.

❧

The purpose of a visual aid is to communicate your ideas, not to display your virtuosity as an artist or wizardry with computer graphics. Visual aids should be simple, clear, and to the point.

—Stephen E. Lucas

❧

2. **Make it simple.** Clarity is critical, a concept that is lost on many speakers. They use text, photographs, cartoons, animation, slides, and video clips in the same presentation. What results is a disjointed smorgasbord of confusing information. Just because you *can* use all these options in your multimedia presentation doesn't mean that you *should*. So don't.

If you overload your presentation, your audience will ignore your message and instead become engrossed in the entertainment: "Wow! I have no idea what the speaker said, but what glitzy graphics!" Your listeners should never have to guess what your point was. Rather than trying to impress your audience with a grandiose spectacle, create a multimedia presentation that illuminates and supports your message. Make it simple, memorable, and understandable.

3. **Choose colors carefully.** Use no more than three harmonizing colors per visual, and maintain consistency throughout your visual aid. If you go wild with color, Confusion and his cousin Chaos will overwhelm your presentation. Also, use distinct color contrasts that make the text easy to read. For example, red and green are not easy to read when combined on a single visual (even at Christmastime), and it can be difficult to distinguish between certain shades of color, such as blue and purple.

4. **Select simple fonts.** Make your fonts simple, consistent, and legible. Use no more than two or three font sizes per visual, with the headings, of course, being largest. If you use too many different sizes or styles (such as this *example* of **excessive font** *styles*), you create confusion. Select fonts that are easy to read from every vantage point in the room. Serif fonts (Present Your Way to the Top!) are suitable for blocks of text, and sans-serif fonts (Present Your Way to the Top!) are useful for headings and titles.

    Avoid compressed (**Present Your Way to the Top!**), decorative (*Present Your Way to the Top!*), and artistic (*Present Way to the Top!*) fonts, because your audience will become frustrated trying to read them. Find a different way to express your individuality and personality. Finally, minimize the use of bold lettering and of all-capital letters. **THEY WILL STAND OUT, BUT CAPS AND BOLD** are challenging to read when they appear in large sections of text.

5. **Title the visuals.** Place a title, or header, at the top of each visual, so that your audience can quickly understand what information you are presenting ("Ten Advantages of Double

Rum-Raisin Ice Cream" or "Broccoli: The Silent Killer"). Set the heading in a larger font to distinguish it from the rest of the text in the visual. Review the guidelines for font sizes in principle 37. And once again, for consistency, use the same size and style of fonts for all the headers in the series of visuals.

❧

Every job is a self-portrait of the person who did it.
Autograph your work with excellence.

—Anonymous

❧

6. **Use uniform transitions.** Don't use a hodgepodge of techniques to introduce new information or to move from one topic or visual to the next. If your text, graphics, and images appear in an unpredictable combination of custom animations, wipes, fades, or cross-dissolves, zipping in from every angle with a flourish of noise, they will become a sideshow. Your distracted audience will stop listening to you ("What speaker? On with the show!") and begin focusing on the entertainment. Make your transitions uniform, smooth, and never distracting.

7. **Check visibility.** Multimedia visual aids pose visibility challenges. If the lights in the room are too bright, if the morning sun causes a glare, if the screen is too small or positioned too low to be visible, or if the lettering or images are minuscule, the members of your audience will be unable to see what you are displaying. They will quickly grow restless and begin to disengage (which is counterproductive), whine (which is contagious), stew (which grows ugly), or repeatedly ask you to explain what is depicted (which will cause you to mumble words that would shock your grandmother).

   The rule is simple: design your multimedia presentation to ensure that it will be visible from every vantage point in the room at any hour of the day. If you cannot do that, select a different visual aid.

8. **Test and retest.** This may sound annoyingly repetitious — because it is — but it cannot be overemphasized: test and retest your equipment, and then, for good measure, test it again. Hardware and software problems are commonplace with complex multimedia programs. Ask any of the bungling speakers involved in the PowerPoint debacle described earlier. Better yet, question the unfortunate souls who were trapped in the audience during that calamity. Never be Pollyannaish or indifferent about your electronic gizmos, because you will eventually be sorry that you were.

   Weeks before you speak, confirm that your equipment is compatible with the equipment you will use at the location where you will speak; frequently it is not. Arrive early on the day of the speech (or even the prior day for that really critical presentation) to set up and test your equipment. Allow enough time before the curtain rises to remedy any problems that you discover.

9. **Adopt a friend.** The sage advice to adopt an AV friend when you are testing your sound system (principle 35) also applies here. If the facility has an on-site AV specialist, make him your bosom buddy. This expert can help you avoid and quickly resolve any multimedia technical problems. He is also typically familiar with the vagaries of the facility's equipment.

   Ask him to be present when you test the equipment. Emphasize his importance to a successful presentation (plead shamelessly, if necessary). To recruit his help, entice him with a reward (a generous gratuity for an important program or a BMW 7 Series for that monumental presentation). Being assured that he can rescue you from the great visual-aid abyss will allow you to breathe much easier; indeed, his mere presence will greatly reduce your anxiety.

10. **Choreograph your presentation.** Speaking while making a multimedia presentation adds an extra layer of complexity, because the timing is crucial. The process should appear effortless to your audience, but this appearance will not just

magically happen; it takes forethought and practice. A speaker who instructs her assistant to just "throw a few slides into a PowerPoint presentation for me" and then presents without practicing or even reviewing the program (boasting, "Piece of cake! I do this all the time, and I could do this in my sleep.") is walking a speaking tightrope without a net.

Bill Gates, the founder of Microsoft, was making a presentation extolling the virtues of his company's latest technology. When he began to demonstrate the product for thousands of technical experts, businesspeople, and members of the news media, it failed. Kaput. Nothing. Shortly thereafter, according to informed sources, Microsoft transferred all the AV technicians involved in that meltdown to another Microsoft office . . . in Antarctica.

The lesson is clear: if one of the world's richest men, with unlimited resources and thousands of the finest technological geniuses at his command, cannot guarantee that his high-tech wizardry will work for him, can you guarantee that it will work for you? Practice.

❧

Success . . . is not often gained by direct effort as by careful, systematic, thorough preparation for duty.

—George S. Boutwell

❧

11. **Secure backups.** Always carry a flash drive with your entire program saved on it in the event that your computer fails and you need to load the program onto a second computer. If feasible, bring a second laptop with the entire program saved on it, or at least know where you can secure another computer in an emergency. You will be thankful that you can quickly switch to Plan B.

12. **Create a contingency plan.** Sometimes, despite your best efforts, the technology fails, and all your sulking will not fix the problem. Like a Ringling Bros. and Barnum & Bailey

Circus, the show must always go on. So, know what you will do other than hide under the head table, bang the equipment, or mumble invectives like a drunken sailor. Devise an alternative plan in the event of a total equipment malfunction.

Be prepared to rely on a more basic visual aid (a flip chart or an overhead projector) if it is appropriate for the size of your audience. In dire circumstances, you may need to proceed without any visual aid.

Does that place a greater burden on you? Certainly. But canceling your presentation is never an option—ever—and forcing your audience to suffer through a lengthy delay while you grapple with the technology is an imprudent decision. Like the hand sanitizer or tissues your mother always insisted you carry, always have a backup plan in your hip pocket.

Check out the recommended resources listed at the end of the book as well as the following excellent Web site, which provides a wealth of information on electronic visual aids:

- Berkeley Digital Library SunSITE Image Finder (http://sunsite2.berkeley.edu:8088/ERF/servlet/ERFmain?cmd=searchResType&resTypeId=14) has thousands of images, including photographs and art, covering such topics as people, history, technology, science, space, and nature.

Mastering all the challenges and nuances necessary to create and use a multimedia presentation skillfully requires extraordinary patience and an exacting eye for detail. But these tools are enthroned at the pinnacle of the visual-aid hierarchy in the speaking world. They can mesmerize, delight, and inspire your audience. And the return on your investment of time and effort is enormous. Your presentations will shine—and who knows: Bill Gates just might call you for advice.

PART VIII

CONFRONT SPECIAL CHALLENGES

Your boss has just leaned over at the company banquet and whispered the five dreaded words you had hoped never to hear: *"Just say a few words."* You glance at the room of over 500 people, and you feel like a trapped animal: your mind is whirring, your heart is thumping, and the room temperature is suddenly soaring. You quickly survey the room for the nearest exit, and you plan your hasty retreat.

ॐ

He said little, but to the purpose.

—Lord Byron

ॐ

The bad news: at some point in your professional or personal life, you will have to speak on the spur of the moment. You may need to comment spontaneously at a client or company meeting or propose a toast at your wayward cousin Rosco's sixth wedding. The good news: if you opt not to barrel out the emergency exit, you can excel in this setting by logically organizing and sharing your thoughts. Read on to learn the secrets.

In a perfect world, your presentations would be flawless, every program would run with absolute precision, and you would encounter nary a snag. It may calm you to envision that speaking utopia, but you had better plan for a few challenges when you speak.

Part VIII is your safety net (or security blanket, if that is more soothing). It contains battle-tested secrets for speaking spontaneously, and rules that will guide you through the minefield of common obstacles that beset speakers.

39

Speak Spontaneously

If no thought
your mind does visit,
make your speech
not too explicit.

—Piet Hein

Law schools use the Socratic method of teaching. It is an experience that most law students (except those with deviant personalities) loathe. It works like this: the professor (the predator) poses a hypothetical question about some obscure legal issue (one that has not been relevant since the *Mayflower* dropped anchor in Cape Cod, but I digress) and then randomly selects from the class a cowering law student (the prey) to respond. The professor relentlessly challenges, probes, and refutes all responses. The student is doomed from the outset, because every answer, even the right one, is wrong. Professors relish this game because it provides a socially acceptable outlet for their sadistic tendencies. Understandably, students, as they are reduced to quivering masses of gelatin, do not share their professors' glee.

This exercise is designed to train law students to listen closely, to quickly analyze what has been said, and to formulate a coherent response immediately. Soon, the students are thinking and speaking like lawyers (and they are then prepared to enter society and wreak havoc by making simple matters hopelessly complex, needlessly confusing, and obscenely expensive).

Although these memories still haunt me, I recognize that the Socratic method was excellent training for speaking spontaneously. Most people never receive similar training. Speaking impromptu nearly immobilizes them. When I conduct an executive presentation skills workshop and solicit participation from the attendees, their reactions are predictable. One attendee immerses herself in her suddenly fascinating handout to avoid all eye contact. Another begins feverishly scribbling something, signaling, "I am busy, so back off!" Still another attendee looks truly pathetic or terrified, and I can almost hear him muttering my own refrain from law school: "Please, please, *please*, dear Lord, don't let him call on me!"

❧

Only talk when it improves the silence.
—Christopher Matthews

❧

The anxiety that improvised speaking causes virtually immobilizes some of you. For many, it is far worse than the typical angst that most speakers experience when giving a prepared speech. Ironically, you speak spontaneously every day in one-on-one conversations (banter on your cell phone, casual exchanges in the hallway), and you do so effortlessly. You listen, respond, gesture, and interact, expressing yourself clearly and logically. But when you are asked to speak in a more formal setting, with people staring at you, your brain is likely to go blank, your body is likely to tense, and mental shutdown is likely to commence.

Eleven Keys to Speaking Spontaneously

You can skip only so many meetings or hide in the restroom stall only so many times to avoid the prospect of speaking spontaneously before people begin to gossip and you begin to slide down the corporate ladder you have been relentlessly climbing. So what can you do? Try these 11 techniques:

1. **Forget perfection.** First, let's demystify the experience of speaking spontaneously. There are probably four people in the world who speak off the cuff flawlessly every time, so the chances that you are one of them are mighty slim. If you have learned that you always have to be perfect when you speak spontaneously, unlearn it now. No one expects you to be a paragon when you are speaking impromptu, so don't place irrational expectations on yourself.

   Unlike with a prepared presentation, where you have ample time to select your words methodically and polish your delivery incessantly (you do both, correct?), you have very little time, or perhaps no time, to formulate an impromptu response. You do not have to say everything you know about your subject, and you may even forget something, but that's fine. Just aim to convey a few thoughts with vigor, in a concise and logical manner.

2. **Anticipate participation.** Before any meeting or gathering where you might be asked to speak, know the terrain and the players. Determine who will be speaking, the nature of the message, and the typical interaction with the audience. Ask yourself: "Is the speaker's topic likely to generate discussion?" "Are these events generally informal, open discussions?" "Does the speaker encourage audience feedback?" "Is the person facilitating the meeting renowned for terrorizing meeting attendees by randomly calling on them?" (Perhaps she is a frustrated former law school professor.)

   Be prepared. Anticipate ways in which you may be asked— or compelled—to contribute. Plan what you might say if you do participate. Do this, and you will sound more confident and organized when you speak. That will amaze your friends and disarm your opposition.

❧

If you would hit the mark, you must aim a little above it.

—Henry Wadsworth Longfellow

❧

3. **Practice.** I know what you're thinking: "Hello, Einstein! Impromptu speaking, by definition, is done on the spur of the moment. How can I practice?"

   Although you cannot practice responses to the *exact* questions you are asked, of course, you can polish and refine your impromptu speaking skills with specific exercises.

   Try this: ask someone to select a topic and designate a position that you have to advocate. What topic the person chooses is not important as long as it is not entirely tasteless. Role-play and address the topic just as you would at a meeting. Take the impromptu training a step further by using the Q&A exercises described in principle 34. This is an excellent way for you to become comfortable with thinking on your feet.

   Record and critique your responses, using the guidelines outlined in principle 21. Then select another topic and repeat the exercise. Over time, you will become more comfortable and, as a result, more convincing.

4. **Formulate responses.** Be an engaged listener, not a detached meeting or program attendee, mindlessly daydreaming, drumming your fingers, and staring at the clock. Focus on what is being said and contemplate how you will respond if questions arise. Ask yourself questions as you listen: "Does that make sense, or is it pure rubbish?" "Do I agree?" "Is the speaker's reasoning persuasive or specious?" "Has the speaker ignored pertinent information?" "Are there viable alternatives?"

   This mental activity will better prepare you to anticipate questions and formulate responses *before* you are asked to participate. Trust me: even a few seconds of forethought provides a distinct advantage. And here's another plus: it minimizes your risk of babbling.

5. **Jot down thoughts.** As others speak, jot down the important points and key words that are mentioned to help you recall what has been said. Include your own commentary. For example, note the speaker's key ideas. Then, next to them, capture your own thoughts by making such simple notations as "Really?" "Why?" or "No way, Numbskull!" (Don't let your neighbor see that last one.)

   If time permits, create a brief outline to provide some structure to your notes. Identify three points that you would make. Doing this will help you organize your thoughts in case you either are called upon or decide on your own to participate. If you just start yammering when you are tapped to speak, without some framework, you are likely to become tangled up beyond salvation.

6. **Build credibility.** When you are asked to make an impromptu comment, don't undermine your credibility or handicap yourself with unnecessary apologies ("Gosh, I am sorry, but I really don't know too much about widgets or gadgets . . ."), excuses ("I haven't had my fifth mug of coffee, so I am not thinking clearly yet . . ."), or defensiveness ("Why are you asking me? Why don't you ask Bernice? She *always* has an opinion . . .").

   Approach these speaking opportunities with gusto and do the very best you can under the circumstances.

   ಶಿ

   If I am to speak for 10 minutes, I need a week for
   preparation . . . if an hour, I am ready now.

   —Woodrow Wilson

   ಶಿ

7. **Act confident.** Your listeners read and react to both what you say and how you say it. They study your facial expressions and body language, listen to the conviction in your voice, and evaluate what they see and hear. So whenever you speak, whether you are delivering a prepared or an impromptu presentation, you should convey unshakable confidence (principle 30).

If you wince, whine, stammer, roll your eyes, pout, or stomp your feet when you are asked to "say a few words," you will undermine your credibility and effectiveness. Instead, stand tall, breathe deeply, smile, and—for dramatic impact— pause before you begin. That behavior sends an unmistakable message to your listeners: "I am knowledgeable and self-assured, and I welcome this opportunity." (You can melt into a puddle after you sit down.)

8. **Deliver an actual speech.** Even when you are speaking spontaneously, you are more likely to be clear and convincing if you structure your comments as you would for a prepared speech (principle 10): a simple opening, two or three points, and a brief summation. Succinct, crisp, structured presentations beat wordy, rambling ones any day.

   For example, suppose that Lloyd, the company health nut, has just advocated eliminating all the vending machines in the employee lounge, because, he contends, they "distribute poison that erodes our brains." You could structure your response to his drivel as follows: First, state your position ("Lloyd is a crackpot, and his suggestion is preposterous . . ."). Second, explain your position ("Although Twinkies and Ding Dongs may create a sugar frenzy, this drastic step will crush employee morale and deprive us of one of life's simple pleasures . . ."). Finally, summarize ("In sum, although cutting out KooKoos might eliminate sugar buzzes and increase the company's productivity, we need to consider less drastic alternatives first, such as firing Lloyd . . ."). This structure will help you make your points quickly and clearly (and rally the junk food addicts).

9. **Use signposts.** Just as with a prepared presentation, your impromptu talk should be organized in a way that helps your listeners follow along. An excellent way to do that is by providing signposts at key junctures, to let your listeners know where you are going and when you are moving from point to point: "There are *three* reasons why the proposal

should die a swift death. *First*, it is ridiculously expensive. *Second*, those of us who will pay for this are ridiculously poor. And *third*, we can afford this luxury only if we forgo eating, since we will have no money left for food, which is disheartening."

After stating your three points in the opening, you give another signal as you reach each of the points: "*Third*, eating trumps luxury . . . ." These signposts focus your comments and help the audience follow along. Today's impatient audiences will not spend much time struggling to understand a jumbled message, so make your talk clear and concise.

10. **Slow down.** Sometimes your speaking anxiety will cause you to jabber, and the jabbering accelerates when you have had virtually no time to prepare. When that happens, you look skittish, and you sound scattered. You are also likely to overlook critical points or to state them so rapidly that they will zip right past your listeners.

Consciously fight this tendency. Pause for a few seconds before you begin speaking and slow down as you are speaking.

❧

He does not say a word more than necessary.

—Charles de Gaulle

❧

11. **Be brief.** Typically, your impromptu presentation should be short. Sometimes a speaker will ramble on and on . . . *and on,* with no end in sight on the speaking horizon. Perhaps she is hoping for a lucid moment, when she might stumble across a clear thought as she struggles to make a point—*any point.* Another speaker mistakenly believes that more words are more convincing. Wrong.

When you are asked to speak off the cuff, it is never an open invitation to blather. In the little time you have, strive to make two or three memorable points, but no more. Have mercy on your audience. Say it succinctly and take your seat.

If you want to enhance your impromptu speaking skills in a cost-effective way and in a nonthreatening venue, join Toastmasters International (www.toastmasters.org). This exceptional international speaking organization has thousands of clubs throughout the world that meet regularly. It was established to give individuals the opportunity to practice speaking and to improve their communication skills. Best of all, you can hone your speaking skills in a safe forum (translation: no boss, no clients, no hecklers).

Use the keys provided in this principle to refine your impromptu speaking skills. They will prepare you not only to *"just say a few words,"* but also to say them with enthusiasm and conviction. You can enhance your image as an expert, score points with your clients and superiors, and maybe even persuade a few people along the way, so plunge in!

40

Overcome the Obstacles

Calamity is man's true touchstone.
—Francis Beaumont and John Fletcher

Imagine a perfect presentation. You exude confidence as you eloquently deliver your speech, exactly as you had planned, while holding your audience's rapt attention from beginning to end. Your thinking is clear and precise, your logic brilliant, and your ideas compelling and fresh. At the conclusion, the members of your audience leap from their seats, applauding in a near frenzy of excitement and showering you with amazing accolades. You decide that you are a fabulous speaker and that speaking is really very cushy. It is a euphoric feeling.

Now, sober up, because here is the more likely scenario: you will occasionally forget portions of your presentation, audience members will distract you, and your audiovisual equipment will betray you. There is a high probability that you will say something that is inaccurate ("When President McCain signed this legislation . . ."), confusing ("What did they say he said about what she said?"), or foolish ("That was a very perspiring message . . ."). You may be stumped by a question, sabotaged by your introducer, or befuddled by logistical problems. Welcome to the real speaking world!

Many events will occur that can fluster you in the best case, or ruin your speech in the worst. I remember well the morning that one company's pinstriped Muckety Muck interrupted my speech because he needed to immediately see Chester, the sluggard employee who was busy in the back of the room tweeting about "one real snoozer meeting" he was sitting in, to fire him. As a rule, a midspeech firing dampens the spirit of any presentation.

It is risky to cross your fingers and hope that the Goddess of Good Fortune will always smile upon you, blessing all your speaking endeavors and protecting you from every challenge. She is just not that reliable. Eventually she will test you, and usually at the worst time. The critical question is whether or not you will be ready.

❧

When I think over what I have said, I envy dumb people.

—Lucius Annaeus Seneca

❧

Five Solutions to Setbacks

You can avoid many problems with careful (bordering on obsessive) planning and preparation. But some challenges, like the five listed here, may be unavoidable despite your best efforts. What follows is a game plan for emerging relatively unscathed and with most of your dignity intact. Flexibility is the key, and praying is not a bad idea in desperate moments. Your goal: to adapt to the situation rather than becoming unglued.

1. **Equipment meltdowns.** Here is the first unavoidable law of speaking: your equipment will fail. That's "will fail," not "may fail." Take the precautionary steps outlined in Part VII so that you can prevent many equipment pitfalls. But sometimes

nothing helps, and your double-crossing equipment just will not work. Sulking, blaming others, or cursing seldom remedies the situation, so here are a few presentation savers:

- Unless you are positive that you can solve the snafu very quickly, take a break. Don't make your audience members wait while you struggle to resolve the problem. And here is a dirty little speaking secret: no audience, in the entire history of speaking (which covers more than a trillion speeches), has ever objected to a break. It is doubtful that yours will be the first. In fact, an extra break will probably enhance your listeners' opinion of your presentation.

- If you cannot get the equipment cart out of the ditch, resort to Plan B (you have one, right?), which might involve quickly replacing the malfunctioning equipment or using a different visual aid.

- If Plan B flops, implement Plan C: proceed without using any visual aid. Packing up and heading home is never an option.

- After the presentation, proceed to Plan D: invest in new equipment.

❧

Public calamity is a mighty leveller.

—Edmund Burke

❧

2. **Cell phone distractions.** If you do not have a cell phone surgically attached to your hip or your ear, on behalf of all speakers worldwide, thank you. The second sure law of speaking: one or more cell phones will ring while you are speaking, even though before you began, you urged your audience to turn them off. Some people would apparently disconnect their own life support system before they would turn off their cell phone and actually be inaccessible for several minutes. That would be much too traumatic.

308 🔊 Present Your Way to the Top

Sometimes a bozo will even answer the call during your presentation and then carry on a conversation. Another simpleton will look around stupidly as his phone rings, shrug his shoulders, and then simply let it continue to ring; apparently he is hoping that everyone else is deaf and will not notice. Violence seems appealing in those moments. How should you deal with this distraction?

- Pause until the ringing stops. Use that opportunity to survey your notes and collect your thoughts. Continuing to talk while the phone is ringing is seldom productive. This delay heightens the peer pressure on the culprit, since everyone in the audience is being inconvenienced by the delay. The audience members may even band together and toss the cell phone (and, if you are lucky, the offender) out the window. Problem solved.

- If the ringing persists, grit your teeth, smile, and politely ask the sinner to place the phone on silent or step out of the room (or the country) to avoid distracting other audience members.

- Enlist the support of the program chairperson at the break to play the "bad cop" role. They have a vested interest in ensuring the program runs smoothly.

3. **Audience unruliness.** Occasionally, audiences might have a few disruptive members. One person is antsy by nature, constantly fidgeting, unable to focus or sit still for more than 30 seconds, especially late in the day. Another is rude, mumbling his sarcastic or snide commentary about your presentation, or passing notes to fellow audience members. Still another is opinionated; she assumes that it is her inalienable right to constantly interrupt your presentation with probing or even antagonistic questions, and to share her perspective.

🔊

Yield not thy neck
To fortune's yoke, but let thy dauntless mind
Still ride in triumph over all mischance.

—William Shakespeare

Once during one of my speeches, an audience member began snoring. That does not boost your confidence. His honking and snorting were amusing but distracting. I fiendishly considered asking everyone else to leave the room, allowing Rip Van Winkle to awaken alone, in a darkened auditorium. Instead, I simply moved closer to him and continued talking. My voice disturbed his slumber, and he awoke, somewhat surprised. He later professed that he really enjoyed my talk. Some speaking days are better than others. Here are several ways to deal with audience distractions:

- Pause, conjure up your most sinister evil eye (such as the one your dad gave you when you backed the family station wagon over his golf clubs), and glare at the offenders. Do this until they finish talking. It will become clear that a few boors are interrupting the program, and audience pressure can be a powerful deterrent.
- Move closer to the distraction. The audience's attention will follow you to the disruption, which often corrects the problem.
- In a nonantagonistic manner (hard to muster when you are seething, I know), smile, and ask the distracting parties if they have a question or maybe an observation that they would like to share with the group. Allow them to speak briefly if they choose to do so, address the comments, and then move on with your presentation.
- Politely suggest that it is difficult for everyone to hear if several people are talking at once, and ask them to hold their comments until after the program. If that does not work and you are feeling feisty, simply muzzle them and toss them into a closet for the remainder of your presentation (most audience members will gladly help you).

4. **Humor that flops.** I have occasionally used humor in my speeches that I felt was simply remarkable. Unfortunately, it was remarkably bad. Sometimes your scintillating wit fizzles. Your colossal punch line may be greeted with deafening silence, and your listeners may stare at you blankly, with

cocked heads, raised eyebrows, and baffled expressions adorning their faces. It is so quiet that you can hear your heart beat. A few compassionate listeners may titter nervously to break the tension, but don't count on it.

Maybe it was just bad timing, maybe your audience was jammed with humorless stuffed shirts, maybe the planets were misaligned, or maybe—just maybe—your humor wasn't funny (yes, I know that is unlikely, but at least consider the remote possibility). When you bomb, you will be gripped by fear. Your face will burn, your palms will sweat, and you will desperately pray that—poof!—you will vanish. Since it is unlikely that you will become invisible, you had better have another plan for bouncing back. Here are a few ideas:

- Ignore your audience's reaction and carry on as if what you said was not intended to be funny.
- Handle it the way professional comedians do when their jokes bomb: poke fun at yourself. "Well, my mom liked it!" "Just a little joke I threw in. Guess it should have been thrown out." or "Don't worry. Some of these are just for me!"[1]
- Tell yourself that you are okay, but your audience is the problem (delusional behavior is allowed in these moments of distress).

5. **The dreaded blank slate.** Speakers have one recurring nightmare: going blank while speaking. It terrifies them, because they are alone on stage and their misfortune is visible for all to see. Occasionally, they will lose their way while speaking, forgetting what they have just said or what they intend to say next. In the worst case, they will forget where they are and why they are there.

❧

The timid man sees dangers that do not exist.

—Publilius Syrus

❧

You may momentarily stumble during your speech for a variety of reasons: your insufficient preparation (for shame!), your spontaneous decision to deviate from your prepared comments, your anxiety, a question that baffles you, or your functioning on two hours of sleep after a wild night at Club Chaos. Whatever the reason, going blank can be slightly embarrassing. Here are several ways to regain your bearings gracefully:

- Pause and refer to your notes or to the visual aid that is currently on display.
- Sip water, adjust your visual aid, or move about the room to stall for time and collect your thoughts.
- Ask for questions from your audience regarding what you have already said in your speech. Address the questions, then simply ask, "Okay, now, where was I?" and hope that some Good Samaritan will clue you in.
- Take a short break to recover (audiences love breaks), if it seems like a logical point to break. Of course, this is not a viable solution if you have gone blank just 12 seconds into your speech.
- Suggest an exercise that will allow you time to recall where you stopped talking. For example, "Pair up with someone sitting close to you, and discuss all the ways you can market this tasty new shrimp ice cream." Or, "Take a moment to list the three most valuable lessons you have learned so far today."
- Playfully tell your audience that you are lost: "Well, it appears that my tongue has gotten ahead of my mind, and it is going to take a moment for my mind to catch up. Where was I, anyway?" Most audience members are eager to pipe up and help, and this disarming admission humanizes you.

&

Whatever happens, look as if it were intended.

—First Rule of Acting

The only sure way never to have to confront a speaking challenge is never to speak. Some people artfully duck every speaking opportunity all the time—a safe choice, but one unlikely to enhance the chances of securing that coveted corner office or VIP reserved parking spot. Be brave. Sure, there are inherent risks, but don't let that discourage you from speaking. If you plan for the unexpected, you can convert a challenge into a golden opportunity to demonstrate your poise and confidence. And who knows? That triumph alone may be enough to generate a standing ovation.

Conclusion

*Nothing in the world can take the place of persistence. Talent will not;
nothing is more common than unsuccessful individuals with talent.
Genius will not; unrewarded genius is almost a proverb. Education will
not; the world is full of educated derelicts. Persistence and determination
alone are omnipotent.*

—Calvin Coolidge

Well, there you have it: how to speak with confidence and conviction,
and for extraordinary results, every time. If it sounds like hard work, it is,
but it is well worth your effort. In today's intensely competitive corporate
world, every presentation truly can make or break your career.

Learning the craft of speaking can be challenging at times and frustrating at others, but also immensely gratifying. Along the way, you will
experience euphoric highs and maybe a few disappointing lows. But the
personal and professional rewards trump any risks—by a wide margin.
Business executives who communicate with confidence and conviction
will see their messages resonate with their audiences and invariably enjoy

a distinct advantage. Rather than glazed looks, they will see engaged audience members, and that is invaluable to any executive, regardless of which rung of the corporate ladder he is standing on. When you see a light—or, if you are fortunate, many lights—spark in the eyes of your listeners, you realize that through your words, you have made a difference. That feeling is priceless. My hope is that I have kindled your desire to become a much better speaker than you are now—indeed, a desire to present in a way that will cause you to truly stand out every time you speak.

Don't settle for mediocrity. No one gets remembered for being average. Worse, in the corporate world, being average can mortally wound your career aspirations. Distinguish yourself from the thousands of speakers who every day, in every conceivable forum, blandly deliver painfully boring presentations. Challenge yourself. Follow this step-by-step guidebook and become a speaker who literally makes her listeners sit upright and spellbound. Prepare for that moment so that when it is showtime you will own the stage. If there was hope for Jell-O Boy, anything is possible. Let your journey begin!

Notes

1. Channel Your Stage Fright

1. Roper Starch, "How Americans Communicate," National Communication Association, www.natcom.org/research/Poll/how_ americans_communicate.htm.
2. David Wallechinsky, Irving Wallace, and Amy Wallace, *The Book of Lists* (New York: Morrow, 1977); quoted in George L. Grice and John F. Skinner, *Mastering Public Speaking*, 4th ed. (Boston: Allyn & Bacon, 2001), p. 44.
3. Stephen E. Lucas, *The Art of Public Speaking*, 7th ed. (New York: McGraw-Hill, 2001), p. 8.
4. Ibid.
5. Garrison Keillor, "Monologue," *A Prairie Home Companion*, Minnesota Public Radio, February 13, 1999; quoted in Grice and Skinner, *Mastering Public Speaking*, p. 44.
6. Carol Burnett, "Ask Them Yourself," *Family Weekly*, January 28, 1979; quoted in Ibid., p. 44.

7. Meryl Streep, interview, *Interview*, December 1988; quoted in Ibid., p. 44.

2. Visualize Speaking Success

1. Vicki Huber, quoted in Stephen E. Lucas, *The Art of Public Speaking*, 7th ed. (New York: McGraw-Hill, 2001), p. 11.
2. Dr. Wayne W. Dyer, interview by author, in Michael Jeffreys, *Success Secrets of the Motivational Superstars: America's Greatest Speakers Reveal Their Secrets* (Roseville, Calif.: Prima Publishing, 1996), p. 62.
3. Lucas, *Art of Public Speaking*, p. 10.
4. Lilly Walters, *What to Say . . . When You're Dying on the Platform* (New York: McGraw-Hill, 1997), pp. xxiii–xxiv.

3. Park Your Ego at the Door

1. Anthony Robbins, interview by author, in Michael Jeffreys, *Success Secrets of the Motivational Superstars: America's Greatest Speakers Reveal Their Secrets* (Roseville, Calif.: Prima Publishing, 1996), p. 24.
2. Les Brown, interview by author, in Ibid., pp. 161, 183.

7. Use These Tools to Get to Know Your Audience

1. Stephen E. Lucas, *The Art of Public Speaking*, 7th ed. (New York: McGraw-Hill, 2001), p. 101.

8. Adopt from the Best Speakers

1. Brian Tracy, interview by author, in Michael Jeffreys, *Success Secrets of the Motivational Superstars: America's Greatest Speakers Reveal Their Secrets* (Roseville, Calif.: Prima Publishing, 1996), p. 122.
2. Dr. Martin Luther King Jr., "I Have a Dream," quoted in Stephen E. Lucas, *The Art of Public Speaking*, 7th ed. (New York: McGraw-Hill, 2001), Appendix B, pp. B7–B10.

9. State Your Purpose

1. John R. Trimble, *Writing with Style: Conversations on the Art of Writing*, 2nd ed. (Upper Saddle River, N.J.: Prentice Hall, 2000), pp. 56–57.

10. Organize for Coherence

1. Patricia T. O'Conner, *Words Fail Me: What Everyone Who Speaks Should Know about Speaking* (New York: Harcourt, 1999), p. 180.

11. Open with a Hook

1. John R. Trimble, *Writing with Style: Conversations on the Art of Writing*, 2nd ed. (Upper Saddle River, N.J.: Prentice Hall, 2000), p. 26.
2. William K. Zinsser, *On Writing Well*, 6th ed. (New York: HarperCollins, 2001), p. 57.

12. Revise, Revise, Revise

1. William Strunk Jr., and E. B. White, *The Elements of Style*, 4th ed. (Boston: Allyn & Bacon, 2000), p. 72.
2. Ibid., p. 23.
3. Ibid., p. 21.
4. Ronald Reagan, "Address to the Nation," January 28, 1986, quoted in Richard L. Johannesen, R. R. Allen, Wil A. Linkugel, and Ferald J. Bryan, eds., *Contemporary American Speeches*, 8th ed. (Dubuque, Iowa: Kendall/Hunt, 1997), pp. 407–408.

13. Harness the Power of Stories

1. Gene Griessman, *Abraham Lincoln on Communication*, DVD, 1992; www.presidentlincoln.com.

16. Close with a Bang

1. General Douglas MacArthur, "Farewell to the Cadets," May 12, 1962; quoted in Richard L. Johannesen, R. R. Allen, Wil A. Linkugel, and Ferald J. Bryan, eds., *Contemporary American Speeches*, 8th ed. (Dubuque, Iowa: Kendall/Hunt, 1997), pp. 403–404.

23. Capitalize on Potent Pauses

1. Isaac Stern, quoted in George L. Grice and John F. Skinner, *Mastering Public Speaking*, 4th ed. (Boston: Allyn & Bacon, 2001), p. 299.

28. Check Your Checklist

1. Lilly Walters, *Secrets of Successful Speakers: How You Can Motivate, Captivate and Persuade* (New York: McGraw-Hill, 1993), pp. 170–171.

29. Focus on Your Audience

1. Joel Weldon, interview by author, in Michael Jeffreys, *Success Secrets of the Motivational Superstars: America's Greatest Speakers Reveal Their Secrets* (Roseville, Calif.: Prima Publishing, 1996), p. 330.

31. Persuade with Passion

1. Anthony Robbins, interview by author, in Michael Jeffreys, *Success Secrets of the Motivational Superstars: America's Greatest Speakers Reveal Their Secrets* (Roseville, Calif.: Prima Publishing, 1996), p. 23.
2. Dr. Wayne W. Dyer, interview by author, in Ibid., pp. 61, 63.
3. Mark Victor Hansen, interview by author, in Ibid., p. 221.

36. Capitalize on Visual Aids

1. Michael E. Patterson, Donald Danscreau, and Dianna Newbern, "Effects of Communication Aids on Cooperative Teaching," *Journal of Educational Psychology* 84 (1992): pp. 453–461.

40. Overcome the Obstacles

1. Lilly Walters, *What to Say . . . When You're Dying on the Platform* (New York: McGraw-Hill, 1997), pp. 3–4.

Bibliography

Bartlett, John. *Bartlett's Familiar Quotations*. 17th ed. Boston: Little, Brown, 2002.

Cialdini, Robert B. *Influence: Science and Practice*. 5th ed. Boston: Allyn & Bacon, 2008.

Cook, John, ed. *The Book of Positive Quotations*. 2nd ed. Minneapolis: Fairview Press, 2007.

DeVito, Joseph A. *Essential Elements of Public Speaking*. 3rd ed. Boston: Allyn & Bacon, 2009.

Ehrlich, Eugene, and Marshall DeBruhl, eds. *The International Thesaurus of Quotations*. 2nd ed. New York: Harper Perennial, 1996.

Fensholt, M. F. *The Francis Effect: The Real Reason You Hate Public Speaking and How to Get Over It*. Oakmont, Calif.: Oakmont Press, 2006.

Fletcher, Leon. *How to Design and Deliver Speeches*. 8th ed. Boston: Allyn & Bacon, 2003.

Frank, Leonard Roy, ed. *Random House Webster's Quotationary*. New York: Random House Reference, 2001.

Garner, Bryan A. *Garner's Modern American Usage*. 3rd ed. New York: Oxford University Press, 2009.

Graves, Robert. *The Long Weekend and The Reader Over Your Shoulder*. Manchester, UK: Carcanet Press, Ltd., 2006.

Grice, George L., and John F. Skinner. *Mastering Public Speaking*. 7th ed. Boston: Allyn & Bacon, 2009.

Heath, Chip, and Dan Heath. *Made to Stick: Why Some Ideas Survive and Others Die*. New York: Random House, 2007.

Jeffreys, Michael. *Success Secrets of the Motivational Superstars: America's Greatest Speakers Reveal Their Secrets*. Roseville, Calif.: Prima Publishing, 1996.

Johannesen, Richard L., R. R. Allen, Wil A. Linkugel, and Ferald J. Bryan, eds. *Contemporary American Speeches*. 8th ed. Dubuque, Iowa: Kendall/Hunt, 1997.

Keillor, Garrison. *A Prairie Home Companion*, Minnesota Public Radio, February 13, 1999. Quoted in Grice and Skinner, *Mastering Public Speaking*.

Knowles, Elizabeth, ed. *Oxford Dictionary of Quotations*. 7th ed. New York: Oxford University Press, 2009.

Lucas, Stephen E. *The Art of Public Speaking*. 10th ed. New York: McGraw-Hill, 2008.

Luntz, Frank I. *Words That Work: It's Not What You Say, It's What People Hear*. New York: Hyperion, 2008.

Moussa, Mario, and Richard G. Shell. *The Art of Woo: Using Strategic Persuasion to Sell Your Ideas*. New York: Penguin, 2008.

Richmond, Virginia P., and James C. McCroskey. *Communication: Apprehension, Avoidance & Effectiveness*. 5th ed. Boston: Allyn & Bacon, 1997.

Strunk, William Jr., and E. B. White. *The Elements of Style—50th Anniversary Edition*. Boston: Longman, 2008.

Torricelli, Robert G., ed. *Quotations for Public Speakers: A Historical, Literary, and Political Anthology*. New Brunswick, N.J.: Rutgers University Press, 2000.

Trimble, John R. *Writing with Style: Conversations on the Art of Writing*. 2nd ed. Upper Saddle River, N.J.: Prentice Hall, 2000.

Venolia, Jan. *Write Right!* 4th ed. Berkeley, Calif.: Ten Speed Press, 2004.

Walters, Lilly. *Secrets of Successful Speakers: How You Can Motivate, Captivate and Persuade*. New York: McGraw-Hill, 1993.

_____. *Secrets of Superstar Speakers: Wisdom from the Greatest Motivators of Our Time*. New York: McGraw-Hill, 2000.

_____. *What to Say . . . When You're Dying on the Platform*. New York: McGraw-Hill, 1995.

Weissman, Jerry. *Presenting to Win: The Art of Telling Your Story*. Upper Saddle River, N.J.: FT Press, 2008.

Zinsser, William K. *On Writing Well, 30th Anniversary Edition: The Classic Guide to Writing Nonfiction*. New York: Harper Perennial, 2006.

Recommended Resources

1. Channel Your Stage Fright

Desberg, Peter. *No More Butterflies: Overcoming Stage Fright, Shyness, Interview Anxiety, and Fear of Public Speaking*. Oakland, Calif.: New Harbinger, 1996.

Fensholt, M. F. *The Francis Effect: The Real Reason You Hate Public Speaking and How to Get Over It*. Oakmont, Calif.: Oakmont Press, 2006.

Grice, George L., and John F. Skinner. *Mastering Public Speaking*. 7th ed. Boston: Allyn & Bacon, 2009.

Jeffreys, Michael. *Success Secrets of the Motivational Superstars: America's Greatest Speakers Reveal Their Secrets*. Roseville, Calif.: Prima Publishing, 1996.

Lucas, Stephen E. *The Art of Public Speaking*. 10th ed. New York: McGraw-Hill, 2008.

Motley, Michael T. *Overcome Your Fear of Public Speaking: A Proven Method*. Boston: Allyn & Bacon, 1997.

Richmond, Virginia P., and James C. McCroskey. *Communication: Apprehension, Avoidance & Effectiveness*. 5th ed. Boston: Allyn & Bacon, 1997.

12. Revise, Revise, Revise

Barzun, Jacques. *Simple and Direct*. 4th ed. New York: Harper Perennial, 2001.

Garner, Bryan A. *Garner's Modern American Usage*. 3rd ed. New York: Oxford University Press, 2009.

Graves, Robert. *The Long Weekend and The Reader Over Your Shoulder*. Manchester, UK: Carcanet Press, Ltd., 2006.

Johannesen, Richard L., R. R. Allen, Wil A. Linkugel, and Ferald J. Bryan, eds. *Contemporary American Speeches*. 8th ed. Dubuque, Iowa: Kendall/Hunt, 1997.

Luntz, Frank I. *Words That Work: It's Not What You Say, It's What People Hear*. New York: Hyperion, 2008.

Merriam-Webster's Manual for Writers & Editors. Springfield, Mass.: Merriam-Webster, 1998.

Strunk, William Jr., and E. B. White. *The Elements of Style*—50th *Anniversary Edition*. Boston: Longman, 2008.

Trimble, John R. *Writing with Style: Conversations on the Art of Writing*. 2nd ed. Upper Saddle River, N.J.: Prentice Hall, 2000.

Venolia, Jan. *Write Right!* 4th ed. Berkeley, Calif.: Ten Speed Press, 2004.

Zinsser, William K. *On Writing Well, 30th Anniversary Edition: The Classic Guide to Writing Nonfiction*. New York: Harper, 2006.

13. Harness the Power of Stories

Davis, Donald D. *Telling Your Own Stories*. Little Rock, Ark.: August House, 1993.

Heath, Chip, and Dan Heath. *Made to Stick: Why Some Ideas Survive and Others Die*. New York: Random House, 2007.

Lipman, Doug. *Improving Your Storytelling*. Little Rock, Ark.: August House, 1999.

Maguire, Jack. *The Power of Personal Storytelling*. New York: Putnam, 1998.

Simmons, Annette. *The Story Factor*. 2nd ed. New York: Basic Books, 2006.

Storytelling Magazine. Published by National Storytelling Network (www.storynet.org/about/magazine.html).

14. Make 'Em Laugh

Carter, Judy. *The Comedy Bible*. New York: Fireside, 2001.

Heltzer, Mel. *Comedy Writing Secrets*. 2nd ed. New York: Writer's Digest Books, 2005.

Robertson, Jeanne. *Don't Let the Funny Stuff Get Away*. Houston: Rich Publishing Company, 1998.

15. Quote for Credibility

Bartlett, John. *Bartlett's Familiar Quotations*. 17th ed. Boston: Little, Brown, 2002.

Ehrlich, Eugene. *The International Thesaurus of Quotations*. 2nd ed. New York: Collins Reference, 1996.

Frank, Leonard Roy, ed. *Random House Webster's Quotationary*. New York: Random House Reference, 2001.

Knowles, Elizabeth, ed. *Oxford Dictionary of Quotations*. 7th ed. New York: Oxford University Press, 2009.

Shapiro, Fred R. *The Yale Book of Quotations*. New Haven, Conn.: Yale University Press, 2006.

Web Sites

Bartleby Online (www.bartleby.com).

The Quotations Page (www.quotationspage.com).

Quoteland.com (www.quoteland.com).

22. Project Vocal Power

DeVore, Kate. *The Voice Book: Caring For, Protecting, and Improving Your Voice*. Chicago: Chicago Review Press, 2009.

Love, Roger. *Love Your Voice: Use Your Speaking Voice to Create Success, Self-Confidence and Star-Like Charisma*. New York: Hay House, 2007.

Vendera, Jaime J. *Raise Your Voice*. 2nd ed. Franklin, Ohio: Vendera Publishing, 2007.

25. Gesture with Conviction

Guerrero, Laura K., Joseph A. Devito, and Michael L. Hecht, eds. *The Nonverbal Communication Reader: Classic and Contemporary Readings*. 3rd ed. Prospect Heights, Ill.: Waveland Press, 2007.

Knapp, Mark L., and Judith A. Hall. *Nonverbal Communication in Human Interaction*. 7th ed. Florence, Ky.: Wadsworth Publishing, 2009.

31. Persuade with Passion

Cialdini, Robert B. *Influence: Science and Practice*. 5th ed. Boston: Allyn & Bacon, 2008.

McCrosky, James C. *An Introduction to Rhetorical Communication*. 9th ed. Boston: Allyn & Bacon, 2005.

Moussa, Mario, and Richard G. Shell. *The Art of Woo: Using Strategic Persuasion to Sell Your Ideas*. New York: Penguin, 2008.

Perloff, Richard M. *The Dynamics of Persuasion*. 3rd ed. Hillsdale, N.J.: Lawrence Erlbaum, 2007.

Walters, Lilly. *Secrets of Superstar Speakers: Wisdom from the Greatest Motivators of Our Time*. New York: McGraw-Hill, 2000.

34. Take Command of "Q&A"

Weissman, Jerry. *In the Line of Fire: How to Handle Tough Questions . . . When It Counts*. Upper Saddle River, N.J.: Prentice Hall, 2005.

36. Capitalize on Visual Aids

Duarte, Nancy. *slide:ology: The Art and Science of Creating Great Presentations*. Cambridge, Mass.: O'Reilly Media, Inc., 2008.

Reynolds, Garr. *Presentation Zen: Simple Ideas on Presentation Design and Delivery*. Berkeley, Calif. New Riders Press, 2008.

Roam, Dan. *The Back of the Napkin: Solving Problems and Selling Ideas with Pictures*. New York: Penguin Group, 2008.

Wilder, Claudyne. *Point, Click & Wow! The Techniques and Habits of Successful Presenters*. 3rd ed. San Francisco: Pfeiffer, 2008.

40. Overcome the Obstacles

Walters, Lilly. *What to Say . . . When You're Dying on the Platform*. New York: McGraw-Hill, 1995.

Index

About the Author

There is no finish line.

—Nike slogan

David Dempsey grew up in a small town in western Nebraska. He began his career as a trial lawyer in Atlanta, Georgia, in 1980. He is a veteran of the courtroom, having tried many cases at both the state and federal levels. In 1986, while practicing law, David also began teaching beginning and advanced public speaking as an adjunct professor at Oglethorpe University in Atlanta. David still continues to teach classes today, and his classes are consistently among the highest rated at the university. One university dean described him as "an amazing resource and an instructor who awakens a skill in people that they did not know they had."

David has spent more than 25 years in the speaking arena as a trial attorney, a university professor, a speechwriter, a professional speaker, an acclaimed author, and a presentation skills consultant. David honed his own speaking talents in the competitive speaking arena. He is the two-time winner of the Toastmasters World Championship of Public Speaking for the State of Georgia.

Today, David is the president and CEO of Neon Zebra, LLC, an executive presentation skills consulting company based in Atlanta. Neon Zebra coaches C-level and senior business executives at global and Fortune 500 companies. David is the "go-to" executive presentation skills consultant when the stakes are high and the results are critical. His straightforward blend of expert advice, hands-on teaching techniques, and real-world experience empowers business executives to inspire, persuade, and truly stand out and be heard every time they speak. His services include speechwriting, one-on-one coaching, communication skills consulting, small group workshops, designing visual aids that *pop!*, and Q&A training.

David is also the author of *Legally Speaking: 40 Powerful Presentation Principles Lawyers Need to Know* (Kaplan Publishing, 2009), a book that shares insights, tips, and proven principles that David learned in his years as a successful trial attorney. This critically acclaimed book has been endorsed by Senator Bob Dole, Governor Carl Sanders, U.S. attorney general Griffin Bell, and Association of Trial Lawyers of America president Mary Alexander, among others.

To learn more about David, Neon Zebra, and the professional services they offer, visit Neon Zebra's Web site, www.neon-zebra.com. You can contact David at Neon Zebra, LLC, 1-800-729-2791 or 770-481-3050, or by e-mail at info@neon-zebra.com.